Immigration and social change
in the Republic of Ireland

MANCHESTER
1824

Manchester University Press

Immigration and social change in the Republic of Ireland

edited by
BRYAN FANNING

Manchester University Press
Manchester and New York

distributed exclusively in the USA by Palgrave

Copyright © Manchester University Press 2007

While copyright in the volume as a whole is vested in Manchester University Press, copyright in individual chapters belongs to their respective authors, and no chapter may be reproduced wholly or in part without the express permission in writing of both author and publisher.

Published by Manchester University Press
Oxford Road, Manchester M13 9NR, UK
and Room 400, 175 Fifth Avenue, New York, NY 10010, USA
www.manchesteruniversitypress.co.uk

Distributed exclusively in the USA by
Palgrave, 175 Fifth Avenue, New York,
NY 10010, USA

Distributed exclusively in Canada by
UBC Press, University of British Columbia, 2029 West Mall,
Vancouver, BC, Canada V6T 1Z2

British Library Cataloguing-in-Publication Data
A catalogue record for this book is available from the British Library

Library of Congress Cataloging-in-Publication Data applied for

ISBN 978 0 7190 7583 4 *hardback*
ISBN 978 0 7190 7584 1 *paperback*

First published 2007

16 15 14 13 12 11 10 09 08 07   10 9 8 7 6 5 4 3 2 1

Typeset in Sabon by
Koinonia, Manchester
Printed in Great Britain
by CPI, Bath

Contents

List of tables and figures

Tables

Figures

Notes on the contributors

Kieran Allen is head of the School of Sociology, University College Dublin. He is the author of a number of books, including *The Celtic Tiger: The Myth of Social Partnership* (Manchester University Press, 2000) and *Max Weber: A Critical Introduction* (Pluto Press, 2004).

Alan Barrett is a Senior Research Officer at the Economic and Social Research Institute, Dublin. His Ph.D. (awarded by Michigan State University in 1994) contained an analysis of the labour market characteristics of immigrants in the United States. Since returning to Ireland in 1994 he has continued his work on immigration and has analysed Ireland's experience. His work in this area has been published in journals such as the *Journal of Population Economics*, *Labour Economics* and the *Economic and Social Review*.

Ciarán Benson is Professor of Psychology at University College Dublin. His books include *The Cultural Psychology of Self: Place, Morality and Art in Human Worlds* (London and New York: Routledge, 2001).

Adele Bergin is a research analyst with the Economic and Social Research Institute in Dublin. She is a graduate of Trinity College Dublin and the University of Bristol. She is working on her doctoral dissertation at the National University of Ireland, Maynooth.

Neltah Chadamoyo is Zimbabwean but resides in Ireland, where she works full-time as a secretary as well as doing a postgraduate Equality Studies course part-time. She is the current chairperson of the board of Africa Centre (2005–06).

Barbara Dooley is head of the School of Psychology at University College Dublin.

Bryan Fanning is a Senior Lecturer in the School of Applied Social Science at University College Dublin. He is the author of *Racism and Social Change in the Republic of Ireland* (Manchester University Press, 2002) and *Evil, God, the Greater Good and Rights* (Edwin Mellor, 2007). He is co-editor of *Ireland Develops: Administration and Social Policy, 1953–2003* (Dublin: Institute of Public Administration), *Theorising Irish Social Policy* (Dublin: UCD Press, 2004) and *Irish Social Policy in Focus* (Dublin: UCD Press, 2006).

Alice Feldman (M.A., Intercultural Communication; Ph.D., Justice Studies, University of Arizona) is a lecturer in the School of Sociology at University College

Dublin and co-ordinator of the Migration and Social Change research initiative at the university's Geary Institute. She also serves in research and advisory capacities with a number of Irish NGOs and statutory agencies involved in work relating to immigration, anti-racism and interculturalism.

Maja Halilovic-Pastuovic is a graduate of the M.Phil. in Ethnic and Racial Studies (2003). Her dissertation was entitled '"Going Home for the Summer": Bosnian Refugee Women in "Intercultural" Ireland'. Maja is studying for a Ph.D. at the Department of Sociology, Trinity College Dublin. Her research examines Bosnian diasporic formations in Ireland, Sweden and Croatia.

Katy Hayward is Research Fellow for the EUBorderConf project, working on the case study of Northern Ireland/Ireland with Professor Antje Wiener. Funded under the EU Fifth Framework programme, this project investigates the role and influence of the European Union in the transformation of border conflicts. A graduate of the University of Ulster at Magee College, Katy was awarded a doctoral research scholarship from University College Dublin, where she completed a thesis on Irish nationalism and European integration in the Department of Politics. Prior to her arrival at Queen's, Katy conducted research for the Identity, Diversity and Citizenship project at the Institute for the Study of Social Change, taught in various departments at University College Dublin and held a research fellowship at the Dublin European Institute. Her book *Nationalism in a European Context: Ireland Reimagined* is published in 2006 by Manchester University Press.

Kevin Howard is a lecturer in social studies at the Dundalk Institute of Technology. Having graduated from Birkbeck College London, he was awarded a doctoral research scholarship from the UCD-based Institute for British Irish Studies, where he completed a thesis on the mobilisation of Irish community activists to secure official recognition of the Irish as an ethnic minority. His primary research interests are in the field of ethnic politics.

Inse Lichtsinn is a graduate of University College Cork, where he is a research assistant in the Department of Applied Psychology.

Piaras Mac Éinrí was Director from 1997 to 2003 of the interdisciplinary Irish Centre for Migration Studies at University College Cork, focusing on Irish and comparative international migration research, a field in which he has lectured and published extensively. He is an adviser to the Dublin-based NGO the Immigrant Council of Ireland and a member of the National Consultative Committee on Racism and Interculturalism. He is a Geography lecturer at the university and is engaged in a number of research projects on Irish immigration and integration policy. He is visiting professor at London Metropolitan University's Institute for the Study of European Transformations for 2004/05.

Siobhán Mullally is a Senior Lecturer in the Faculty of Law, University College Cork. She has lectured at the university of Hull and the University of Peshawar in Pakistan. She has held visiting appointments at Cornell Law School, Harvard Law School, Sydney La School and the National University of India Law School. She has worked as an adviser and consultant to UN bodies and international NGOs in East Timor, Kosovo, Afganistan and Pakistan. She has published widely in the fields of human rights law, immigration and refugee law and gender and law.

Fidèle Mutwarasibo works with the Immigrant Council of Ireland as the Information and Research Officer. Originally from Rwanda, he arrived in Ireland in 1995 and became an Irish citizen in 2003. Since 2000 he has researched, written/ co-written a number of publications and articles on integration, rights and obligations, community development, cultural diversity and political participation of immigrants and ethnic minorities in Ireland. He is a founding member of Africa Solidarity Centre, a support group for the African diaspora in Ireland. He is on the steering committee of the Discovery Initiative of the Church of Ireland. He sits on a number of other advisory committees and is a regular contributor of papers on diversity in Ireland at national and European level. He is in the process of registering to the Ph.D. programme in the Sociology Department, University College Dublin. His working title for the research is 'Social Capital a Seedbed for the Emergence of Immigrant/Ethnic Minority Leaders (Élites) in Ireland'.

Dermot Ryan is a lecturer in the School of Psychology, University College Dublin. He holds a master's degree in sociology from the National University of Ireland, Maynooth. After completing a higher diploma in Psychology at University College Dublin he went on to complete a Ph.D. in Psychology at the same institution under the supervision of Professor Ciarán Benson and Dr Barbara Dooley (head of the School of Psychology). His doctoral research project examined psychological stress among of forced migrants living in Ireland. It was the first longitudinal study of its kind to be conducted at an international level.

Vera Sheridan is a lecturer in the School of Applied Language and Intercultural Studies in Dublin City University, where she teaches language and intercultural studies. She has researched adult second language acquisition as well as the process of long-term cross-cultural adaptation by members of the Vietnamese community in Ireland. Her interests focus on immigrant entrepreneurship, narrative, literature and exile and representations of cultural difference in literature. Aspects of her research on the Vietnamese community have already been published as well as literacy materials for asylum seekers learning English as a second language, a project funded by the EU Social Fund and the Department of Education, among others.

Abel Ugba is a lecturer in the School of Social Sciences, Media and Cultural Studies, University of East London. Until 2006 he taught Social Theory at the Department of Sociology, Trinity College Dublin. He is researching the role of Pentecostal beliefs/practices in identity formation among African immigrants in Dublin for a Ph.D. dissertation. He has written extensively on immigrants in Ireland both in the popular press and for academic and research purposes. His most recent report, *A Quantitative Profile Analysis of African Immigrants in Twenty-first-century Dublin*, was published in 2004. He trained and worked as a journalist in Nigeria and Ireland. He was one of the publishers and the pioneering editor of *Metro Eireann*, Ireland's multicultural newspaper.

Angela Veale, Ph.D., is a lecturer in Applied Psychology at the National University of Ireland, Cork. Her research and publications in Ireland and internationally focus on youth and families in adversity, in particular asylum seekers and separated children in Ireland and the reintegration of war-affected children and psycho-social interventions in post-conflict contexts elsewhere. She is researching youth and political involvement in post-conflict contexts, and continuing research on the experiences of asylum seekers and processes relating self and culture.

Acknowledgements

Many people helped to make this book possible – too many to name. Manchester University Press were a joy to work with, as were (most of the time) each of the contributing authors. All deserve gratitude for putting up with me as editor. My own contributions would not have been possible without their help and the help of others in Irish universities and of NGOs preoccupied with the issues and debates addressed in this book. In one way or another I have stood on the shoulders of the Irish Centre for Migration Studies, the Irish Refugee Council, the Equality Authority, Pavee Point, the Irish Travellers' Movement, the Irish Council for Civil Liberties, Amnesty International, Metro Eireann, the Immigrant Council of Ireland, Africa Solidarity Centre and the Combat Poverty Agency. I owe much to my colleagues and students at the School of Applied Social Science at University College Dublin, who have given me something almost priceless: a great place to work. I am indebted to the friends and colleagues who have encouraged me. Tom Garvin, Andreas Hess, Jim O'Brien, Gabriel Kiely, Tim Mooney, Ronnie Moore, Fidèle Mutwarasibo and Michael Rush stand out. My debt to my family, Joan Maher, Caitriona, Eilis and Ellie, is beyond measure.

Dedicated to Kay Maher

1

Introduction

Bryan Fanning

Immigration and Social Change in the Republic of Ireland was planned as a companion volume to *Racism and Social Change in the Republic of Ireland*. The earlier book addressed developments during the nineteenth and twentieth centuries as a crucial context for thinking about racism in present day Ireland. Its perspective was that of an individual author. No such overview is yet possible when it comes to thinking through the rapid social changes resulting from recent immigration. Instead, this book presents the efforts of a number of writers well placed to address some of the multi-faceted changes that are taking place within Irish society. Inevitably it is a multidisciplinary text. Contributors are drawn from the fields of political science, sociology, social policy, psychology, geography, linguistics, law and economics. The book addresses a range of social, economic and institutional processes that affect the lives and life chances of immigrants as well as emerging debates about the integration of immigrants within Irish society. By necessity it addresses a range of conceptual approaches to rights, law, citizenship, racism, integration and multiculturalism that are being brought to bear on thinking about immigration in Ireland and elsewhere. However, to a considerable extent chapters are also grounded in research undertaken about the lives and needs of immigrants, the barriers they encounter and their contributions to twenty-first-century Irish society.

The Irish past is littered with hidden and secret Irelands. The business acknowledging and addressing these has long been a fraught one. Emigration swept social problems aside whilst ideologies of faith and fatherland swept them under the carpet. A litany of past institutional abuses of vulnerable people has recently to light. These were caused, to no little extent, by a societal inability to come to terms with uncomfortable realities that were known by many yet somehow discounted. The unveiling of any unacknowledged abuse, exploitation or discrimination often begins with the witness of participants, the efforts of activists to promote debate and those of researchers to understand what is going on. This book draws upon a fast growing literature and body of research on immigrant communities, some of it by immigrants, some by activists and some by academics. Much of this concerns inequalities and barriers encountered by immigrants that need to be acknowledged and addressed if they are to be integrated within Irish society.

The changes wrought by immigration are both pronounced and subtle. Walk around the centre of Dublin and you will see amidst the fly posters for nightclubs ones for Polish elections; the presumption perhaps being that some voters will slip over to Warsaw or Kracow on polling day by CIE coach or Ryanair. In 2005 the *Evening Herald* newspaper began to publish a weekly supplement in Polish. Yet interviews with Polish immigrants in the Irish media – prompted by a 2005 feature in the Polish edition of *Newsweek* on the 'hellish experiences' of some Poles in Ireland – suggest many are no less marginal than past generations of emigrant Irish navvies. Stop on a Sunday to buy flowers outside the Catholic Church in Harolds Cross and you might notice that the church is now a Russian Orthodox one. New and reassigned places of worship abound. The mobile phone chatter on the Dublin omnibus has become multi-lingual. Many bus drivers and taxi drivers are immigrants. Immigrants have become ubiquitous in the service and construction industries and commonplace in many other sectors. Yet the opposite pertains within the public sector where immigration policy is formulated. The recruitment practices of the civil service make it particularly unrepresentative of the diversity of Irish society. The removal in 2005 from the selection criteria for the Gardai of a qualification in the Irish language was replaced with one for any second language got rid of an obvious institutional barrier. Many other areas of the public sector have yet to follow suit. However, the health services have depended on the skills of immigrants for longer than other sectors of the Irish economy. This reality was disregarded in the politics of the 2004 Referendum on Citizenship, where nativist distinctions between 'nationals' and 'non-nationals' and a government campaign for 'commonsense' citizenship prevailed alongside claims that immigrants were exploiting Irish maternity hospitals. The political parties at the apex of prevalent top-down debates about immigration are still, by and large, monocultural entities. These exemplify a profound disconnection between official Ireland and an increasingly diverse real one.

Immigration and Social Change in the Republic of Ireland opens with a chapter by Bryan Fanning that seeks to relate debates about racism to debates about rights. In the Irish case legislation prohibiting discrimination on the basis of race coexists with a raft of laws and administrative rules that sanction discrimination against non-citizens. Such discriminations tend to be ignored in the narrow debate about racism that has become institutionalised in the Irish state and within mainstream politics. In this context new distinctions have emerged between the political, economic and social rights of citizens and of those exempted from citizenship. The subsequent chapter by Siobhan Mullally analyses the case law and constitutional changes that have set the ground rules for belonging to Irish society. Its specific focus is on the removal of the citizenship birthright from Irish born children of immigrants in 2004.

The next three chapters examine in different ways the economic context of recent immigration. Chapter 3 by Katy Hayward and Kevin Howard evaluates the campaign by the Irish state to encourage the return migration of former emigrants. Within this campaign those with the skills deemed necessary to feed the Celtic Tiger were targeted selectively. Here, according to Hayward and Howard, a desire to control immigration and social change resulting from immigration could be detected. Alan Barrett and Adele Bergin examine the contribution of immigration to the Irish economy. The big picture outlined by Barrett and Bergin is one within which immigrants are proportionally more likely to be educated to degree level than Irish citizens, to be employed in the professional and technical sectors and not significantly more likely to be engaged in out-of-hours employment or shift work. At the same time immigrants are not employed to the level suggested by their educational qualifications and they are far less likely to be members of trade unions. The following chapter by Kieran Allen seeks to contextualise well documented cases of immigrant worker exploitation. Allen, like Hayward and Howard, draws attention to the prevalence of free-market ideology within Irish immigration policy. The authors of both chapters identify processes of stratification shaped by market-oriented policies of selective targeting. In the case of prospective Irish returnees there was less of a welcome for those with low skills.

Asylum seekers have become almost invisible within debates about immigration. They are also excluded from the terms of reference of broader social policy debates. For example, the punitively low cash benefits received by those in direct provision, identified from the outset as a cause of extreme poverty, were not increased between 2000 and the time of writing in 2006. State policies of isolating asylum seekers from the mainstream of Irish society through enforced poverty and dependence are only part of the problem. Inse Lichtsinn and Angela Veale examine the efforts of Nigerian asylum-seeker lone mothers to negotiate cultural differences in building new lives for themselves and their children. The chapter by Dermot Ryan, Ciaran Benson and Barbara Dooley presents a series of six compelling case studies of experiences of post-migratory psychological trauma amongst people whom the authors describe as forced migrants. The asylum process is often described as a state akin to limbo, a place where lives are on hold. It is one where people can experience extreme isolation, unnecessary poverty, neglect and cruelty that exacerbates what, for some, have been profound levels of pre-migratory trauma. By any standard this limbo amounts to an unpromising starting place for new lives in a new place.

Two chapters address the experiences of relatively long-established Vietnamese and Bosnian immigrant communities and as such offer important lessons for future integration policies. A further chapter on African Pentecostals addresses the experience of more recent immigrants. Chapter 9 consists of an interview by Vera Sheridan of Tuyen Pham, who was a teenager when he came to Ireland in 1979 as a programme refugee. The interview traces his experiences in Ireland from that time to the present. It examines issues of family reunification, education, the difficulties of integration and the different perspectives of older and younger generations within the Vietnamese community. The following chapter by Maja Halilovic-Pastuovic offers a critique of the reception and resettlement scheme put in place for Bosnian programme refugees by the Irish state from the early 1990s. Again the chapter examines questions of integration and adaptation, with emphasis on how Bosnians have found their own ways of negotiating their position within Irish society. Integration debates in Ireland as elsewhere tend to be top-down. Such debates neglect the extent to which immigrants are often required to depend on the shelter of own communities. The American sociologist Robert Putnam distinguishes between 'bridging' forms of social capital and an exclusionary or 'bonding' form of social capital. The lesson of Irish history is that solidarities based on religious affiliation can be sectarian. Yet, as Abel Ugba demonstrates in his chapter on African Pentecostals in Ireland, the mutual supports that they provide for each other also provide a bridge to participating in Irish society.

Two chapters examine the challenges facing immigrant-led organisations in the Republic of Ireland. In Chapter 12 Neltah Chadamayo, Bryan Fanning and Fidele Mutwarisibo describe a study by the Africa Solidarity Centre of responsiveness by Irish political parties to immigrants and ethnic minorities undertaken prior to the 2004 elections and referendum. Irish political parties more than most Irish institutions do not reflect the now diverse make-up of Irish society. The findings of the ASC study suggest that they find it difficult to conceive of immigrants as potential supporters let alone as members or candidates. Such monocultural politics have meant that much of the debate about immigration has been confined to the margins of Irish public life. In Chapter 13 Alice Feldman charts the recent growth of immigrant-led organisations. In Ireland, as elsewhere, contemporary patterns of migration have catalysed new debates about national identity and citizenship, inclusion and belonging, equality and difference. Such debates are taking place most vociferously in what Feldman describes as the Third Sector. Here, immigrant 'newcomers' may assert and represent themselves, acting as social and economic entrepreneurs, building alliances and ultimately effecting change in advance of wider institutional support or advances, often prior to gaining citizenship status.

The final two chapters examine different aspects of debates about integration. While immigration policy and immigration developments in general (who is coming, how many, why, under what conditions?) are very much in the news in Ireland, there has been relatively little explicit discussion how immigrants should be integrated into Irish society. While the word itself, as well as such related terms such as multiculturalism, interculturalism and diversity, has since entered popular discourse, there has been insufficient debate about the precise meanings of such terms and their implications for public policy. At the same time these topics are now hotly contested in a number of other EU member states. The multicultural model championed by liberal thinkers such as Bhikhu Parekh has come under criticism in Britain, while in the Netherlands the murders of Pym Fortuyn and Theo Van Gogh have led to some questioning of the Dutch approach to diversity. In France the debate on the wearing of the hijab and other 'ostentatious' forms of religious expression has concluded, after well over a decade, with a law, passed by a majority on the left and on the right, which bans such practices outright. Piaras Mac Éinrí's chapter explores the implications of such debates for the development of an Irish approach to integration. The final chapter by Bryan Fanning explores the role of Irish social policy in promoting the integration of immigrants. Within Irish social policy debates a family resemblance can be seen between social inclusion goals and integration goals. The thesis at the heart of Irish anti-poverty policy is that people may be excluded from activities that are considered the norm for other people in society due to inadequate income and resources. Debates about integration emphasise the urgent need to remove institutional barriers that inhibit full participation in society. The experiences of other countries point to the long-term costs of failing to address such barriers.

2

Racism, rules and rights

Bryan Fanning

This chapter locates Irish responses to immigration within broader twenty-first-century debates about citizenship and rights. Societal racism and ethnocentrism continue to be mobilised within populist political responses to immigration in an era where anti-racist and rights-based approaches to social problems are often endorsed by the political mainstream. In this context new distinctions have emerged between the political, economic and social rights of citizens and of those exempted from citizenship. The rights of some non-citizen groups are increasingly defined in terms of their membership of administrative categories. Notably, the last decade has witnessed the growing racialisation of human beings administratively defined by their inclusion in the distinct human rights category of 'asylum seeker' under the United Nations Conventions relating to the Status of Refugees (1951). What is striking is that this has occurred at a time when social and legal norms opposed to racism and some other forms of discrimination have never seemed so strong.[1]

Efforts to challenge racism in the politics and social policies of many Western states have been bounded by presumptions about citizenship. Anti-racist and multiculturalism paradigms have often presumed that those being culturally, economically and politically discriminated against were citizens. For example, during the 1990s a focus on concepts such as institutional racism sought to redress barriers to egalitarian citizenship caused by racist and cultural bias in the delivery of welfare goods and services to citizens from black and minority ethnic communities. The problem with this paradigm is that it ignores discriminatory responses to persons deemed not entitled to many such goods and services. Forms of discrimination sanctioned by legislation, such as the lesser benefits entitlements of asylum seekers or non-citizen immigrants are all too easily excluded from debates about racism and inequality. Nation-states in the current era of global migration still discriminate between citizens and non-citizens notwithstanding some reciprocal entitlements to domicile, employment or welfare services result from agreements between nation-states or international conventions emphasising universal human rights. In the Irish case this discrimination is a particularly pressing issue because a large proportion of immigrants (who now amount to a significant proportion of Irish society) are recent ones. As the proportion of non-citizens living in Irish society increased so too have rules that distinguish their rights and entitlements of those from citizens become more pronounced.

The fragility of rights

The lineage of present-day conceptions of human rights includes Thomas Paine's declaration of the rights of man. This in turn was rooted in John Locke's natural law-influenced conception of natural rights. The refinement of essentially *a priori* notions of inalienable rights occurred alongside the development of a tradition of legal positivism that represented the law as a system of rules and disparaged beliefs in rights, as Jeremy Bentham put it, as 'nonsense on stilts'.[2]

Paine's achievement as a theorist of the American and French revolutions was to deepen understandings of the consequences of believing in rights within Western democracies. This could be seen in his opposition to slavery in America. In a 1775 polemic published in Pennsylvania he railed against justifications of slavery by 'Christians', suggesting, in keeping with the Gospel according to St Matthew, that if they were enslaved 'it might convince more than Reason or the Bible'.[3] At that time there were about half a million slaves in the thirteen states.[4] The first ever anti-slavery society, the Society for the Relief of free Negroes unlawfully held in Bondage, was founded in the wake of Paine's article. Its members championed a Bill against slavery in the Pennsylvania legislature. Its preamble, written by Paine, argued that all men however distinguished in feature or complexion were the work of an Almighty Hand. It argued that slaves were deprived of 'the common blessings that they were by nature entitled to'.[5] The Western tradition of rights, exemplified by Paine and by the Abolitionists, was built on religious foundations. However, those foundations seemed increasingly shaky as the Enlightenment progressed. Theistic beliefs in rights came to the fore at a time when these had begun to lose their philosophical credibility. As put by Jeremy Waldon:

> the morality of rights seemed naïve, simplistic and irrelevant to the complexity of the problems of nineteenth century society. The industrial revolution was viewed largely in terms of a play of forces which were to be understood sociologically, not ethically. And for the democratic revolution, in England and elsewhere, was fought for on the basis of the greatest

happiness of the greatest number, rather than individual human rights. Social determinism, the sociology of ideas, legal positivism and utilitarianism: in the midst of these theoretical currents, the rights of man seemed hopelessly out of their depth.[6]

Rights languished until the twentieth century in the shadow of the big ideas of modernity. They were rejuvenated in the wake of the Holocaust through international conventions such as the Universal Declaration of Human Rights (1948). Their imaginative, rhetorical and ideological appeal has grown steadily since that time.[7] Yet international debates about human rights have relied heavily on eighteenth-century claims about the rights of man, notably Paine's and the French Declaration of the Rights of Man and the Citizen.[8] Waldon suggests that to call these *human* rights was about defining the scope of the claims being made rather than addressing how these might be justified.[9] The problem of justification is primarily an ontological problem of 'believing in rights'. Yet the idea of human rights, however shaky the stilts upon which it stands, emerged in response to distinct social changes and events such as the Holocaust which made all too apparent the failures of legal norms within modern societies. The subsequent expansion of conceptions of rights by Western states to include hitherto marginalised groups such as black and ethnic minorities, women, gays and lesbians and people with disabilities was a sociological one. It was grounded in shifting social norms that impacted politically upon the making and interpretation of laws. The broad consensus referred to Waldon is by no means a universal one. Nor can it ever be understood as a permanent or irreversible one. Rights can be extended or undermined.

So much depends then on normative understandings of the status of rights. Within jurisprudence a tradition of positive law theory that essentially understands the law as a system of rules has vied with a natural law one that emphasises the priority of principles. The sorts of criticisms Bentham made about Locke's understanding of natural rights are echoed in twentieth-century jurisprudence, where interpretations of constitutions and arguments about the validity of economic, political and social rights are determined by the courts. Present-day debates between legal positivism and rights-based approaches to law are exemplified by two influential texts. *The Concept of Law*, by H. L. A. Hart, outlined an essentially positivist understanding of legal theory. *Taking Rights Seriously*, by Ronald Dworkin, emphasised the centrality of principles in the interpretation of law.[10]

Dworkin defined a 'principle' as 'a standard that is to be observed, not because it will advance or secure an economic, political or social situation deemed desirable, but because it is a requirement of justice or fairness or some other dimension of morality'.[11] In effect he challenged legal positivism as an empirical account of how legal decisions were actually made.[12] He argued that it was a fallacy to imagine that the law could or does exclude principles or remain apolitical. He also maintained that positivist theory offered an impoverished account of 'those puzzling, hard cases that send us to look for theories of law', since it ignored the question as to which principles were to count and to what extent.[13] Dworkin observed that if two rules of law clashed the decision as to which one was valid hinged upon considerations that went beyond the rules.[14] Where no clear rule could be located then a judge had to use his discretion to decide the case by what in essence amounted to a new piece of legislation or by somehow denying that judicial discretion existed. This, he argued, posed a problem for positive law theory in so far as it was unclear about the authority of the discretion that was invoked in such a situation.[15]

Hart argued that it was not necessary to believe in some *a priori* moral goals to empirically accept a 'minimum content natural law' of necessary and useful rules concerning individual and collective welfare.[16] Hart's minimum content natural law was a sociological account of how the law reflected prevailing understandings of morality:

> The law of every modern state shows at a thousand points the influence of both the accepted social morality and wider moral ideals. These influences enter into law either abruptly and avowedly though legislation, or silently and piecemeal through the judicial process ... No 'positivist' could deny these facts, or that the stability of legal systems depends in part upon such types of correspondence with morals. If this is meant by the necessary connection of law and morals, its existence should be conceded [17]

Hart considered that belief in a moral order constituted a social fact. This of itself had a bearing upon the possibilities for justice that affected interpretation of the rules of laws. It amounted to a notion of natural justice writ small epitomised by presumptions that the rules of law should be fairly applied and that like cases should be treated alike. Justice in its simplest form was justice in the application of the law. Hart identified a deeply embedded prevalent normative idea of justice at work in interpretations of Western law: 'Indeed so deeply embedded in modern man is the principle that *prima facie* human beings are entitled to be treated alike that almost universally where the laws do discriminate by reference to such measures as colour or race, lip-service at least is still widely paid to this principle.'[18]

However, Hart carefully qualified this observation. He pointed out that his reference to 'lip service' was meant to disparage the notion that a principle could be anything other than a social value or norm.[19] Not only were principles ontologically problematic, they could also be mobilised to endorse injustice. Aristotle's natural law doctrine of natural slavery was a case in point. Any invocation of moral principle in the pursuit of justice could backfire. Principles, no less than rules, were a two-way street. Hart was predominantly concerned with the possibilities for justice in the administration of the law.

For Hannah Arendt the big practical problem with human rights was the absence of a 'right to rights'.[20] The grammar of rights could, at best, be understood as a set of norms (the way we reason) that have come to have a greater influence on interpretations of rules of law. However, they have mostly done so within the confines of nation-states. Arendt agreed with Edmund Burke's view that rights spring from membership of a nation-state rather than from the human condition. Those exempted in one way or another from citizenship found no protection in the abstract naked-ness of being human. As she put it in *The Origins of Totalitarianism*, 'The survivors of the extermination camps, the inmates of concentra-tion and internment camps, and even the comparatively happy stateless people could see without Burke's arguments that the abstract nakedness of being nothing but human was the greater danger.'[21] Human rights depended, as such, upon what states (and their citizens) would or would not do about them.

Within modern articulations of human rights such as the Universal Declaration of Human Rights (1948) or the European Convention on the Protection of Human Rights and Fundamental Freedoms (1952) two particular formulations predominate.[22] The first of these is 'everyone has the right to …'. The second is 'no one shall be …'. These are exemplified by Article 29.2 of the Universal Declaration of Human Rights, which states:

> In the exercise of his rights and freedoms, everyone shall be subject only to such limitations as a determined by law solely for the purpose of securing due recognition and respect for the rights and freedoms of others and meeting the just requirements of morality, public order and the general welfare in a democratic society.

Here the notion that the rights of individuals are inseparable from duties towards other members of the community, specifically a duty not to infringe their human rights, amounts to a communitarian rather than individualist ethos. There is more to this notion than merely having rights against the state. An emphasis on mutual responsibility to ensure the rights of others as distinct from passive obedience to states respon-sible for handing down rights is suggested. As such, not all rights are understood to be absolute. Even those considered to be inalienable are subject to various limitations.

The sorts of dilemmas that result from the relationship between rights and citizenship (the basis of rights to rights) highlighted by Arendt in the post-World War II era are no less pertinent in the present era of globalisation. So too are the moral dilemmas evident in the willingness of rights-loving citizens to reduce the rights and entitlements of asylum seekers and other categories of migrants. In particular, the last decade has demonstrated the willingness by nation-states to increase inequalities between the rights of migrants and citizens in response to populist politics. This has been accompanied in recent decades by new restrictions upon the right to citizenship of immigrants.[23] Such responses highlight a disjuncture between human rights and citizen rights and the extent to which meaningful rights are still rooted in citizenship. For example, the enlargement of the European Union in 2004 to include ten new states improved the rights of migrants from these to other European countries but, at the same time, some of the original member states, including Ireland, passed legislation that reduced the rights of such migrants to social protection.

Rules and racism

Bureaucracies are archetypically concerned with classification and sorting human beings. The legal systems of the nation-state distinguish between citizens and non-citizens. Administrative categories determine the entitlement of people to welfare, education and health care. Ideas about race and ethnicity continue to circumscribe the lives of human beings. For instance, in recent years the category of asylum seeker has become a vilified one in many Western countries. Laws have been passed in various countries that removed various rights from people so administratively categorised. As a result it has recently become natural that asylum seekers have lesser welfare and education rights or that they be excluded from the remit of policies aimed at addressing poverty and disadvantage. Within the administrative logic of such systems human beings become defined by the categories they find themselves placed in. Rules are rules. As Raul Hilburg argued in *The Destruction of the European Jews* the Holocaust became administratively possible when the Nuremberg Laws established a legal definition of a Jew.[24]

Max Weber argued that human objects of bureaucratic tasks cease to be subjects of moral demands.[25] Moral considerations and social solidarity become subordinated to organisational goals and legal rules. Such bureaucratic rationality is evident within the administrative and decision-making processes of Western societies where these affect groups such as immigrant workers, refugees, citizen welfare recipients as well as persecuted minorities. The way in which refugees or immigrants are administratively classified determines whether or not they are to be regarded as members of the society within which they live. Gradations of rights between citizens and non-citizens, immigrant 'guest' workers, undocumented workers, refugees and asylum seekers have emerged in a number of Western countries that as recently as a century ago operated few restrictions on immigration. In effect, these are the result of placing human beings in different administrative boxes. Under the logic of citizenship it becomes 'natural' that the non-citizen should not have social and economic rights. Citizenship, then, becomes the 'wall, the barrier which protects an abstract national community. Citizenship grants privileges to those who belong at the very same time as it denies them to the non-citizen. Most expressions of prejudice and intolerance, most strategies of rejection, are based on the boundaries that have been traced around citizenship.'[26]

A large body of research in a wide range of societies has illustrated how racism interacts with other social and political processes to produce distinct forms of 'racialised' inequality.[27] The concept of racialisation describes the ways in which racist ideologies and beliefs function as a mechanism for demarcating defined groups, such as ethnic minorities, in ways that legitimise their marginalisation or social exclusion. It describes processes whereby specific groups of people are 'constructed' as a 'type' with reference to a limited number of physical and cultural characteristics. Their actual or assumed behaviour, abilities and values are then explained by reference to those selected features.[28] Racism, then, is an imprecise term often loosely used to describe a collection of interrelated prejudices, beliefs and ideologies which assume the biological or cultural inferiority of distinct groups. Racism can be broadly defined as referring to any beliefs or practices which attribute negative characteristics to any group of persons, either intentionally or unintentionally, on the basis of supposed 'race' or ethnicity within the context of differential relations of power.[29] The term 'racism' can be also used to describe a tendency to portray the cultures and ways of life of minority ethnic groups as inferior or as threatening to those of majority groups in society.[30] It is used to describe negative attitudes and practices towards persons because of their membership of groups perceived to differ in physical or cultural characteristics from the perceiver. The ethnicity paradigm, which developed from the 1970s, extended accounts of racialised discrimination to include groups who experienced this on the basis of cultural difference.[31]

Racism, as such, describes a number of interlocking discourses which emerged in turn, were superimposed upon each other, and which can be seen to persist within ideological and everyday understandings of social difference. For example, the UNESCO Declaration on Race and Racial Prejudice emphasised the role of structural and institutional barriers in producing racist barriers in society. It defined racism to include racist ideologies, prejudiced attitudes, discriminatory behaviour, structural arrangements and institutional practices 'resulting in racial inequality'. It notes that racism 'is reflected in discriminatory provisions in legislation or regulations and discriminatory practices as well as in antisocial beliefs and acts'.[32] Racism finds expression in the rules and structures of organisations, social norms and legislation. The Apartheid system institutionalised overt legal discrimination against non-whites from 1948. Hitler institutionalised discrimination against the Jews through the Nuremberg Laws. In both these cases 'racial' categories became legal ones and became vehicles of overt discrimination. Such overt racist discrimination has been challenged in the West in the decades since the Holocaust. Examples include international conventions on human rights, desegregation legislation in the United States and, crucially, shifts in social norms where overt expressions of racist beliefs became less and less acceptable.

From institutional racism to structural racism

The institutional racism paradigm that developed following the McPherson inquiry into the death of Stephen Lawrence presumed that those experiencing inequality were citizens.[33] The consequences of institutional racism include unequal access to services and unequal outcomes on the basis of ethnicity. Services configured towards the cultures, expectations and needs of majority groups which wittingly or unwittingly neglect those of minority ethnic groups are likely to produce unequal outcomes for minority ethnic groups. It is important to distinguish such institutional barriers from structural ones where immigrants formally have lesser entitlements or no entitlements.

For example, a complex interplay between institutional and structural forms of discrimination can be identified in Irish social work responses to unaccompanied minor children. Such asylum-seeker children have the same statutory right to child protection as others covered by the Children Act 1991 introduced following Ireland's ratification of the UN Convention on the Rights of the Child (1989). An emphasis on children's rights under international law can be traced to Article 25 of the Universal Declaration of Human Rights (UDHR), adopted by the United Nations in 1948, which proclaimed that childhood was entitled to special care and assistance and that all children should enjoy the same social protection. Articles 22 and 25 of the UDHR affirmed that *all* individuals have the right to an adequate standard of living, including clothing, housing, medical care and necessary social services. These rights were further affirmed along with the right to seek asylum under the 1951 UN Convention relating to the Status of Refugees, ratified by the Irish state in 1956. Subsequently, specific reference to the social, economic and cultural rights of refugee and asylum-seeking children was set out within the text of the Declaration of the Rights of the Child (1959). The International Covenant on Civil and Political Rights (ICCPR), adopted in 1966, also includes statements about children's rights (Article 24). The Covenant proclaims that children are entitled to special care, assistance and protection on the basis of their status as minors. No distinction is made between the rights of refugees, asylum seekers and citizens of signatory countries under the terms of these conventions.[34]

In practice, however, distinctions can be identified in how care and protection is extended to different groups. For example, in the Irish case, the care of unaccompanied minors is subject to the same legislation as citizen children yet broader structural barriers shaping responses to asylum seekers have contributed to institutional discrimination or double standards. A Seanad (Senate) debate in December 2003 (on the appointment of an Ombudsman for Children) noted reports of the institutional neglect of unaccompanied minors ('separated children seeking asylum') in the care of the state.[35] For example, one centre from September 2002 accommodated sixty-six young people aged from twelve years upwards. These generally shared rooms with one or more other young people and had minimal facilities and support. No qualified care workers were employed on site. As put by a voluntary sector social worker working with asylum seekers in February 2003, 'there is no care'. She described the level of support provided by Health Board social workers and project workers to the children as minimal.[36] All this breached National Standards for Children's Residential Centres (1995) setting out requirements for management, staffing, monitoring, children's rights, statutory care plans, child protection, education, health safety and the role of social workers.[37] In essence, unaccompanied minors in care were exempted from procedures and practices that emanated from commitments to children's rights.

The National Standards explicitly stated that young people should have a room of their own and that centres must have age-appropriate play and recreational facilities. There was also a requirement that the Health Board (since 2004 the Health Services Executive) must be satisfied, by undertaking a proper risk assessment, that centres are safe and secure places for young people to live in. Research commissioned by the Health Services Executive published in 2005 formally acknowledged disparities between provision for separated children seeking asylum and other (citizen) children in the care system. At the time of the study (2004) older children typically lived in hostels 'not under the oversight of the Social Services Inspectorate' rather than residential children's homes.[38] The Health Services Executive acknowledged that by 2005 some 250 separated children seeking asylum who were in care had gone missing and expressed concern that some of these children had been trafficked for prostitution.[39]

The potential institutional neglect of unaccompanied minors cannot be separated from government policies that marginalise asylum seekers within Irish society. In 2000 'direct provision', a separate welfare system for asylum seekers, was introduced. This removed existing entitlement to universal social assistance administered by the Health Boards. Direct provision weekly rates of payment at just €19.05 per adult and €9.53 per child were far less than those for other categories of welfare recipient in equivalent circumstances. Whist rates of mainstream benefits were increased on an annual basis, direct provision rates remained unchanged year on year from 2000 to the time of writing (2006). This ran contrary to the spirit of the UN Convention on the Rights of the Child (1989).[40] For instance, Article 24 of the convention set out the 'right' of all children to benefit from social security.

Unsurprisingly, a number of studies have identified detrimental conse-quences of so differentiating between asylum-seeker children and their families and other vulnerable groups in Irish society. Research under-taken in Cork during 2001 identified extreme child poverty and social exclusion amongst asylum seekers on direct provision resulting from lesser welfare entitlements and accommodation deprivation.[41] Research undertaken in Dublin during 2001 found that the inadequately nutri-tious diet available for women in direct provision caused difficulties in breast feeding. Women in hostels tended to give up breast feeding within a few weeks of the birth of their babies.[42] Research undertaken in Counties Sligo, Leitrim and Donegal during 2003–04 identified food poverty amongst asylum seekers due, in part, to (low) levels of 'direct provision' benefits.[43]

In the case of unaccompanied minor children the social work system administers regulatory distinctions between the entitlements of asylum seeker and citizen children. Christie's account of Irish social work responses to unaccompanied minors draws upon Bauman's description of the welfare state as a gardening state.[44] Within this analogy social workers are depicted as maintaining borders and regulating the growth of the different parts of the 'garden' or, more specifically, by using social work practices to integrate families and individuals within society using techniques of moralisation, normalisation and tutelage. In so far as social work may reflect the dominant culture the social control role can be affected by cultural differences and by racism. For example, assessments relating to child protection are likely to be affected by attitudes to and understandings of clients from black and ethnic minorities amongst social workers. However, it is also shaped by normative understandings of rights and administrative stratifications between the entitlements of different groups.

Non-citizens with lesser rights and entitlements encounter structural barriers to participation in society that may compound institutional barriers resulting from racism. Firstly, they may be categorised by the state as outside the remit of a range of policies and programmes aimed at tackling disadvantage. Secondly, they may be excluded from official equality discourse, that is, excluded from how inequalities in society are conceptualised and discussed in official research, reports and within the remit of policies. This can be seen as a form of ideological exclusion whereby asylum seekers and other non-citizen groups are deemed not to be part of Irish society. In this context, social policy considerations may become subordinate to policies of excluding such groups or of limiting their rights and entitlements. The marginalisation of asylum-seeker children and the potential exclusion of other categories of child migrants within the National Children's Strategy was exemplified by how the text of the strategy links children's rights to citizenship:

> An Ireland where children are respected as young citizens with a valued contribution to make and a voice of their own; where all children are cherished and supported by family and wider society; where they enjoy a fulfilling childhood and realise their potential.[45]

In December 2001 I sought to raise the problem of asylum-seeker child poverty with the then Minister for Children, following a speech she had made about children's rights. She replied that she was not the Minister for those children. They were, she said, the responsibility of the Minister of Justice Equality and Law Reform.[46] She was correct in so far as that Minister had administrative responsibility for the welfare of asylum-seeker children. However, one consequence of such administrative practices was the perception that such children were exempt from commitments to children's rights. This perception also applied within the National Children's Strategy where there was some discussion of the needs of refugees but none of asylum seekers. Arguably, the administrative presumption was that asylum-seeker children were outside the remit of the National Children's Strategy.

Bridges and walls

The tensions between rules and rights evident within such examples of structural discrimination have deepened in recent decades. Present-day constitutional, legislative and administrative norms affecting the treatment of non-citizens have developed over time. Commitments to extending the rights and entitlements of non-citizens resulted from the ratification of international conventions. Yet the main thrust of recent legislation shaped by international norms and national political responses to immigration has often been to circumscribe rights and entitlements. Political responses to refugees in Ireland mirrored those in other parts of 'fortress Europe'. Social policy systems of entitlement for non-citizen immigrants became subordinated to the control imperatives of border policies.[47] New forms of institutional and structural discrimination emerged. Older ones, to a considerable extent, persisted.

Immigration first became regulated by the Aliens Restriction Act 1914. This and the Restriction Amendment Act 1919 formed the basis of the Aliens Act 1935. Provision within the 1935 Act covering ministerial powers of deportation was found to be unconstitutional in 1999. In essence Section 5.1(e) of the 1935 Act had delegated to the Minister power to deport aliens contrary to the 1937 Constitution which vested the sole and exclusive power of making laws for the state in the Oireachtas (Parliament). A 1999 Supreme Court ruling on deportations noted how, under the Aliens Act 1935 in the absence of established criteria that set out the basis on which refugee applications should be determined, decisions were vulnerable to prevailing political pressures as well as to prejudices of various institutional actors within the Department of Justice:

> The Aliens Act, 'not the slightest degree unclear or unambiguous' empowered the Minister of Justice to exclude and deport not merely particular aliens but whole categories of aliens determined by their nationality or class. ... The change effected in the law by Section 5.1e of the Act was not a conferring on the state of an absolute power to deport aliens. It already had that power. But it was now to be exercised by the Minister.[48]

The 1935 Act effectively gave the Minister 'absolute and uncontrolled' discretionary power to deport individual aliens or categories of them, including racial or ethnic groups.[49] In effect, this power was wielded by officials. The Department of Justice adopted a policy of discriminating against Jewish refugees after the Anschluss. This persisted during the Holocaust and remained in place until the 1950s. In effect the Aliens Act 1935, though unconstitutional, allowed legal distinctions between Jews and others to be employed by the Irish state. The Irish state did not, as did Nazi Germany, adopt a legal definition of a Jew. However, it did adopt an administrative one that drew on the criteria of the Nuremberg Laws to make decisions about refugees.

The administrative criteria adopted by the Department of Justice in 1938 resulted from the effective devolution of refugee policy to a voluntary body, the Irish Co-ordinating Committee for the Relief of Christian Refugees.[50] It was agreed that the Co-ordinating Committee would take responsibility only for sifting applications and would put forward names to the department that they were satisfied were 'suitable in every way'. As stated in a memorandum of 16 November 1938, 'These proposals relate only to Christians with Jewish blood. The Co-ordinating committee are of opinion that this country should confine its efforts to such persons as there are adequate funds subscribed by the Jewish communities in other countries to deal with the cases of practising Jews.'[51] In a detailed 1939 article T. W. T. Dillon, the secretary of the Co-ordinating Committee, described what was now the policy of the Department of Justice – and, as then legally interpreted, the policy of the Irish state – using racial categories employed in the Nuremberg Laws. Dillon advocated a policy of admitting Christian refugees defined under the Nuremberg Laws as non-Aryan 'hybrids' or *mishlinge* (those with Jewish ancestry who had converted to Christianity). In essence, applications Catholic converts from Judaism were to be supported but not unconverted Jews.[52] The Irish Jewish community were told that 'the only refugees who are admitted to this country are persons whose cases are recommended to the Minister by the Irish Co-ordinating Committee for Refugees'[53] Institutional antisemitism persisted during the Holocaust and the policy remained in place into the next decade. The contribution of individual officials to discrimination against Jews can be identified—notably in civil servant memoranda authored by Peter Berry of the Department of Justice.[54] Berry was hardly the dispassionate Weberian bureaucrat just following orders. He was regarded as a friend by the Jewish politician Robert Briscoe. Members of the Jewish community with whom he mixed socially were unaware of his antisemitism.[55] Nor was he the single bad apple in the barrel as suggested in 2003, on Ireland's first Holocaust memorial day, by Michael McDowell, Minister of Justice Equality and Law Reform, in his 'apology' on behalf of the department to the Irish Jewish community. Institutional racism reflects societal norms as well as individual prejudices. The mechanics of exclusion experienced by Jewish refugees resulted from a combination of antisemitism and administrative practices and legislative discretion that allowed overt discrimination.

In 1956 the Republic of Ireland ratified the UN Convention relating to the Status of Refugees (1951). The result was only a partial break with the past. No legal or administrative infrastructure to fulfil Ireland's obligations under the convention was put in place until the 1990s. Institutional responses to refugees and asylum seekers (a distinction created by the 1951 convention) continued to be framed by pre-Convention legislation, notably the Aliens Act 1935. These responses continued to be shaped by pre-Convention expectations that refugees should not be a burden upon the state. Such expectations persisted even as rights and entitlements to refugees were being extended over time on a piecemeal basis. Slow shifts in state practices relating to refugees occurred over several decades within a framework designed to exclude certain categories of aliens.[56] Overt policies of discrimination, such as those encountered by Jews, became unfeasible within the context of an obligation to admit all those who sought refugee status. Obligations to extend social rights were gradually addressed. In the decades after the 1950s responses to cohorts of Chilean and Vietnamese refugees were guided, to a considerable extent, by pre-Convention thinking.

Specific legislation to address obligations under the 1951 convention was passed in 1996, immediately prior to a significant expansion in the number of applications for refugee status. The resultant situation mirrored what occurred in 1956, when political enthusiasm for the 1951 Convention was undermined by difficulties in living up to the obligations it imposed.[57] Abstract principles were one thing, the presence of real Hungarian refugees was another. The government quickly backtracked on commitments to admit more than the initial cohort accommodated in Clare in November 1956 in the face of resistance by the Hungarians to authoritarian administrative practices.[58] In both the 1956 and the 1996 decisions, in principle, to extend the rights of refugees and the responsibilities of the state unravelled when found to be 'unworkable' in the absence of adequate infrastructure. In the latter case a rise in the number of asylum seekers was used to justify non-implementation of much of the Act.

In June 1997 the Aliens Act 1935 was amended so as to increase the power of immigration officers to determine whether 'aliens' should be allowed to enter the country.[59] A preoccupation with discouraging asylum seekers from coming to Ireland persisted within subsequent legislation introduced in response a perceived asylum crisis. A new Deportations Bill was quickly introduced to allow deportations to resume after deportations under the Aliens Act were found to be unconstitutional in 1999. The resultant Illegal Immigrants (Trafficking) Act 2000 made it harder to apply for asylum. The Act introduced sanctions against those who aided asylum seekers to enter the state without recognising that many refugees were forced to use illegal means in order to flee persecution. It defined a 'trafficker' as a person who 'organises or knowingly facilitates the entry into the state of a person who he or she knows or has reasonable cause to believe to be an illegal immigrant'. An 'illegal immigrant' in turn was defined as a 'non-national who enters or who seeks to enter the state unlawfully'. As such, the Act criminalised asylum seekers without proper papers and imposed 'carrier liability' upon those who assisted them. Under Article 2 of the Act 'a person who organises or knowingly facilitates the entry into the state of a person whom he or she knows or has reasonable cause to believe to be an illegal immigrant or a person who intends to seek asylum shall be guilty of an offence'. The Act specified strict penalties, including fines and sentences of up to ten years' imprisonment. Carrier liability undermined the right to seek asylum. It imposed fines on airlines and shipping companies that brought asylum seekers to Ireland. In effect, it devolved authority for deciding who should be allowed to enter the state upon airlines and shipping companies. In this context, many asylum seekers had to risk exploitation by traffickers. In December 2001 eight Kurdish asylum seekers – six men and two young boys – died in transit inside a freight container bound for the port of Waterford after a fifty-three-hour journey.

Political hostility to asylum seekers from the late 1990s resulted in a number of measures to discourage applications for asylum by removing rights and entitlements. With the introduction of 'direct provision' in 2000 social policy became an instrument of border policy. Lesser welfare entitlements for asylum seekers were defended as necessary to tackle the asylum 'crisis' of the presence of asylum seekers. Subsequently the right of all Irish-born children to citizenship came under political scrutiny. In 1987 the High Court determined, in *Fajujonu* v. *Minister of Justice* that asylum seekers and other immigrants with Irish-born children were entitled to leave to remain for the benefit of their children.[60] This was interpreted by the court as a right of Irish-born children of non-citizens to live in Ireland with their family that allowed the regularisation of a significant number of asylum seekers and other immigrants with Irish-born children.[61] A 'policy decision' was made to begin to refuse leave to remain to asylum-seeker families in the knowledge that this would trigger a further test case in the Supreme Court.[62] In April 2002 the Fajujonu ruling was successfully (from the government's point of view) overturned in the High Court (*Lobe v. Minister of Justice*). On 23 January 2003 the Supreme Court upheld this ruling. In essence the Supreme Court ruled that the Irish citizen child of non-citizens could be deported with its parents unless the non-citizen parent agreed to be deported without their child.[63] This ruling was effectively superseded by the June 2004 Referendum on Citizenship that removed the existing birthright to citizenship from the Irish-born children of non-citizens.

The Irish Nationality and Citizenship Act (2001) superseded the Aliens Act (1935). Significantly it systematically replaced the term 'alien' in Irish legislation with 'non-national'. The term was used by the Department of Justice Equality and Law Reform in security debates, in reports about crime, human trafficking and illegal immigration, and by the Department of Enterprise and Employment to describe immigrant workers. By 2004 the 'national/non-national' dualism had become the prevalent common-sense conceptual framework for debates about immigration. The 2004 referendum undermined a definition of social membership set out in Article 45.1 of the 1937 Constitution, which states: 'The state shall strive to promote the welfare of the whole people by securing or protecting as effectively as it may a social order in which justice and charity inform all the institutions of the national life'. Here a concept of domicile entitlement, distinct from citizenship, was emphasised. It had been articulated in social welfare legislation that referred to 'every person in the state' rather than citizens of the state.[64] The Irish response to immigration has been to extend differences between the rights of citizens and those of non-citizens. It has done so through legislation which undermined previous norms of extending entitlement to non-citizens (based on domicile) and which countered presumptions of universal human rights.

One month prior to the 2004 referendum the enlargement of the European Union assured the residence status of some immigrant workers on non-transferable work permits. The workers who benefited – some 35%[65] – became less vulnerable to workplace exploitation. However, the Irish government used the occasion to remove a range of social security entitlements from new immigrants and their families for an initial two-year period. Amongst these, the Social Welfare (Miscellaneous Provisions) Act 2004 removed entitlements to children's allowances and other non-contributory payments previously available on a universal domiciliary basis from non-EU citizens.

Conclusion

The exclusion of some categories of new immigrants from political, economic and social rights has been identified as an expression of populist politics and racism. However, the discriminations encountered by some categories of immigrant are part of a wider partial unravelling of post-World War II human rights norms. The irony in the Irish case, as elsewhere, is that these are to some extent excluded from the remit of rights based approaches to social policy, the implementation of anti-discriminatory legislation and consideration within national anti-racist policies. Official anti-racism policies and emphasis on rights-based approaches to discrimination coexist with the undermining of immigrant rights. Debates about poverty, social exclusion and even the integration of minority groups remain anchored in the paradigm of citizenship. Goals of promoting equal opportunity within citizenship coexist with the use of citizenship as a mechanism of exclusion. Institutional racisms within citizenship persist but they are augmented by structural racisms fostered by stratified rights and entitlements on the basis of citizenship entitlement. Legal and administrative distinctions between citizens and non-citizens have become a site of racism and ethnic discrimination. However, beliefs about 'race' or 'ethnicity' are no longer the sole basis of discrimination. Status itself has become racialised. Asylum seekers in Ireland (persons from dozens of countries and ethnic groups) have been demonised as a category. That said, links with older manifestations of racism remain evident. Racialised claims about asylum-seeker 'baby tourists' were mobilised in support of the 2004 citizenship referendum.[66] The specific 'baby tourists' emphasised as exploiting Irish health services were black Africans. Yet the principal discourse within which the politics of the referendum played out was a populist distinction between 'nationals' and non-nationals'. The term 'non-national' transcended official use by government Ministers and civil servants to become the prevalent one used by the media and the general public to denote all non-Irish others. Within the jurisdiction of the Irish state 'non-national' also implied a sense of statelessness – that most dangerous of conditions emphasised by Hannah Arendt – in so far as immigrants living in Irish society were depicted as not part of it.

Notes

1 M. C. McGraw, 'Human Rights in a Global Age: Coming to Terms with Globalisation', in T. Evans (ed.), *Human Rights Fifty Years On: A Reappraisal* (Manchester: Manchester University Press, 2001), p. 201.

2 From a text first published in France in 1816. See J. Bentham (1843), 'Anarchical Fallacies; being an Examination of the Declaration of Rights issued during the French Revolution', in J. Waldron (ed.), *Nonsense upon Stilts: Bentham, Burke, Marx and the Rights of Man* (London: Methuen, 1987), p. 53.

3 T. Paine (1775), 'African Slavery in America', in M.C. Conway, *The Writings of Thomas Paine* I, *1774–1779* (New York: AMS Press, 1967), pp. 5–6.

4 Published in 1775 under the pen name 'Justice and Humanity' in *The Pennsylvania Journal; and the Weekly Advertiser*. See J. Keane, *Tom Paine: A Political Life* (London: Bloomsbury, 1995), pp. 99, 194–5.

5 T. Paine (1790), 'The Rights of Man', in M. C. Conway (ed.), *The Writings of Thomas Paine* II, *1779–1792* (New York: AMS Press, 1967), p. 29. A

watered-down version of the Bill was passed in 1780. J. Keane, *Tom Paine* (London: Bloomsbury, 1995), p. 195.

6 Waldon, *Nonsense upon Stilts*, p. 153.

7 F. Robinson, 'The Limits of a Rights-based Approach to International Ethics', in Evans (ed.), *Human Rights Fifty Years On*, p. 59.

8 O. O'Neill, *Faces of Hunger: An Essay on Poverty, Development and Justice* (London: Allen and Unwin, 1986), pp. 103–4.

9 Waldon, *Nonsense upon Stilts,* p. 163.

10 R. Dworkin, *Taking Rights Seriously* (London: Duckworth, 1977).

11 Ibid., p. 22.

12 Ibid.

13 Ibid., p. 45.

14 Ibid., p. 27.

15 Ibid., p. 34.

16 H. L. A Hart, *The Concept of Law* (Oxford, Clarendon, 1994), pp. 188–200.

17 Ibid., pp. 204–5.

18 Ibid., p. 162.

19 Ibid.

20 H. Arendt, *The Origins of Totalitarianism* (London: Allen and Unwin, 1961), p. 294.

21 Ibid., p. 299.

22 J. Finnis, *Natural Law and Natural Rights* (Oxford: Clarendon, 1999), p. 212.

23 C. Joppke, 'How Immigration is changing Citizenship: a Comparative View', *Ethnic and Racial Studies*, 22: 4 (1999), pp. 629–52.

24 R. Hilberg, *The Politics of Memory: The Journey of a Holocaust Historian* (Chicago: Ivan R. Dee, 1996).

25 M. Weber, *The Protestant Ethic and the Spirit of Capitalism* (New York, Scribner, 1958), p. 182.

26 M. Peillon, 'Strangers in our Midst', in E. Slater and M. Peillon (eds), *Memories of the Present: A Sociological Chronicle of Ireland, 1997–1998* (Dublin: Institute of Public Administration, 2000), p. 111.

27 J. Solomos and L. Back, *Racism and Society* (London: Macmillan, 1996), p. 65.

28 R. Miles, 'Racialisation', *Dictionary of Race and Ethnic Studies* (London: Routledge, 1996), p. 307.

29 S. Hall, 'Racism and Reaction', in Commission for Racial Equality (ed.), *Five Views of Multi-racial Britain* (London: Commission for Racial Equality, 1978).

30 M. Barker, *The New Racism* (London: Junction Books, 1981).

31 S. Cornell and P. Hartmann, *Ethnicity and Race: Making Identities in a Changing World* (Thousand Oaks, CA: Pine Forge Press, 1998), p. 17.

32 United Nations Educational Scientific and Cultural Organisation (UNESCO), General Conference, 27 November 1978, Declaration on Race and Racial Prejudice, Article 2.

33 The McPherson report defined institutional racism in the following terms:
   'The collective failure of an organisation to provide an appropriate and
   professional service to people because of their colour, culture or ethnic
   origin. It can be seen in processes, attitudes and behaviour which amount to
   discrimination through unwitting prejudice, ignorance thoughtlessness and
   racist stereotyping which disadvantage ethnic minority people.' W. McPherson, *The Stephen Lawrence Inquiry: Report of an Inquiry by Sir William
   McPherson of Cluny* (London: Stationery Office, 1999).
34 J. Stapleton and B. Fanning, 'Refugee and Asylum-seeking Children: a
   Rights-based Perspective', in Barnardo's (ed.), *Diversity in Early Childhood*
   (Dublin: Barnardo's, 2002), p. 26.
35 Senator Henry, *Seanad Eireann,* 17 December 2003.
36 B. Fanning, 'Asylum-seeker and Migrant Children in Ireland: Racism, Institutional Neglect And Social Work', in D. Hayes and B. Humphries (eds), *Social
   Work and Immigration* (Manchester: Jessica Kingsley, 2004), pp. 210–16.
37 Department of Health and Children (2002), *National Standards for Children's
   Residential Centres* (Dublin: Official Publications), p. 2.
38 P. Conroy and F. Fitzgerald, *Separated Children Seeking Asylum Research
   Study 2004: Health and Educational Needs*, Executive Summary (Dublin:
   Eastern Health Print), p. 9.
39 *Irish Times,* 'Asylum-seeking Children exploited, warns HSE: Separated
   Children taken back into Care after Abuses', 21 November 2005.
40 The UN Convention on the Rights of the Child (1989) reaffirmed and
   expanded upon the rights outlined in previous Conventions. Article 2 of the
   Convention states that all children should be entitled to basic rights without
   discrimination. Article 3(1) states that the best interests of children should be
   a primary consideration in all actions concerning children (whether undertaken by public or private social welfare institutions, courts of law, administrative authorities or legislative bodies). Other articles specify a right to
   the highest attainable standard of health and to have access to health and
   medical services (Article 24), a right to benefit from social security (Article
   26), a right to an adequate standard of living with a duty on the state to assist
   parents, where necessary, in fulfilling this right (Article 27), a right to education and access to appropriate secondary education (Article 28.1) and a right
   to participate in leisure, recreational and cultural activities (Article 31). The
   Convention applies to all children within the jurisdiction of the state.
41 B. Fanning, A. Veale and D. O'Connor, *Beyond the Pale: Asylum Seeker
   Children and Social Exclusion* (Dublin: Irish Refugee Council, 2001).
42 P. Kennedy and J. Murphy-Lawless, *The Maternity Needs of Refugee
   and Asylum-seeking Women* (Dublin: Applied Social Science Research
   Programme, University College Dublin, 2002).
43 S. Manandhar, S. Friel, M. Share, F. Hardy and O. Walsh, *Food, Nutrition and
   Poverty amongst Asylum Seekers in North West Ireland* (Dublin: Combat
   Poverty Agency, 2004).
44 Z. Bauman, *Modernity and Ambivalence* (Cambridge: Polity, 1991), cited
   in A. Christie, 'Responses of the Social Work Profession to Unaccompanied

Children seeking Asylum in the Republic of Ireland', *European Journal of Social Work*, 5: 2 (2002), pp. 187–98.

45 National Children's Strategy (2001), *Our Children: Their Lives* (Dublin: Official Publications), p. 10.

46 At the book launch of A. Cleary, M. Nic Ghiolla Phadraig and S. Quin, *Understanding Children* I–II (Dublin: Oak Tree Press, 2001).

47 T. Kostakopoulou, *Citizenship, Identity and Immigration in the European Union* (Manchester: Manchester University Press, 2001), pp. 148–9.

48 *Laurentiu v. Minister of Justice*, Supreme Court, 1999. See *Irish Times*, 21 May 1999.

49 Ibid.

50 National Archives of Ireland, Dublin (NAI), Department of An Taoiseach (DT), 16 November 1938.

51 Ibid.

52 T. W. T. Dillon, 'The Refugee Problem', *Studies*, 28: 111 (1939), pp. 402–14.

53 D. Keogh, *Jews in Twentieth-Century Ireland* (Cork: Cork University Press, 1998), p. 143.

54 National Archives, NAI, DT, S11007, 23 February 1953.

55 The Jewish Fianna Fail TD Robert Briscoe regarded Berry as a friend. Ben Briscoe in response to a paper that I presented on Ireland's response to the Holocaust, B. Fanning, 'Ireland's response to the Holocaust', *Irish–Israel Friendship League*, 12 February 2003.

56 Fanning, *Racism and Social Change*, pp. 96–7.

57 E. Ward, '"A big show-off to show what we could do": Ireland and the Hungarian Refugee Crisis of 1956', *Irish Studies in International Affairs*, 8 (1996), pp. 131–41.

58 Fanning, *Racism and Social Change*, pp. 88–94.

59 Ibid., p. 104.

60 The Fajujonus, a Moroccan and Nigerian married couple with two Irish-born children, had successfully contested a deportation order under the Aliens Order (1946) on the basis that their children were Irish citizens. The Fajujonus argued successfully that their children, as Irish citizens, had a right to family life, in accordance with the rights of the child under the Irish constitution. Article 40 of the Irish constitution sets out the personal rights of citizens. Article 41 sets out the rights of the family (notably 41.1.1, 'The state recognises the family as the natural primary and fundamental unit group of society, and as a moral institution possessing inalienable ... rights, antecedent and superior to all positive law'). Article 42 refers to the rights (and duties) of parents to provide for the religious and moral, intellectual, physical and social education of their children.

61 For example, some 4,071 people were granted 'leave to remain' in 2002. Some 75% of these (3,123) had applied for asylum.

62 D. O'Connell and C. Smith, 'Citizenship and the Irish Constitution', in U. Fraser and C. Harvey (eds), *Sanctuary in Ireland: Perspectives on Asylum Law and Policy* (Dublin: Institute of Public Administration, 2003), p. 265.

63 The Supreme Court ruling in *Lobe* v. *Minister of Justice, Equality and Law Reform* (2003) effectively limited the residence rights of the Irish-born children entitled to citizenship whose parents are neither Irish or EU country citizens.

64 For example, the Social Welfare (Consolidation) Act 1993 set out a statutory right to supplementary welfare allowance (SWA) that extends beyond citizenship. Section 171 of the Act states that 'Subject to this Act, every person in the state whose means are insufficient to meet his needs and the needs of every child dependant of his shall be entitled to SWA.'

65 47,549 work permits were issued in 2003. Of these 9,723 were issued to migrants from the Baltic states and 6,883 were issued to persons from other EU accession states. E. Quinn and G. Hughes, *Policy Analysis Report on Asylum and Migration: Ireland, 2003 to mid-2004* (Dublin: Economic and Social Research Unit, 2004), p. 6.

66 B. Fanning and F. Mutwarasibo, 'Nationals/non-nationals: Immigration, Citizenship and Politics in the Republic of Ireland', *Ethnic and Racial Studies*, 30:3 (May 2007).

3

Children, citizenship and consitutional change

Siobhán Mullally

How we distribute membership in our human communities has been described as 'the most important good'.[1] Citizenship laws provide us with models of membership. They define the terms on which we belong – or not – to political communities, allocating both the benefits of membership and the brutalities of exclusion. Debates on the meaning and scope of citizenship have been at the heart of political discussions in Europe and elsewhere for many decades. In Ireland, it is only in recent years, however, that we have begun to debate the meaning of citizenship and the criteria for membership in the nation-state. In June 2004, a referendum on citizenship was held in Ireland. The referendum and subsequent constitutional amendment led to restrictions being imposed on the constitutionally protected right to citizenship by birth.[2] It was the second referendum on citizenship to be held in Ireland in recent years. In 1998, following the Belfast Agreement[3] and multi-party negotiations in Northern Ireland, a new Article 2 was inserted into the Irish Constitution affirming the entitlement of anyone born within the 'island of Ireland' to Irish citizenship.[4] A new Article 3 was also inserted into the Constitution, recognising the 'diversity of identities and traditions on the island of Ireland'.[5] This moment of inclusion, however, was short-lived. The Belfast Agreement and subsequent constitutional changes coincided with increasing immigration in Ireland, both North and South. This coincidence was described by the Irish Supreme Court as an 'accident of history'.[6] It is an 'accident' that has led to significant changes in the concept of citizenship and in the legal protections afforded to migrant families within the State.

The citizenship referendum followed a period of heated debate on the meaning of citizenship and the terms on which migrant families would be allowed to remain in Ireland. In 1989, the Supreme Court ruled in the *Fajujonu* case that Irish citizen children had the right to the 'company, care and parentage' of their parents within a family unit.[7] Subject to the exigencies of the common good, this right could be exercised within the State, with parents asserting a choice of residence on behalf of their children. Following on from the *Fajujonu* judgement, non-national parents were routinely granted the right to remain in Ireland on the basis of the children's right to the 'company, care and parentage' of their parents. This practice was to change in early 2003. In January 2003, the Supreme Court ruled in the *L.* and *O.* cases that the automatic right of residence granted to the parents of Irish-born children, regardless of the legal status of the parents, could no longer be sustained.[8] The common good required that restrictions be imposed on citizen children's right to family life and to their right to the 'company, care and parentage' of their parents within the State. At the time of the Supreme Court judgement, more than 11,500 applications for residence from parents with Irish citizen children were pending. The judgement provoked widespread confusion and fear amongst migrant families. Predictions that the Supreme Court's judgement would stem the flow of inward migration to the State, however, failed to materialise. The government decided, therefore, to take further action. In June 2004, a referendum was held to amend the Constitution so as to restrict the entitlement to citizenship for children born to non-national parents. By a majority of almost four to one, the electorate voted to amend the Constitution, removing the right to citizenship from future generations of Irish-born children who could not demonstrate generations of belonging to the State.

The debate on the meaning and limits of citizenship in Ireland raised questions of fundamental rights not only under Irish constitutional law but also under the European Convention on Human Rights (ECHR), incorporated into Irish law in 2003.[9] Before changes were introduced into the Irish law of citizenship, the European Court of Justice was also to add its voice to the debate. The judgement of the European Court of Justice in *Chen* v. *Secretary of State for the Home Department*[10] added a further twist, highlighting the protections afforded to EU citizens and the family unit under EU law. These protections, as we shall see, may ultimately prove stronger than those afforded by the ECHR.

Ireland is not the only State that has grappled in recent times with the right to citizenship by birth and the entitlements to family life that come with such a claim. In both the United Kingdom and Australia the *jus soli* principle has been significantly restricted. In the US, Canada and elsewhere, while the *jus soli* principle continues to apply, citizen children born to undocumented migrant parents are subject to *de facto* deportation, their right to membership of the nation-state 'postponed' because of the legal status of their parents.[11] In challenges to deportation proceedings involving such children, the perspective of the child as a bearer of rights is marginalised, with disputes turning largely on the balancing of

States' interests in immigration control against the residence claims made by migrant parents.[12] This pattern is reflected in recent legal developments in Ireland. Despite the 'strongly entrenched' constitutional provisions on the family[13] and repeated affirmations of the 'best interests of the child',[14] the Irish courts and the electorate have deferred to the State's inherent right to control and limit immigration.

Citizenship, family life and the 'anchor' child[15]

As many commentators have noted, the principles of *jus soli* and *jus sanguinus* are anachronistic in the context of liberal democratic States which have, in other areas of the law, moved away from ascribing status on the basis of criteria such as blood and soil.[16] In the context of citizenship laws, however, most States continue to make a formal legal connection between entitlement to membership in a political community and circumstances at birth. In Irish law, the principles of both *jus soli* and *jus sanguinis* are applied in determining entitlement to citizenship.[17] The principle of *jus soli* was given constitutional recognition in 1998 following multi-party negotiations and a peace agreement in Northern Ireland. This constitutional recognition reflected the lingering significance of territoriality to the process of nation-building. The 1937 Constitution of Ireland, *Bunreacht na hÉireann*, had left open the question of how citizenship was to be allocated, providing only that citizenship status would be determined in accordance with law.[18] It was presumed that the *jus soli* principle of citizenship by birth would continue to apply as part of the inherited body of common law. In 1956, the Irish Nationality and Citizenship Act was passed, providing for citizenship by birth or descent. The primary concern within the legislature was to ensure that all those born in the island of Ireland would be entitled to citizenship. Citizenship laws could transcend the partition of the island into North and South. The still nascent project of nation-building required an open and inclusive concept of citizenship. Emigration and depopulation were threats to the project of nation-building and so the *jus sanguinis* principle, allowing citizenship by descent, was also provided for. This inclusive concept of citizenship was not all-embracing, however. From the beginning, debates on the meaning and significance of citizenship in Ireland were deeply racialised. Speaking on the passage of the Irish Nationality and Citizenship Act in 1956, Deputy Esmonde noted that while the entitlement to citizenship by birth was desirable, 'in one sense', such an entitlement also carried with it a 'certain amount of danger'. There were, he noted, 'a great number of people [in the world] who would be undesirable to us in Ireland'. Esmonde's comments reflect an assumed commonality within the Irish nation and a denial of the humanity of the stranger. This assumption and denial was to continue to surface in debates on immigration and citizenship in Ireland.

Historically a land of emigration, debates on immigration and citizenship did not become central to political debate until recent years. Despite the absence of debate, however, a steady body of case law was developing, exploring the rights and obligations of non-nationals living within the State. Ireland's jurisprudence on fundamental rights is steeped in the traditions of natural law. Steeped as they were in the jurisprudence of natural law, one would have expected that the legal notion of citizenship would not have greatly influenced the Irish courts' determinations on the rights of non-nationals within the State. In the case of *Northants Co. Council v. ABF*,[19] a case involving an adoption order, Hamilton J based his judgement on natural law theory, stating:

> The natural law is of universal application and applies to all human persons, be they citizens of the State or not, and it would be inconceivable that the father of the infant child would not be entitled to rely on the recognition of the family contained in Article 41.[20]

In many cases, however, a concern to protect the State's 'inherent right' to control immigration trumped the claims to fundamental rights made by non-nationals. This concern has been particularly evident in debates surrounding the rights of residence claimed by undocumented migrants with Irish citizen children. While the children acquired citizenship by birth, the precise nature of their birthright and the terms on which they belonged to the Irish nation was much disputed. The case of *Osheku v. Ireland*[21] was one of the earliest to deal with the right to family life in the context of immigration decisions. Gannon J, speaking for the High Court, concluded that the fundamental rights protected by the Constitution were not absolute. In an oft-quoted statement, he defended a quintessentially State-centred view on the limits and scope of fundamental rights. There were, he said, 'fundamental rights of the State itself as well as fundamental rights of the individual citizens, and the protection of the former may involve restrictions in circumstances of necessity on the latter'.[22] In a statement that reflects the exclusionary impulse behind the nation-state, he noted that the 1935 Aliens Act reflected the philosophy of the nation-state: 'Its unspoken major premise is that aliens have, in general, no right to be on the national territory.'[23] As we shall see, it is this exclusionary impulse that has guided, or misguided, legislative and judicial responses to the claims made by migrant families in Ireland.

The position of children born in Ireland with non-national parents was the subject of greatest debate in 1990 decision of the Supreme Court, *Fajujonu v. Minister for Justice*.[24] The *Fajujonu* case involved a husband

and wife, of Nigerian and Moroccan nationality respectively. The couple were living in Ireland, without documentation. Their presence in Ireland had come to the attention of the Minister for Justice when a local community group sought a work permit on behalf of Mr Fajujonu. Mr Fajujonu was asked to make arrangements to leave the State. It was this request, coupled with the fear that a deportation order would follow, that ultimately gave rise to the proceedings before the Supreme Court. When the matter finally came before the Supreme Court, Mr and Mrs Fajujonu had been resident in the State for more than eight years. The third named plaintiff, their eldest daughter, Miriam Fajujonu, was born in Ireland and a citizen by birth. The Fajujonus had two further Irish citizen children. In the Supreme Court, their challenge centred on the manner in which ministerial discretion was exercised and on the need to take into account the two most salient features of the Fajujonus' case: (1) the length of time during which the parents had been resident within the State and (2) the fact that the children were Irish citizens. The constitutional rights of their family unit, they argued, could be infringed only for 'very compelling reasons'.

Finlay CJ, speaking for the majority of the Supreme Court, concluded that a citizen child had a constitutional right to the 'company, care and parentage of their parents within a family unit'. Subject to the 'exigencies of the common good', this was a right, he held, which could be exercised within the State. Particular emphasis was placed on the Fajujonus' residence for 'an appreciable time' within the State. Finlay CJ did not deny that the Minister could deport a family with citizen children, if an interference with a constitutional right was necessary in the interests of the common good. Any such interference, however, would be possible, he concluded, only after 'due and proper consideration' and only where a 'grave and substantive reason' associated with the common good could be established. Walsh J, concurring with the majority judgement, placed greater emphasis on the rights of the family as a constitutionally protected unit and the need to protect the integrity of the family. The children, he said, were of tender age, requiring the society of their parents. In the particular circumstances of this case, to move to expel the parents would be inconsistent with the constitutionally protected rights of the family.[25]

The findings of the Supreme Court and, in particular, the judgement of Walsh J reflect the cardinal value of citizenship for a child: 'the ability to enjoy the company, care and parentage of their parents within a family unit within the State'.[26] Following on from this judgement, applications for residence from undocumented migrant parents were routinely granted. However, over the next decade, the migration context in Ireland was to change drastically. The number of non-national parents claiming residence on the basis of Irish citizen children increased from approximately 1,500 in 1999 to over 6,000 in 2001.[27] At the beginning of 2003, more than 11,500 applications for residence from undocumented migrant parents were pending with the Ministry. As the number of families claiming residence rights increased, political pressure to deny these claims grew. Bowing to this pressure, the Minister for Justice Equality and Law Reform began to refuse or stay applications in late 2002, leading finally to the Supreme Court judgement in the *L.* and *O.* cases in January 2003.[28] By this time, the right to citizenship by birth had been enshrined as a constitutional right, following the *Belfast Agreement* and the Nineteenth Amendment to the Constitution Act 1998.

The *L.* and *O.* cases involved two families of Czech Roma and Nigerian origin, each with Irish citizen children. Deportation proceedings were commenced against *L.* and *O.* following the failure of their asylum applications. Seeking a judicial review of the deportation orders, *L.* and *O.* both asserted the right to exercise a choice of residence on behalf of their citizen children, and on behalf of their children claimed the right to the company, care and parentage of their parents within the State. The significance of the questions raised in the case was not lost on the Court, as each of the seven-member bench delivered separate and lengthy opinions. The majority of the Supreme Court distinguished the *Fajujonu* case on the basis of the length of time the parents had lived within the State and the changing context of immigration in Ireland since then. Using the terms of Finlay CJ's judgement in *Fajujonu*, the majority of the Supreme Court concluded that neither family had been within the State for 'an appreciable time', such as to give rise to a right to residence. The denial of the parents' claims to residence, the Court concluded, did not breach any constitutionally protected rights of the citizen children or the family unit. Keane CJ distinguished the nature of citizenship claims enjoyed by children and adults. While an adult citizen had an automatic right to reside in the State, he said, the position of minors was 'significantly different'.[29] The right to reside within the State could not vest in a minor until she or he was capable of exercising such a right. And, while the parents could assert a choice of residence on behalf of their citizen children, any claims made by the parents were subject to the exigencies of the common good. The requirements of the common good are defined by the Court solely with reference to the State's interest in controlling immigration and in maintaining the 'integrity of the asylum system', specifically the Dublin Convention (Dublin 1). Both *L.* and *O.* had originally submitted asylum applications in the UK prior to coming to Ireland. The UK had accepted responsibility for the determination of their asylum claims. As the dissenting judgements noted, however, the Dublin Convention provides a mechanism for allocating responsibility for asylum claims. It does not, however, preclude a State from accepting an asylum claim even though an applicant has previously submitted a claim elsewhere within the EU.

The *L.* and *O.* cases also raised questions concerning the constitutional commitment to protecting the 'inalienable and imprescriptible' rights of the family. Article 41 of the Constitution assigns the family an exceptionally important status and role in the 'welfare of the Nation and the State'. The rights of the family are described in the constitutional text as being 'antecedent and superior' to all positive law, including, this would suggest, to immigration and asylum law. Ireland's commitment to the protection of the family unit has frequently been invoked as a marker of Ireland's distinct national identity.[30] In *McGee* v. *Attorney General,* Walsh J noted that the family, as the 'natural primary and fundamental unit group of society', had rights that the State could not control.[31] In the *L.* and *O.* cases, however, the Court concluded the State's right to control immigration and to safeguard the integrity of the asylum and immigration systems took priority over any claims asserted by undocumented migrant family units. Only certain kinds of families, it would seem, are deserving of the constitutional protection afforded by the very entrenched provisions on family life.

The findings of the Supreme Court in the *L.* and *O.* cases stand in marked contrast to the Court's deference to the family unit in previous cases. Just one year earlier, in the *N.W.H.B.* case, Keane CJ held that the family, because it derives from the 'natural order', was endowed with an authority that the Constitution itself recognised as being superior even to the authority of the State. He went on to argue that the Constitution outlawed any attempt by the State to usurp 'the exclusive and privileged role of the family in the social order'.[32] In the same case, Murphy J noted that the express terms of the Constitution relegated the State to a subordinate and subsidiary role.[33] The circumstances that could justify intervention by the State in the family unit, he said, must be exceptional indeed. Such exceptions have been found to arise where the best interests of the child required intervention. In the *L.* and *O.* cases, however, this line of reasoning was turned on its head, with the State's interest in immigration control invoked to challenge the exercise of parental authority and to undermine the child's best interests.

The Court's judgement suggests the possibility of a *de facto* postponement of citizenship for many children. Postponing the right to residence significantly impacts on the quality of a child's citizenship right, denying the child's constitutionally protected right to be 'part of the Irish nation' and to share in the nation's 'cultural identity and heritage'.[34] As both Fennelly J and McGuinness J noted in their dissenting judgements, a child is either an Irish citizen or not. Once the right to citizenship by birth is recognised, the quality of a child's right as a citizen should not be affected by the 'fortuity' or otherwise of her or his birth to undocumented migrant parents.[35] The findings set out in the majority judgement are deeply problematic, not only in terms of the consequences for the many families affected by the judgement but also in terms of the reasoning applied by the Court. The Court had been careful to emphasise that although the routine practice of granting residence could no longer be sustained, each case would need to be considered on its merits. How the merits of individual cases were to be determined, however, was left unclear. In July 2003, the government announced that applications for residence from non-national parents with Irish citizen child would, henceforth, be considered only in the context of deportation proceedings.[36] Applications for residence would no longer be accepted and those pending with the Minister of Justice Equality and Law Reform would not be processed. More than 11,500 migrant parents were now left in a legal limbo, uncertain as to their status within the State or as to their future prospects for residence. Despite the Supreme Court judgement and change in practice, however, migrant women and men continued to travel to Ireland and to give birth to their children within the State. Predictions that the Supreme Court's judgement would stem the flow of inward migration to the State failed to materialise. The government decided to take further action, and in April 2004 the government announced its intention to hold a referendum on a proposed constitutional amendment which would restrict the right to citizenship by birth where a child was born within the State to non-Irish nationals.

The Twenty-seventh Amendment of the Constitution Bill 2004 proposed that a new section be added to Article 9 of the Constitution to read as follows:

> 9.2.1 Notwithstanding any other provision of this Constitution, a person born in the island of Ireland, which includes its islands and its seas, who does not have, at the time of his or her birth, at least one parent who is an Irish citizen or entitled to be an Irish citizen is not entitled to Irish citizenship or nationality, unless otherwise provided for by law.

The proposal provoked widespread controversy. To being with, the constitutional provision recognising birthright citizenship had been inserted into the Irish Constitution following the peace agreement in 1998 and multi-party consultations involving all political parties in Northern Ireland. The Irish government was now unilaterally proposing to undo this constitutional change. In response to criticisms from political parties in Northern Ireland and the Joint Committee of the Human Rights Commissions,[37] the British and Irish governments issued an interpretive declaration, stating that the 1998 Belfast Agreement (including the British–Irish and Multi-party agreements) was not intended to extend birthright citizenship to the children of undocumented migrants. The potential of citizenship clauses both to include and to exclude was evident in the governments' joint declaration. Assurances were given that exceptions would be made for children born 'on the island of Ireland' to British national parents. The concern with territoriality and nation-building remained, but the nation was defined in exclusive terms.

The speed with which such fundamental changes were to be introduced also attracted criticism. As the Irish Human Rights Commission pointed out, any proposal for significant legal change, particularly a change in the fundamental law of the State, should be premised on a full consideration of the consequences of such a change.[38] The onus to demonstrate that pressing social need and the proportionate and non-discriminatory nature of the proposed response lay with the government but had not, in its view, been discharged. Many questions concerning the nature of citizenship and the rights attaching to citizenship were not addressed by the government's proposal or even discussed. The Constitution Review Group and many commentators have noted that the constitutional protections afforded to non-citizens remain shrouded in uncertainty and confusion.[39] Against this background, the consequences, in terms of rights protection, of removing one category of children from entitlement to citizenship was unclear. It was also pointed out that the proposed changes were discriminatory, imposing restrictions on one category of citizens who were deemed to have no substantial historical or familial connection to Ireland while failing to address the citizenship entitlements of other equivalent groups, including those who acquired citizenship by descent. If the State's primary concern was immigration control, entitlement to citizenship by descent opened up citizenship status to much greater numbers than did the application of the *jus soli* principle.

The uncertainty concerning the constitutional protections afforded to non-citizens and non-citizen children, in particular, is compounded in Ireland by the failure to incorporate international human rights treaties and the strict dualist approach adopted with regard to Ireland's international human rights obligations and to norms of customary international law.[40] Both the UN Convention on the Rights of the Child and the International Covenant on Civil and Political Rights impose obligations on the State that were potentially undermined by the government's proposed referendum. The obligation to be guided by the 'best interests of the child' is one of the core principles of the CRC and the obligation not to discriminate against a child on the basis of his or her nationality, birth or social origin is enshrined in many human rights treaties, including the Convention on the Rights of the Child and the International Covenant on Civil and Political Rights. In the government's proposal, however, the perspective of the child was strikingly absent. Rather the proposal reflected an overriding concern with parental status and immigration control. The failure to incorporate many human rights treaties into domestic law lessens the possibility of raising legal arguments in deportation or other proceedings on the basis of such treaties.

Despite the concerns expressed, however, the constitutional referendum was held on 12 June 2004. By a majority of almost four to one, the electorate voted to amend the Constitution, removing the right to citizenship from future generations of Irish-born children who could not demonstrate generations of belonging to the State. The Irish Nationality and Citizenship (Amendment) Act 2004, enacted just six months later, provides that children born to non-nationals will acquire citizenship by birth only if one parent has been lawfully resident within the State for a period of three years or more.[41] The annotated Bill refers to this period as being the same as the residence period for naturalisation of non-national spouses who are married to Irish citizens. Refugees or any other person with an unrestricted right of residence are exempt from the three-year residence requirement.[42] However, periods of time spent within the asylum process or on student visas will not be counted and the position of persons with 'temporary leave to remain' on humanitarian or other grounds, remains unclear. No provision is made to regularise the status of children born to undocumented migrant parents who remain in the State for a substantial period of time. Neither is any provision made to regularise the position of non-national parents with children born after the Supreme Court judgement in the *L.* and *O.* cases.

The position of migrant families with citizen children born prior to the commencement of the 2004 Act was finally addressed in January 2005, when the government announced the introduction of a new set of procedures to assess residence applications.[43] Although the move to end the uncertainty surrounding the legal status of many immigrant families has been welcomed, the process has attracted criticism and is likely to be the subject of legal challenge. Of particular concern is the requirement for applicants to sign a declaration on family reunification, stating that they are aware that the granting of permission to remain in the State 'does not in any way give rise to any legitimate expectation' that family members living abroad will be given permission to remain in the State.[44] The declaration raises, yet again, the question of whether and how citizenship status ensures protection of the right to family life, both under the Irish Constitution and under the ECHR. To date, there is little to suggest that the 'best interests of the child' will be the primary concern in any decision on residence. Announcing the introduction of the new proposals, the Minister for Justice Equality and Law Reform, Michael McDowell, stated that residence would be granted only to those parents who could show that they had 'not been involved in criminal activity' and were 'willing to commit themselves to becoming economically viable'.[45] As yet it is unclear how a criminal record that arose in an applicant's country of origin will be considered or whether this reference will be limited to non-political crimes. The requirement of 'economic viability' raises questions as to whether a parent who is unable to be economically self-sufficient will be denied residence. This requirement echoes the distinctions made recently by the ECJ in the *Chen* case, where the Court was asked to adjudicate on the meaning and scope of EU citizenship and the right to family life of an EU citizen child.[46]

Citizenship, family life and European human rights law

Prior to the citizenship referendum, a further legal twist was added to the debate, this time by EU law. Mrs Chen, a Chinese national and mother of a Chinese national child, went to Northern Ireland to give birth to her second child, Catherine. Catherine acquired Irish citizenship by virtue of being born on the island of Ireland. Mrs Chen and her daughter, Catherine, subsequently moved to Cardiff, Wales, and applied for a long-term residence permit. Their application was refused. On appeal, the immigration appellate authority referred the case to the ECJ for a ruling as to whether Community law conferred a right of residence in the UK upon Catherine and her mother. Advocate General Tizzano, issuing his opinion on 18 May 2004, concluded that a young child who is a national of a Member State has a right to reside in another Member State so long as he or she has sickness insurance and sufficient resources not to become 'an unreasonable burden' on the public finances of the host Member State.[47] In addition, he concluded that to deny Mrs Chen's right to residence in the UK would render Catherine's right of residence totally ineffective. The Advocate General's opinion was upheld by the ECJ in its ruling on 19 October 2004. The Court dismissed the United Kingdom's argument that Mrs Chen had improperly exploited Community law by deciding to give birth in Northern Ireland so as to secure Irish and consequently EU citizenship for her daughter. The Court rejected the United Kingdom's submission, concluding that the United Kingdom was attempting to impose additional conditions on the acquisition of rights arising from the grant of nationality by another Member State.[48]

The Court's judgement reflects one of the fundamental inequalities in Community law. Catherine and her mother, if not independently wealthy, could not have availed themselves of the freedoms of Community law under either Article 18 EC or Directive 90/364. Catherine's status as a citizen of the Union could not ensure 'the cardinal value of citizenship',[49] the right to reside in the country of which one is a national. That right was subject to having sufficient independent resources not to become 'an unreasonable burden' on the host State. Despite these limits, however, the *Chen* judgement does go some way towards recognising the networks of relationships into which a child is born and his or her dependence on those relationships for the effective vindication of Community rights. This relational understanding of the EU citizen recognises, albeit with many limitations, a citizen child's right to family life. In contrast, the Irish Supreme Court, in the *L.* and *O.* cases, was willing effectively to deny the children's right to residence within the State by deporting their carers and subjecting the children to *de facto* deportation. Despite the well entrenched family life and fundamental rights provisions in the Irish Constitution, Community law, with its relatively underdeveloped rights jurisprudence, ultimately granted the citizen child greater protection than did Irish constitutional law. In response to the *Chen* case, the Irish government argued that its decision to hold a referendum on citizenship was vindicated by the judgement. Comity with other EU Member States required the government to take action to restrict the acquisition of Irish nationality and hence of the status of EU citizen. No such steps were taken, however, to impose restrictions on the much larger category of persons entitled to acquire citizenship by descent under Ireland's citizenship laws and the operation of the *jus sanguinus* principle.

The extent to which the *Chen* judgement can be relied on by other Irish citizen children with third-country national parents remains unclear. The difficulty lies in the peculiar Community law requirement that a case must involve a transborder element before the its protections are triggered. EC law does not apply to situations that are internal to a Member State. With the emergence of the concept of EU citizenship, it was hoped that this requirement would no longer persist, resulting as it does in a kind of reverse discrimination against those who remain within the borders of one Member State. The case of *Mary Carpenter* v. *Secretary of State for the Home Department*[50] has expanded the protection afforded to family unity by Community law by recognising a transborder element in a case that might have been argued to be internal to the Member State. The ECJ concluded that the deportation of Mrs Carpenter (a national of the Philippines) would be detrimental to the Carpenters' family life and to the conditions under which Mr Carpenter (a British national) exercised a fundamental freedom – the freedom to travel to other Member States and to provide advertising services. Mrs Carpenter acted as a mother to Mr Carpenter's two children from a previous marriage. Mrs Carpenter had applied for a residence permit but was refused. By denying Mrs Carpenter's application for residence the United Kingdom would prevent him from exercising a fundamental freedom protected by Community law and would violate the fundamental right to family unity protected as a general principle of EC law. The Carpenter case has attracted widespread commentary and both negative and positive critiques. It expands the protection afforded by Community law and limits the discretion of Member States, exposing also the arbitrariness of the lingering requirement of a 'transborder' element against a background of attempts to establish a European polity. The Carpenter case is also significant from an ECHR perspective. In its analysis under Article 8 of the ECHR, the Court concluded the proposed deportation would constitute an interference in the Carpenters' right to family life. The fact that the family's residence in the United Kingdom was not based on a legal entitlement was not decisive to the question of what constituted an unreasonable interference in family life. Here, we see that family life trumps the State's interest in immigration control, a finding that stands in marked contrast to Irish Supreme Court's conclusions in the *L.* and *O.* cases. The Citizenship[51] and Family Reunification Directives[52] add little to the existing protections afforded by Community law or by the ECHR. Indeed, in the case of the Family Reunification Directive, these protections are potentially undermined, with Member States permitted to opt out and restrict the scope of family reunification rights on many dubious grounds. Earlier drafts of the Citizenship Directive had removed the necessity of the transborder element to trigger the protections of Community law. In the final draft, however, no changes are made, suggesting the continuing relevance of transborder movement for many third country and EU nationals.

The ECHR, in particular Article 8, has also played a significant role in immigration debates in Contracting States. When the *L.* and *O.* cases came before the Irish Supreme Court, Ireland had not yet incorporated the ECHR into domestic law.[53] The Supreme Court, none the less, examined the jurisprudence arising under the Convention, the appellants having invoked the protections afforded by Article 8 to support their claim to family unity and to residence within the State. As Fennelly J noted, however, the case law of the ECHR 'does not provide an easy or automatic answer to any particular case of suggested violation of Article 8 ECHR'.[54] To date, the jurisprudence of the European Court of Human Rights offers only limited protection to migrant families. In *Poku* v. *UK*[55] the European Commission noted that factors such as immigration control and considerations of public order could justify exclusions or deportations that might otherwise amount to denials of the right to family life. In *Yousef* v. *UK*[56] the Commission again found against the applicant, despite evidence submitted on his behalf demonstrating a 'strong and affectionate bond between the father and the child'.[57] The Commission's findings display a strong moralistic tone and a disapproval of Yousef's behaviour while in the UK: he was unemployed, had a minor criminal conviction, and had failed to maintain consistent contact with his son because of his 'relationship with a second British woman'.[58] Missing from the Commission's findings is a recognition of the damaging impact that deportation proceedings would have on Yousef's son. In *Berrehab* v. *the Netherlands*[59] the Court found the Netherlands to be in violation of the applicant's right to respect for his family life. Berrehab had lost his right to residence in the Netherlands on the breakdown of his marriage to a Dutch citizen. In finding in his favour, the Court noted that he had been living and working in the Netherlands continuously for six years and had maintained strong links with his Dutch citizen child, including through contributions to her maintenance and education. The Court's reasoning is marked more by concern to reward Berrehab's good behaviour than to ensure protection of the child's best interests. A similar concern can be seen in the more recent case of *Ciliz* v. *the Netherlands*,[60] where a Turkish national was denied the opportunity to develop an ongoing relationship with his Dutch son because of the initiation of deportation proceedings against him. Finding that the State had both a positive obligation to ensure that family life can continue between parents and children and a negative obligation to refrain from measures that might cause family ties to rupture, the Court held that the Netherlands had interfered with Ciliz's right to family life and were in violation of their duties under Article 8. Again, however, more attention was paid to the behaviour of the parent than to the particular interests and needs of Ciliz's son. In *Al-Nashif* v. *Bulgaria*[61] the perspective of the children involved is again absent from the Court's judgement. In this case, although the Court found that the deportation proceedings against Al-Nashif constituted an arbitrary interference with his right to family life, there is little discussion in the case of the impact of the State's actions on the citizen children involved.

In *Mahmood* v. *Secretary of State for the Home Department*,[62] a case that was heavily relied on by the Irish Supreme Court, Lord Phillips MR concluded that removal or exclusion of one family member from a Contracting State would not necessarily infringe Article 8 provided that there were 'no insurmountable obstacles' to the family living together in the country of origin of the excluded family member.[63] The ordinary hardship endured in any deportation or expulsion proceedings was not enough to engage the protection of Article 8. Missing from Lord Phillips's findings is any recognition of the need to apply a child-centred perspective in assessing the degree of hardship endured in deportation proceedings. The disputes arising are characterised primarily as involving conflicting claims between undocumented migrant parents and the Contracting State. The recognition of the child as a bearer of rights in such cases would, of course, transform the terms of the debate. As yet, this has not happened. In *Sen* v. *the Netherlands*,[64] however, we see a potentially significant shift in the jurisprudence and practice of the European Court, from the 'only way' test applied in *Ahmüt*[65] and *Gül*,[66] to a 'most suitable way' test. The *Sen* case arose from a refusal by the Netherlands to grant admission to the twelve-year-old child of Turkish parents, both of whom were legally resident in the Netherlands. The Court explored the positive obligations on a Contracting State in relation to family reunification cases and refused to draw negative inferences from the parents' decision to leave their child behind in Turkey. The issue to be decided was, what is the most suitable way (*le moyen le plus adéquat*), for the family members to continue their life together. The Court in *Sen* followed the position adopted by Judge Marten in his dissenting opinion in *Ahmut,* that is, that a more generous approach should be adopted in family reunification cases. As such, the shift in the Court's approach may not have been of assistance to *L.* and *O.,* even if it were considered by the Irish courts. The application of the 'most suitable way' test is likely to be of relevance, however, in any challenges to the procedures introduced to allow non-national parents of Irish citizen children to apply for residence and, in particular, to the declaration on family reunification.[67] In *Solomon* v. *the Netherlands* the European Court held that the absence of any assurance that a non-national would be given a permanent right of residence would weigh heavily against a claim that the State is subject to a positive obligation to permit family reunification.[68] Much will turn on how the Irish courts, and perhaps the European Court, will interpret State practice over the last two years and the significance of such declarations frequently made in the face of pending deportation proceedings. The admissibility decision of the European Court of Human Rights in *Chandra* v. *the Netherlands*[69] suggests a possible return to the 'only way' test, highlighting the continuing deference of the Court to the State interest in immigration control. In this case, the children concerned had strong linguistic and cultural links with Indonesia and two of the children had attained the age of majority by the time of final decision. The Court pointed out that Article 8 'does not guarantee a right to choose the most suitable place to develop family life'.

Concluding remarks

Debates surrounding the right to citizenship by birth raise crucial questions as to how States allocate the benefits of political membership. How we answer the question 'Who belongs?'[70] has profound implications for the rights and duties assigned to those within the jurisdiction of a State. The 'social fact of attachment'[71] that gives rise to citizenship is presumed to correspond with a place within which a citizen is entitled to make certain claims, one of the most fundamental of which is the right to reside within that place. For citizen children, however, this right is frequently denied, the protection of a child's claim to reside within a State made dependent on the legal status and behaviour of her or his parents. The devices of exclusion that have been put in place in recent legislative and constitutional changes ensure that future generations of children, born to immigrant parents will continue to be denied a sense of belonging in the State.

Notes

1 M. Walzer, *Spheres of Justice* (Oxford: Robinson, 1983), p. 29.
2 See Twenty-seventh Amendment of the Constitution Act 2004 (Irish Citizenship of Children of Non-national Parents).
3 See Agreement between the Government of the United Kingdom of Great Britain and Northern Ireland and the Government of Ireland (British–Irish Agreement) and the Agreement reached in Multi-party negotiations (Belfast Agreement), concluded 10 April 1998, reproduced in (1998) 37 ILM 751. See also British–Irish Agreement. See generally C. Harvey and S. Livingstone, 'Human Rights and the Northern Ireland Peace Process', *European Human Rights Law Review*, 1999, pp. 162–77; C. J. Harvey (ed.), *Human rights, Equality, and Democratic Renewal in Northern Ireland* (Oxford: Hart Publishing, 2001); Colin Harvey, 'Governing after the Rights Revolution', *Journal of Law and Society*, 27 (2000), pp. 61–97.
4 See Nineteenth Amendment to the Constitution Act 1998. The full text of Article 2 of the Constitution of Ireland (as amended) reads: 'It is the entitlement and birthright of every person born in the island of Ireland, which includes its islands and seas, to be part of the Irish nation. That is also the entitlement of all persons otherwise qualified in accordance with law to be citizens of Ireland. Furthermore, the Irish nation cherishes its special affinity with people of Irish ancestry living abroad who share its cultural identity and heritage.'
5 See Article 3 of the Irish Constitution, inserted following the enactment of the Nineteenth Amendment of the Constitution Act 1998.
6 See *L. and O.* v. *Minister for Justice, Equality and Law Reform*, [2003] IESC 1 (23 January 2003) *per* Fennelly J, para. 451. See generally C. Breen, 'Refugee

Law in Ireland: Disregarding the Rights of the Child Citizen, Discriminating against the Rights of the Child', *IJRL* 15: 4 (2003), pp. 750–85.

7 *Fajujonu* v. *Minister for Justice* [1990] 2 IR 151; [1990] ILRM 234.

8 See *L. and O.* v. *Minister for Justice, Equality and Law Reform*, [2003] IESC 1 (23 January 2003).

9 European Convention on Human Rights Act 2003.

10 Case C-200/02, *Chen* v. *Secretary of State for the Home Department*, 19 October 2004.

11 See *Perdido* v. *INS* 420 F.2d 1179; 1969 US App. LEXIS 9566. For a comparative review of legal practice in cases involving the deportation of citizen children and migrant parents see S. Mullally, 'Citizenship and Family Life in Ireland: asking the Question "Who belongs?"', *Legal Studies*, December 2005.

12 This point is forcefully made by Jacqueline Bhabha, 'The Citizenship Deficit: on being a Citizen Child', unpublished paper (copy of file with the author).

13 See Article 41 of the Constitution of Ireland, *Bunreacht na hEireann*.

14 See *North Western Health Board* v. *W. (H.)* [2001] IESC 70 (8 November 2001); *DPP* v. *Best* [1999] IESC 90; [2000] 2 IR 17; [2000] 2 ILRM 1 (27 July 1999); *Western Health Board* v. *M. (K.)* [2001] IESC 114 (21 December 2001).

15 In the *L. and O.* cases, counsel arguing on behalf of the appellant families described their citizen children as 'anchors' tying the remaining family members to the State. See *supra* n. 6, *per* Hardiman J, paras 293–6.

16 See A. Schachar, 'Children of a Lesser State: Sustaining Global Inequality through Citizenship Laws', in S. Macedo and I. M. Young (eds), *Child, Family and State*, Nomos LXIV (New York: New York University Press, 2002), pp. 345–97. Schachar argues that citizenship should be viewed as a property right, with important implications for allocating valuable resources. Allocating citizenship on the basis of the 'naturalising veil of birthright', she argues, is arbitrary and hides the important distributive implications of citizenship decisions (p. 381).

17 Irish Nationality and Citizenship Act 1956.

18 Article 9 of the Constitution of Ireland.

19 [1982] ILRM 164.

20 Ibid., p. 166.

21 [1986] IR 733.

22 Ibid., p. 746.

23 Ibid., p. 745.

24 *Supra*, n. 7.

25 In a statement that is likely to have relevance to many families facing deportation proceedings in the future, Walsh J went on to point out that deportation proceedings could not be taken against a family that included citizen children simply because of poverty, particularly where that situation of poverty was induced by the absence of a work permit.

26 Bhabha J, *supra*, n. 12, p. 13.

27 See 'What's to befall these Irish children?', *Irish Times*, 9 April 2002.

28 *Supra*, n. 6.
29 Ibid., *per* Keane CJ, para. 34.
30 Judgement of 26 October 1988, 13 EHRR 186.
31 [1974] IR 284, at p. 310.
32 *North Western Health Board* v. *HW and CW* [2001] 3 IR 622.
33 Ibid., p. 732.
34 See Article 2, *Bunreacht na hÉireann, supra*, n. 4.
35 *Supra*, n. 6, *per* Fennelly J, para. 495. Fennelly J's judgement echoes the findings of the US Supreme Court in *Phyler* v. *Doe*, 457 US 202 (1982), where the court held that a child's right to access State-funded education should not be denied because of the undocumented status of her parents – the so-called 'corruption of blood' principle. This principle could equally apply in the context of a citizen child's right to residence within the State of which she or he is a national. It was, however, given little weight by the majority in the *L*. and *O*. cases.
36 Department of Justice, Equality and Law Reform, 'Notice to Non-national Parents of Irish-born Children', 18 July 2003, available at www.justice.ie/ 80256E01003A21A5/vWeb/pcJUSQ5YHLJR-en.
37 The Joint Committee issued the following statement: 'In so far as the Irish Government's proposal impacts on Article 2 of the Irish Constitution, which was amended in order to allow the Good Friday Agreement to come into force, the Joint Committee believes that the proposal ought to be considered in the manner indicated in paragraph 7 of the section of the Agreement dealing with Validation, Implementation and Review. That paragraph requires the two Governments to consult with parties in the Assembly if relevant legislation [such as the Irish Nationality and Citizenship Acts] requires amendment.' See Joint Committee Statement on Proposed Citizenship Referendum, Wednesday 28 April 2004, available at www.ihrc.ie/home /wnarticle.asp?NID=91&T=N&Print.
38 Human Rights Commission, Observations on the Proposed Referendum on Citizenship and on the Twenty-seventh Amendment to the Constitution Bill 2004, 25 May 2004, available at www.ihrc.ie/documents/documents .asp?NCID=6.
39 See *Report of the Constitution Review* (Dublin: Government Stationery Office, 1996).
40 See *Kavanagh* v. *Governor of Mountjoy Prison, the Special Criminal Court, the DPP, the Minister for Justice Equality and Law Reform and the Attorney General*, 29th, [2001] IESC 11 (1 March 2001), *Horgan* v. *An Taoiseach and others* [2003] IEHC 64 (28 April 2003).
41 Section 4, 'Citizenship of Children of Certain Non-nationals'.
42 Section 4(2)(d).
43 Department of Justice Equality and Law Reform, 'Minister announces Details of Revised Arrangements for Residence', 14 January 2005, available at www.justice.ie.
44 See Department of Justice Equality and Law Reform, application form IBC/05.

45 Department of Justice Equality and Law Reform, 'Minister announces Revised Arrangements for processing Claims for Permission to Remain from Parents of Irish-born Children', 14 December 2004.

46 *Supra*, n. 10.

47 See Article 1(1) of Directive 90/364.

48 *Supra*, n. 10, para. 39.

49 See Bhabha J, *supra*, n. 12.

50 [2002] ECR I-6279.

51 Parliament and Council Directive 2004/58/EC of 29 April 2004 on the right of citizens of the Union and their family members to move and reside freely within the territory of the Member States amending Regulation (EEC) No. 1612/68 and repealing Directives 64/221/EEC, 68/360/EEC, 72/194/EEC, 73/148/EEC, 75/35/EEC, 90/364/EEC, 90/365/EEC and 93/96/EEC, [2004] OJ L229/45.

52 Council Directive 2003/86/EC of 22 September 2003 on the Right to Family Reunification, [2003] *OJ* L 251/12. See generally Cholewinski, 'Family Reunification and Conditions placed on Family Members: Dismantling a Fundamental Human Right', *European Journal of Migration and the Law* (2002), p. 271.

53 See European Convention on Human Rights Act 2003, signed by the President on 30 June 2003.

54 *Supra*, n. 6, at p. 44.

55 [1996] 22 EHRR CD 94.

56 Application No. 14830/89, decision adopted on 30 June 1992, European Commission of Human Rights.

57 Ibid.

58 Ibid., para. 43.

59 ECtHR, 21 June 1988, Series A, No. 138 (1988), 11 EHRR 322.

60 Application No. 29192/95, judgement 11 July 2000, EHRR 2000, p. 623.

61 Application No. 50963/99, judgement of 20 June 2002.

62 [2001] UKHRR 307.

63 Ibid., p. 329.

64 ECtHR, 21 December 2001, Application No. 31465/96 (2003) EHRR 7. See generally S. van Walsum, 'Comment on the Sen Case: how wide is the Margin of Appreciation regarding the Admission of Children for purposes of Family Reunification?', *European Journal of Migration and Law* (2002), p. 1; C. Forder, 'Family Rights and Immigration Law: a European Perspective', [2003] 3 IJFL, p. 2. See also *J.M.* v. *Netherlands*, ECtHR, 9 January 2001, Application No. 38047/97.

65 ECtHR, 28 November 1996, Reports of Judgements and Decisions 1996–VI, p. 2017, Application No. 21702/93 (1997), EHRR 62.

66 *Gul* v. *Switzerland*, Application No. 23218/94, ECtHR, 19 February 1996, Reports of Judgements and Decisions 1996–I, p. 159

67 *Supra*, n. 44.

68 *Solomon* t. *Nederland*, ECtHR, 5 September 2000, Application No. 44328/98.

69 Decision of 13 May 2003, Application No. 53102/99.
70 See J. Carens, 'Who belongs? Theoretical and Legal Questions about Birth-right Citizenship in the United States', *University of Toronto Law Journal*, 37 (1987), p. 413; ibid. Aliens and Citizens, 'The Case for Open Borders', *Review of Politics*, 49 (1987), pp. 251–73.
71 See *Nottebohm* case (*Lichenstein* v. *Guatemala*), Second Phase, 1951–1955, ICJ Rep. 4.

4

Cherry-picking the diaspora

Katy Hayward and Kevin Howard

Large-scale immigration and emigration constitute two of the most visible and dramatic forms of social change. Whether through the arrival of significant numbers of the 'visibly different' or the abandonment of once-populated areas, migration presents great challenges to the societies affected and their respective political elites. In the 1980s, after the hiatus of the 1970s, Irish migration once again resumed its familiar pattern – heading outwards from Ireland. Despite over six decades of independence and over a decade of membership of the European Economic Community (EEC), Irish politicians repackaged the resumption of emigration not as evidence of national failure but as a consequence of utility-maximising individuals seeking the best return on the sale of their labour in the global market place. Older, highly emotive constructions of emigration as exile and concomitant images of the diaspora longing to return to the homeland were discounted. As MacLaughlin has shown, Irish elites sanitised emigration in the 1980s, reconstructing it as economic voluntarism.[1] The aim of this chapter is to show how this notion of voluntarism is undermined and contradicted by the way the State mobilised the emotive discourses of blood and soil to persuade people to return to the homeland.

As the economy began to grow rapidly from the mid-1990s it became apparent that, left to their own rationally made choices, the Irish abroad might not return in sufficient numbers to meet the demands of the Irish labour market. While it is to be expected that employment agencies will seek people abroad to fill internal labour shortages, this chapter uncovers the vigour with which the State itself got behind labour recruitment. Figure 4.1 shows the relative resurgence of the Irish component of the immigrant population in the period mid-1998 to mid-2001. It is this period that makes up the central focus of this chapter. Our aim is to explore a correlation between the relative resurgence of Irish returnees and the Irish State's proactive recruitment policy amongst the Irish diaspora. We show the elasticity and instrumentality in the deploy-

Figure 4.1 Irish citizens as a percentage of immigrants, 1991–2004

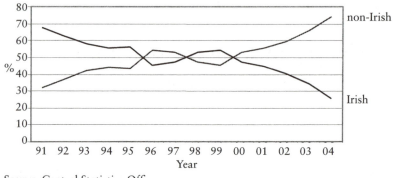

Source: Central Statistics Office

ment of notions of ethnic consanguinity to cherry-pick suitable labour from amongst the wider Irish diaspora. We present an analysis of how, through the National Training and Employment Agency (FÁS), the Irish government ran a global, multi-million-pound campaign to persuade people with skills to sell to relocate to Ireland. In particular we focus on efforts at proactive recruitment, namely the 'Jobs Ireland' campaign (1998–2002) of FÁS and its presentation in the ethnic Irish media. The Irish government aimed to manage the types of people that were needed to fill the gaps in the labour market. This particular 'type' was sought in places as far afield as Newfoundland, Sydney, Britain and South Africa on the principle grounds of enticing 'our' people to 'come home'.

Turning to Ireland's 'strategic reserve of Irish professionals abroad'[2]

A small token of the Irish government's regret at not being able to provide full employment opportunities for its graduates in the 1980s was the establishment of the International Network for Ireland in 1989. The Network was funded by FÁS and established the High Skills Pool with liaison officers in the United Kingdom, the United States, Germany, Denmark, Holland, and Japan.[3] Given the outlook for the Irish economy at the time, the function of the Network – to 'link up graduates with jobs and business opportunities in Ireland' – originally had far more symbolic than practical significance.[4] Within a decade, the Irish government was responding to its own myth of the 'Ryanair generation' as emigrants through ambition and opportunism (rather than simple necessity) by turning to its expatriates as a potential resource.[5] In 1996, Forbairt (later merged into Enterprise Ireland) developed a programme targeting 'Irish emigrant communities abroad' to entice potential entrepreneurs back to

Ireland to establish businesses.[6] However, economic growth was so rapid in Ireland that, within two years, the obstacle to further expansion was not lack of enterprise but of labour. FÁS was requested by the government to formulate a strategy to meet this demand and, as its domestic training programmes were simply unable to satisfy the skills deficit, it sought to target skilled workers abroad and facilitate their relocation to Ireland.[7] Although the target and rationale of the International Network for Ireland (to draw on qualified Irish emigrants as a labour resource) still appealed, a much larger and better resourced scheme was required, given that job vacancies were now plentiful and urgent. The solution proffered was Jobs Ireland – FÁS's flagship programme – as it 'repositioned itself as a proactive player in the recruitment sector' on the international stage.[8]

The Jobs Ireland programme had strong support from the highest levels, as seen in the fact that it was financially supported by the government with a grant of IR£4million for 2000–02.[9] With this backing FÁS was able to develop three core instruments for attracting 'job-ready, skilled and experienced workers to Ireland' under the Jobs Ireland programme.[10] First, it launched www.jobsireland.com, an interactive Web site for potential employees to view job vacancies in Ireland and to submit their CVs. This Web site built on the successful model of the 'Opportunity Ireland' Web site (sponsored by Enterprise Ireland in association with the Department of Enterprise Trade and Employment and aimed at 'attracting IT emigrants back to Ireland') and broadened it to cover a range of sectors.[11] Linked with this was the creation of a database for the use of Irish employers with job vacancies which included the résumés of those who registered an interest in working in Ireland, either through the Web site or at a Jobs Ireland exhibition. Such exhibitions formed the other crucial dimension of Jobs Ireland, namely its 'overseas awareness and recruitment campaign' involving roadshows in targeted international cities.[12] Supported by the Jobs Ireland promotional strategy, this campaign worked from the assumption that 'There is a major pool of Irish and other people working abroad who might be interested in working in Ireland if they were given more information on Ireland and assistance from bodies such as FÁS.'[13]

The Jobs Ireland campaign

FÁS conceived the Jobs Ireland campaign to attract 'the overseas labour which our burgeoning economy requires' as a follow-on to the success of the Industrial Development Authority (IDA) in attracting inward investment from overseas. The campaign was viewed as a crucial competitive advantage for Ireland, giving it 'the edge' in competing for 'that increasingly scarce economic resource: labour'.[14] The campaign began with a focus on recruitment for information technology and construction in 1999. It soon expanded to include such sectors as engineering, financial services, tele-services and tourism; by 2001 it was recruiting for vacancies in retail and health care.[15] The Jobs Ireland exhibitions included seminars, information distribution (booklets, slide shows, posters) and a variety of promotional stands hosted by different companies. This format replicated that of similar events hosted by different agencies in the late 1990s, such as the 'Expo Ireland', 'High Skills Pool' and 'Opportunity 1999/2000' exhibitions. The Jobs Ireland roadshows began in 1999 with exhibitions in London, Brussels, Cologne and Hamburg. In 2000 the campaign extended in Britain (to include Manchester and Birmingham) and in Europe (to include Hanover and Prague), as well as Newfoundland, the United States and South Africa. In 2001 Australia, New Zealand, Moscow, Bombay, and North America were targeted, as well as additional locations within Britain and the European Union. The active Jobs Ireland campaign lasted until early 2002, by which time signals from the Irish economy weakened confidence in the sustainability of its growth and the campaign was deemed to have 'successfully achieved its objectives'.[16]

> [Jobs Ireland aims] to inform Irish people or people of Irish descent of the employment opportunities in Ireland with a view to encouraging them to return to this country.[17]

The publicity strategy for Jobs Ireland centred on targeting media organisations, advertising in the local print and broadcast media, and inviting interested journalists to accompany the roadshows. The targeting of the Irish diaspora is reflected in the particular use of the *Irish Voice* in the United States and *Irish Post* in Britain, where articles regularly appeared (and in some cases repeatedly) both directly and implicitly supporting the Jobs Ireland campaign. The *Irish Post* also did a good job in advertising job fairs for Jobs Ireland occurring around the world, as well as across Britain,[18] encouraging a positive response from its readers[19] and writing warm reviews of the events.[20] Indeed, the *Irish Post* itself (the major media outlet for Irish emigrants in Britain, with weekly circulation figures of around 26,800) took a proactive step to recruit Irish emigrants for jobs in Ireland through a reader service begun in January 2000:

> Interested in returning to live and work in Ireland? Take advantage of our great new service! Fill in the following information and mail it back to us and we will keep you up to date with job opportunities in Ireland.[21]

The focus on the Irish diaspora was also reflected in the choice of advertising locations and methods for Jobs Ireland. For example, the roadshows were publicised in 'Irish pubs, cultural centres and Irish Associations', the New York exhibition was held on St Patrick's Day in order to take advantage of the media interest, and FÁS booked advertising during broadcasts of the All Ireland championships in Britain, Europe and the United States.[22] The *Jobs Ireland* magazine, the first issue being published in January 2001, was distributed through all Irish embassies and consulates, as well as at the recruitment fairs.[23] The core focus on Irish expatriates is particularly evident in marketing strategies for Jobs Ireland concentrated in Ireland itself. For example, the use, particularly around the time of the Christmas holidays, of poster campaigns at airports and ferry ports[24] and a series of radio and television campaigns 'aimed at educating both skilled and interested emigrants about the increasing number of job opportunities'.[25] As a recruitment specialist commented on the job fair in Dublin in January 2001: 'The ideal thing is to get people who are back in Ireland visiting and have an emotional attachment to the country.'[26] Publicity for Jobs Ireland in the Irish national media was maintained throughout the year in an effort to rouse 'home-based family members of such job-seekers' to encourage them to return.[27] The genera-tion of 'a huge public awareness in Ireland of the campaign' also served to encourage potential employers to direct enquiries to FÁS.[28]

Targeting Irish expatriates: 'young, gifted and gone!'[29]

The implicit hierarchy in the type of immigrants sought to join the Irish labour force at this time (1998–2002) is reflected in the course taken by the Jobs Ireland campaign. What began with a clear focus on skilled Irish expatriates soon moved to include members of the Irish diaspora (partic-ularly in Britain, but also in Europe and North America), then spread to welcome qualified non-nationals from Britain, EU member States, East European States (including Russia), and then English-speaking States (including India).[30] The original (although certainly not exclusive) focus on skilled Irish-born workers who emigrated in the 1980s and 1990s is reflected in the way in which job opportunities are presented. For example, a supplement in the *Irish Post* (14 November 1998) on 'Jobs in Ireland' is subtitled 'A returner's guide'. The Jobs Ireland campaign was explicitly described by FÁS in an advertisement in 1999 as a 'world-wide campaign to attract emigrants home'.[31] Nonetheless, it is evident that Irish blood alone was not qualification enough to be welcomed with open arms. What made the Irish people who had left in the 1980s and 1990s (the so-called 'Ryanair generation') so attractive were their 'skills and experience gained while living abroad'.[32] The target was 'the maximum number of qualified Irish workers abroad' and much store was placed on the qualifications of the workers recruited.[33] A spokesperson for Hewlett-Packard, for instance, acknowledged, 'We know that a lot of people want to come back,' but added that they were 'looking for the cream of Irish graduates, preferably with a lot of experience.'[34] There is undoubtedly a degree to which the egos of both parties are being massaged in such messages – 'Ireland, Europe's fastest growing economy, is looking for bright energetic people like you to fill positions in a wide range of areas'[35] – but there is a certain element of exclusivity in the target audience of this discourse. Going on these assumptions, government Ministers were unequivocal in their identification of the target audience for Jobs Ireland whom they were 'particularly trying to encourage' to 'come home'.[36] Minister Noel Dempsey said explicitly that the purpose of the job fairs was to 'attract back many of those who left'.[37] Tánaiste Mary Harney was even more firm in her exhortation to readers of the *Irish Post*: 'There will never be a better time to return to Ireland ... I say to people who are thinking about it: Stop thinking about it and make the decision to come home.'[38]

This direct emotional appeal is echoed in the language used in advertisements aimed at potential employees. The following advertisements were displayed in the *Irish Post*, which has an active readership of Irish-born and second- and third- generation Irish men and women. They indicate an assumption that the potential employees for all types of jobs in Ireland – financial control, HGV drivers, health care, information technology, manufacturing, warehouse staff, etc. – are those who would be returning to their homeland: 'Your country needs you,'[39] 'Interested in returning to work in Ireland?',[40] 'Returning to Ireland in 1999?',[41] 'Returning home?',[42] 'Coming Home?',[43] 'Ag teacht abhaile?',[44] 'Time to go home!',[45] 'Wild geese, come home!'.[46] By early 2000 it was believed that 'the pool of potential returning emigrants in Britain and America is becoming exhausted';[47] there was consequently a shift in the emphasis of the Jobs Ireland campaign, moving from Irish expatriates to the wider Irish community abroad.

Targeting the wider Irish diaspora: 'Bringing them all back home'[48]

Although the reach of the Jobs Ireland roadshows widened internationally in the years 2000 and 2001, the choice of locations to host the events (such as Liverpool, Boston and Sydney) reflect a continuing emphasis on the Irish diaspora as the target audience. As reported in the *Irish Post* in 2000:

Thousands of first-, second- and third-generation Irish attended [the Jobs Ireland fair in Manchester], eager to grasp the opportunity of returning to live and work in the booming Celtic Tiger economy.[49]

Even in European cities, such as Munich and Berlin, the Jobs Ireland campaign was explicitly 'focused on the Irish community living and working there' and was intended to 'encourage them to look at the opportunities now available to them in Ireland'.[50] The decision to initiate the Jobs Ireland campaign across the Atlantic (beginning in Newfoundland) encapsulates the instrumentality of appeals to primordial attachments. The rationale is clear: 'with over 44,000 unfilled vacancies, Ireland must look to its expatriates and suitably qualified EU and Newfoundland citizens'.[51] The symbolic importance of beginning the North American campaign in St Johns was that it was 'closer to Ireland, both geographically and culturally' than any other city.[52] It was thus anticipated that 'Irish employers will find a genuine welcome in this, the home of the "forgotten Irish" who have lived here since the seventeenth century'.[53] The Newfoundland campaign exemplifies the extent to which certain assumptions about primordial Irishness infused this recruitment drive based on economic and business needs. As Ireland's visiting Minister for Science and Technology Noel Treacy put it: 'basically we are talking about our own people here ... These are the children whose forefathers [no mothers, it seems] left Ireland many, many years ago.'[54] In the publicity of the Jobs Ireland event, for example, Newfoundland was described as 'the fourth Aran Island' and it was asserted: 'Many places claim a cultural affinity with Ireland, but few can do with as much authenticity as Newfoundland.'[55]

The concentration on Irish communities abroad as a resource pool reflects a fundamental belief that members of the Irish diaspora, no matter how far removed in terms of distance and time, will fit in better to life in Ireland than those with no connection with the country. To illustrate the point, there are three indicators of this thinking in the representative biographies in the *Jobs Ireland* magazine (January 2001): an emphasis on accent,[56] cultural affinity, and a romantic image of Ireland. First, one of the most obvious markers of being a member of the Irish diaspora is an Irish accent. *Jobs Ireland* features a twenty-seven-year-old German management team leader who 'speaks with a thick Irish accent, and looks and sounds like he never left Ireland – whereas in fact he has been here for just under three years'.[57] Presumably a major reason for the strength of his Irish accent is that his mother is from Dublin. Together these qualify him to be described as 'more Irish than the Irish themselves'.[58] Secondly, to follow on from the Newfoundland case, a programmer who moved from St Johns to work for the Bank of

Ireland says that she has found it easy to settle in Dublin because 'The culture is very similar to that in Newfoundland and I never once heard a bad thing about it [Ireland].'[59] A third way in which members of the Irish diaspora are seen as fitting easily into Ireland is their 'passion for Ireland', whether built on personal experience of the place or not.[60] For example, an Australian doctor 'whose grandfather hails from Ireland' is quoted as saying that he always wanted to visit Ireland because of 'the whole myth of the place'.[61] Picture-postcard Ireland, it seems, becomes a reality to these happy immigrants who love their jobs,[62] have settled in well,[63] have no regrets,[64] and would recommend the move to others.[65] Media reports aimed that the Irish in Britain proclaimed the 'Reality of old dream of returning'.[66]

Appealing to the target audience

There were two dimensions to the Jobs Ireland campaign. The first dimension addressed the personal aspects of such a move (why you are right for Ireland) and the second dealt with the attractiveness of Ireland as a destination (why Ireland is right for you). This section of the chapter considers both of these in turn. First, the personal appeal to potential employees (which again were primarily assumed to have a strong affinity with Ireland) concentrated on emphasising that they would 'fit in' to Ireland for both romantic and rational reasons. Romantic notions of 'coming home' are constantly reinforced in the publicity surrounding the Jobs Ireland events. For instance, the chief executive of Smurfit Media UK attending such an event in London took the opportunity to empha-sise the emotional dimension of return migration. 'We should not lose sight of the fact that these job fairs are not just a commercial enterprise but the fulfilling of a dream for many. It is a wonderful feeling to be going back.'[67]

Barely explicable but powerful emotive reasons for 'coming home' were highlighted repeatedly in material aimed at potential employees, because this was clearly viewed as a 'clincher' for the Jobs Ireland campaign in comparison with other recruitment drives. An example of this was a story in the *Jobs Ireland* magazine about an Irish-born business analyst who moved from Boston to Dublin:

> Since his quiet childhood days in the rural parish, he has lived in some of the biggest and densely populated cities in the world's busiest economic centres. He goes back to Limerick regularly and it would be hard to find a nicer environment in the world, he says, 'There are not many places like the Galtee mountains.'[68]

A second dimension within the promotional literature emphasised returning to one's roots to be among family and childhood friends. For instance a twenty-four-year-old from Longford in Ireland was described as having 'spent two years in London ... before she got the very inviting opportunity to return to Ireland, where her mum, dad, three brothers, two sisters and a host of friends lived'.[69]

'Back for good'[70]

The sense of 'belonging' and the assurance that the change in Ireland's economic fortunes is non-reversible are two principles in the Jobs Ireland campaign that were confirmed in the frequently reiterated notion that the return to Ireland should be a permanent move. Nowhere was this more clearly illustrated than in the slogan of the recruitment drive run by the Construction Industry Federation ('an industry that is transient by its very nature') between 1997 and 1999: 'Back for good.'[71] This is supported by testimonies in *Irish Post* articles aimed at Irish expatriates. (Irish men are twice as likely as the rest of the population to work in the construction industry in Britain.)[72] For example, a building contractor who had himself come back to Ireland after working in the English Midlands is quoted as saying he would be 'delighted to welcome home' builders for good: 'All my ground-workers came back from England and have stayed.'[73] The presentation of a move back to Ireland as a decision to settle contrasts with the image of Irish expatriates' experience abroad (no matter how long for) being essentially career-building/educational ventures. Most of the biographies of the Irish diaspora in the *Jobs Ireland* (January 2001) magazine affirmed Ireland as the ideal final destination: 'I will be here for good now. Ireland is a great place to live'; 'the home bird has come back to roost for the foreseeable future and is very content with her lot'.[74]

'Your chance of a new life in Ireland'[75]

It is definitely worth coming over. ... Ireland has one of the fastest-growing economies in Europe, so there are lots of opportunities here and its [sic] great fun.[76]

The presentation of Ireland as a land of opportunity is encapsulated in advertisements in the *Irish Post*. Catch phrases for the umbrella campaigns such as Jobs Ireland ('Your chance of a new life in Ireland'; 'Ireland: the right place to build your career', 'Your future in Ireland')[77] were echoed in the slogans of advertisements from individual companies, such as 'Opportunities in Ireland!!!'[78] and 'Yes, Ireland is booming and we need you!'[79] The images used in correspondence with this discourse are clear and powerful. For example, the *Irish Post* supplement on the Expo Ireland exhibition contained two different advertisements featuring a stylised map of Ireland with slogans stamped across it; one read 'Employers waiting' and the other 'Jobs in Ireland'.[80] The opening speeches made by government Ministers at Jobs Ireland exhibitions promoted the theme of a Celtic Tiger Ireland, barely recognisable from just a few years before. This new Ireland was 'one of Europe's most dynamic countries' which is 'pushing out the boundaries on e-business', 'a tourist magnet' with 'the best job-creation record of any OECD country'.[81] Ireland, readers were assured, has now become 'an attractive place to which to come to live and work'[82] where they would be offered 'serious earning potential and a quality of life that has made Ireland famous the world over'.[83]

Most of the publicity for the Jobs Ireland campaign would not have looked out of place in a Bord Fáilte publication. Quality of life in Ireland, according to the publicity in the Jobs Ireland programme, centres on unquantifiable factors that make Ireland a tourist attraction in the first place. For example, the stereotype of a laid-back lifestyle was reinforced through testimonies that 'there is zero stress. The work is important, but the main thing about Ireland is the social side. There are less stress levels here, whereas in Britain the job dictates life.'[84] One of the clearest discrepancies between the image of Ireland being presented and the actual environment people were being recruited to work in lay in the fact that the vast majority of the exhibition stands at the Jobs Ireland roadshows were taken by large corporations based in Dublin and there was little representation of companies or agencies based outside Dublin. Yet idealised images of rural Ireland were routinely used by Jobs Ireland to tug at the heartstrings of Irish graduates abroad. Three excellent examples of this were to be found in the first issue of the *Jobs Ireland* (January 2001) magazine alone. On the first page there was a FÁS advertisement headed 'Your next opportunity is in Ireland', beside which were photographs of government buildings in Dublin, a dolmen, presumably in the west of Ireland, and a nondescript dilapidated farm house at the foot of a hill.[85] Further on in the magazine (p. 7) was a quotation from the chairman of the Industrial Development Authority proclaiming that 'Ireland is experiencing the Golden Age. Changes in both the Irish Economy and Society have wholly changed from insular to dynamic.' This quotation was placed over a full-page photograph of a rugged Irish coastline bathed in golden sunlight, the only sign of life being a few desolate farmsteads and a scattering of sheep. Romantic imagery is common in publications aimed at diasporic groups.[86] Nonetheless, the fact that no attempt is made to match the message with more apt contemporary images of

Ireland indicates that the Jobs Ireland campaign not only used the myth of the Emerald Isle to sell the Celtic Tiger but actively disregarded the discrepancy between myth and reality.

'Your country needs you'[87]

A final core tactic employed in the Jobs Ireland campaign was to present the recruitment drive as an urgent and vital attempt to sustain the Irish economic boom. In this way, the Jobs Ireland campaign was not merely putting attractive opportunities to the qualified Irish workers abroad, it was simultaneously putting the onus on them to ensure the future well-being of their homeland. The keenness of this message escalated in the year early 1999 to early 2000. For example, the Opportunity Ireland campaign in spring 1999 concentrated on the information technology sector, which was presented as the lynchpin of the Celtic Tiger: 'The skills shortage in high-tech industries in Ireland has become so acute that the government fears that it may be a serious threat to the Celtic Tiger.'[88] The Jobs Ireland campaign expanded the recruitment focus, and with it the weight of responsibility: 'The Irish economy could be a victim of its own success unless enough skilled workers are found to cope with the labour shortages.'[89] By early 2000 the editorial in the *Irish Post* sounded a warning that if people did not go home to fill the Tiger's vacancies then the Tiger might be threatened, thereby possibly removing any future chance of return. [90] The editorial also suggested that not only did future economic growth in Ireland depend upon a positive response to this 'great opportunity for second and third-generation Irish people to live and work in Ireland', it also offered 'the best chance yet' for these generations to enable their parents as well as their own children to 'return home'.[91]

Conclusion

The style and tone deployed in attempts to attract workers to feed the Celtic Tiger economy depended very much on the potential respondents. Recruitment amongst the non-Irish focused on economic rationality: Ireland was an arena of opportunity for people with the right kind of labour to sell. In this way, non-national immigration *into* Ireland was constructed in precisely the same way as Irish emigration *out of* Ireland had been in the 1980s. On the other hand, recruitment amongst the Irish diaspora, particularly amongst the very people who had left in the 1980s, was a qualitative appeal to ethnic consanguinity. Put simply, the time of exile was over and dream of returning home could at last be realised. At times this went even further: the exhortation to 'think with the blood' and return to Ireland was a patriotic duty. The appeal to ethnic belonging contrasts sharply with the construction of migration as a rational choice, thus highlighting the flexibility and indeed instrumentality of this kind of emotive discourse.

The recruitment campaign for Jobs Ireland centred on the selective targeting of a particular type of immigrants and used particular images of Ireland to attract them. Although it was clear that they were being invited to contribute to the Irish economy, it was their Irish identity rather than their skills that made certain workers targets for the campaign. This was borne out in the use of traditional, idealised, and patriotic propaganda about Ireland as part of efforts to project a new vibrant and dynamic country. The fact that Ireland's economic success was seized upon as an opportunity to invite emigrants to return is one thing. The targeting of members of the Irish diaspora – however far removed – to fill gaps in the job market is quite another. The campaign to recruit skilled Irish professionals abroad indicates a desire to control immigration and thus to control the extent and nature of social change that it would engender. This desire to preserve certain cultural ideals whilst cultivating economic growth is not only a key to the Irish government's approach to return migration. The government's response to the challenge of immigration as a whole may be said to centre on a similar endeavour to juggle national ideals and economic pragmatism.

Notes

The authors wish to acknowledge the assistance (particularly in the provision of sources) of individual members of FÁS who were directly involved in the Jobs Ireland programme, especially Dermod O'Byrne. However, the interpretation of those sources contained in this chapter is entirely and solely that of the authors.

1 Jim MacLaughlin, 'Changing Attitudes to "New Wave" Emigration? Structuralism versus Voluntarism in the Study of Irish Emigration', in A. Bielenberg (ed.), *The Irish Diaspora* (London: Pearson Education, 2000), pp. 317–30.
2 Extract from High Skills Pool brochure quoted in 'The Irish Abroad', *The Irish Emigrant*, 11 March 1990, issue No. 162.
3 Ibid.
4 Richard Bruton, Minister for Enterprise and Employment, 'Returned emigrant business projects', Written Answers, Dáil Éireann, Vol. 460, 25 January 1996.
5 This so-called 'myth of voluntarism' is encapsulated in the interview given by Brian Lenihan, as Ireland's Minister for Foreign Affairs, given to *Newsweek* magazine (13 October 1987) while visiting the US: 'I don't look on the type of emigration we have today as being of the same category as the terrible emigration of the last century ... [Emigration] is not a defeat because the

Irish hone their skills and talents in another environment; the more they develop a work ethic in a country like Germany or the US, the better it can be applied in Ireland when they return. After all, we can't all live on a small island.'

6 Government appeals for investment from Irish business people abroad were high-profile and continued after the start of the Celtic Tiger, helping to feed the image of a new, economically dynamic Ireland. For example, the Tánaiste Mary Harney launched the IDA-sponsored *Business Influence* magazine in London, which celebrated the 'growing number of successful Irish people' and publicised 'the numerous investment opportunities in Ireland' ('Tánaiste to praise influential Irish', *Irish Post*, 27 February 1999).

7 'Short History of the Jobs Ireland Programme, 2000–2002' (source: FÁS).

8 'Overview of the Jobs Ireland Programme', March 2001 (source: FÁS).

9 'Short History of the Jobs Ireland Programme, 2000–2002' (FÁS). The fact that this is more than twice that given to the Díon fund to support Irish community groups in Britain itself shows the preference given to one particular type of expatriate in government policy towards the Irish diaspora.

10 Press release on Jobs Ireland programme, 1999 (source: FÁS).

11 The 'Opportunity Ireland' campaign of 1999 sought to 'bring back 2,000 highly qualified graduates to Ireland' and was specifically 'aimed at the "brain drain" generation of 1980s graduates who left Ireland because of lack of opportunity and who are now thinking of returning home for either personal or professional reasons' ('Young, gifted and gone!', *Irish Post*, 20 March 1999).

12 These exhibitions were modelled on the High Skills Pool jobs fairs which were held by the International Network for Ireland in Dublin at Christmas time. Quotation from press release on Jobs Ireland campaign in Newfoundland (source: FÁS).

13 'Overview of the Jobs Ireland Programme', March 2001 (source: FÁS).

14 'Immigration will remain High', FÁS press release, 2001 (source: FÁS).

15 FÁS Jobs Ireland first information brochure, 1999, and FÁS press release on Jobs Ireland programme, 1999.

16 Extract from correspondence with D. O'Byrne, FÁS (July 2005).

17 'Short History of the Jobs Ireland Programme, 2000–2002' (source: FÁS).

18 For instance, the articles anticipating the job fairs in Birmingham ('Jobs fair set for Birmingham', 14 October 2000) and Liverpool '60,000 Jobs on offer' (3 February 2001) and the supplements on Expo Ireland, September 1999 (*Irish Post*, 12 June 1999) and, in January 2000, the seven-page feature on the forthcoming Opportunity 2000 event in Dublin.

19 'Visitors to Expo who are interested in working and living in the Republic are encouraged to bring their CVs with them as there will be many vacancies' ('Where to get help', *Irish Post*, 24 April 1999); 'Smurfit Media, the publishers of the *Irish Post*, is joining forces with FÁS to encourage Irish people here [in Britain] to return home' (editorial, *Irish Post*, 12 February 2000).

20 For example, 'Jobs show success' (30 September 2000), 'Fair is just the job' (16 December 2000), 'Jobs fair success in Liverpool' (3 March 2001).

21 Advertisement, *Irish Post*, 8 January 2000.
22 'Overview of the Jobs Ireland Programme', March 2001 (source: FÁS); 'Work this way', *Irish Post*, 12 June 1999.
23 'Introduction by An Tánaiste', *Jobs Ireland* magazine, January 2001, p. 3.
24 'Work this way', *Irish Post*, 12 June 1999.
25 'Calling emigrants home', *Irish Post*, 14 November 1998.
26 'Stay and work here', *Irish Post*, 6 January 2001.
27 'Overview of the Jobs Ireland Programme', March 2001 (source: FÁS).
28 Extract from correspondence with D. O'Byrne, FÁS (July 2005).
29 Headline of article on Opportunity Ireland, *Irish Post*, 20 March 1999.
30 This preference weighting is reflected in the choice of fourteen employees carefully selected for inclusion in the first issue of the *Jobs Ireland* magazine (January 2001). Of these, five were Irish-born recent returnees, three were members of the Irish diaspora (two second-generation and one third-generation), three were European, two were Indian and one was Canadian (Newfoundland).
31 'Work this way', FÁS advertisement, *Irish Post*, 12 June 1999.
32 'Short history of the Jobs Ireland Programme, 2000–2002' (source: FÁS).
33 Ibid.
34 'Home offers to graduates', *Irish Post*, 24 April 1999.
35 *Jobs Ireland* magazine, January 2001, p. 2.
36 Mary Harney, Tánaiste, extract from speech at Jobs Ireland fair, London, cited in the *Irish Post*, 20 May 2000.
37 Quoted in 'Come home: we need you', *Irish Post*, 16 December 2000.
38 Quoted in 'Britain gets Irish job fair', *Irish Post*, 12 February 2000.
39 Slogan on *Irish Post* 'Returner's Guide', 12 June 1999.
40 Advertisement for St James's Hospital, *Irish Post*, 29 August 1998.
41 Advertisement for Action Recruitment, *Irish Post*, 12 June 1999.
42 Advertisement for Corrib Food Products, *Irish Post*, 12 June 1999.
43 Advertisement for i.ce Group, *Irish Post*, 12 June 1999.
44 ('Coming home?') Advertisement for Grafton Recruitment, *Irish Post*, 2 December 2000.
45 Advertisement for Shamrock Agency, *Irish Post*, 18 June 1998.
46 Advertisement for Quinn Richardson Recruitment, *Irish Post*, 12 June 1999.
47 Managing director of High Skills Pool, quoted in *Irish Post*, 6 January 2000.
48 Headline of article on Jobs Ireland initiative in Newfoundland, *Irish Post*, 25 March 2000.
49 Editorial, *Irish Post*, 30 September 2000.
50 'Jobs Ireland German campaign begins', press release, June 1999 (source: FÁS).
51 Statement by the Public Affairs Manager of FÁS, quoted in press release on Jobs Ireland campaign in Newfoundland (source: FÁS).
52 Extract from press release on Jobs Ireland campaign in Newfoundland (source: FÁS).

53 Extract from press release on Jobs Ireland campaign in Newfoundland (source: FÁS).
54 Noel Treacy, *Irish Post*, 29 April 2000.
55 'Bringing them all back home', *Irish Post*, 25 March 2000.
56 An article in the *Irish Post* ('Irish accent is good for business', 28 September 1998) captures the discourse of a complete about-turn in the experience of Irish people in Britain from the 1980s, when an Irish accent was seen as a liability, to the 1990s, when it was being seen as 'good for business'.
57 'PK, Teleservices', *Jobs Ireland* magazine, January 2001, p. 4.
58 Ibid.
59 'MM, Banking in Ireland', *Jobs Ireland*, p. 6.
60 'CM, Electronics', *Jobs Ireland*, p. 17.
61 'TM, Nursing and medical healthcare', *Jobs Ireland*, p. 15.
62 '"I love the job. If someone offered me a job with a higher salary, I wouldn't leave here," he smiles', 'PK, Teleservices', *Jobs Ireland*, p. 4. '"I like this job very much, it is perfect. Ireland is so beautiful"', 'MD, Tourism, hotels and catering', *Jobs Ireland*, p. 22.
63 'She found it very easy to settle in Ireland and felt more than welcome when she arrived into her new work and social environment', 'BS, Teleservices', *Jobs Ireland*, p. 5.
64 'He has absolutely no regrets and would encourage others thinking to do likewise [*sic*]', 'PK, Teleservices', *Jobs Ireland*, p. 4.
65 'There is lots to do here and I would highly recommend moving to Ireland, especially people from Canada [*sic*]', 'MM, Financial Services', *Jobs Ireland*, p. 6. 'Not content with having packed and left Boston to start a new life in Ireland, H. has been boasting of Ireland's and his company's charms, to former colleagues in Boston, and is trying to poach them to work in Ireland too', 'HB, Information Technology', *Jobs Ireland*, p. 9.
66 Headline in *Irish Post* for report on Opportunities 2000 exhibition, January 2000.
67 'Fair is just the job', *Irish Post*, 16 December 2000.
68 'HB, Information Technology', *Jobs Ireland*, p. 9.
69 'EL, Financial services', *Jobs Ireland* January, p. 19.
70 Quotation from 'HB, Information Technology', *Jobs Ireland*, p. 9.
71 'Builder's boom', *Irish Post*, 27 March 1999.
72 *Irish Post*, 8 August 1998.
73 'Builder's boom', *Irish Post*, 27 March 1999.
74 'CM, Electronics', *Jobs Ireland*, p. 17; 'EL, Financial services', *Jobs Ireland*, p. 19.
75 Headline in *Irish Post* for report on Jobs Ireland fairs in Britain, 2 December 2000.
76 'PK, Teleservices', *Jobs Ireland*, p. 4.
77 *Jobs Ireland* advertisements, *Irish Post*, 2, 9 December 2000 and 21 January 2001.
78 CRC International Hotel and Catering advertisement, *Irish Post*, 12 June 1999.

79 Freedom Recruitment advertisement, *Irish Post*, 4 September 1999.
80 *Irish Post*, 12 June 1999.
81 Extracts from the official opening speech by Noel Dempsey, the Minister for the Environment and Local Government, FÁS Jobs Ireland London exhibition, 9 December 2000.
82 Ibid.
83 *Jobs Ireland*, p. 2.
84 'MM, Financial Services', *Jobs Ireland*, p. 46; 'CM, Electronics', *Jobs Ireland*, p. 17.
85 *Jobs Ireland*, p. 2.
86 For example, in October 1998 the *Irish Post* produced a supplement on buying property in Ireland. Entitled 'Home from home', the supplement was advertised over a photograph of a woman in simple traditional costume (black dress, white apron) sitting sewing outside the stable door of a white thatched cottage.
87 Slogan on *Irish Post* 'Returner's Guide', 12 June 1999.
88 'Young, gifted and gone', *Irish Post*, 20 March 1999.
89 'Work this way', FÁS advertisement, *Irish Post*, 12 June 1999.
90 Editorial, *Irish Post*, 12 February 2000.
91 Ibid.

5

The economic contribution of immigrants in Ireland

Alan Barrett and Adele Bergin

Given the scale of immigration into Ireland in recent years and the fact that it is a new dimension to Ireland's demographic experience, it is clear that there is much to learn about the characteristics of immigrants and their impacts. In this context, this chapter has four broad and inter-related objectives. First, we provide information on the characteristics of Ireland's immigrant population and in particular the characteristics that impact upon their participation in the labour market (the next two sections). Second, we provide an indication, at least to the limited degree allowed by the data available, of the degree to which the nature of employment differs across immigrants and the Irish-born population (the section following). Third, and again within the constraints implied by the data used, we look at the issue of job search techniques used by unemployed immigrants and assess differences with the Irish-born unemployed (penultimate section). Finally, we provide an estimate of the impact on Ireland's economy of the recent immigrant inflow, along dimensions such as wages, unemployment and output.

The analysis presented builds on research presented in Barrett and Trace (1998),[1] Barrett *et al.* (2002)[2] and Barrett *et al.* (2005).[3] In this series of papers the authors have used information from the Labour Force Surveys and the Quarterly National Household Surveys of the Central Statistics Office to provide descriptive information on the population of immigrants. They have also used this information in economic modelling exercises, whereby estimates of the economic impact of immigrants have been produced. This chapter extends this work by (1) using more recent data (Quarterly National Household Survey of 2004, second quarter), (2) using the data more broadly to look at issues neglected in the earlier work and (3) basing the impact estimates on the most recent inflows.

Before proceeding with the main focus of the chapter, it is useful to provide information on both the stock and flow of immigrants in Ireland, since the sizes of the immigrant stocks and inflows are obviously pivotal in determining impacts. Looking firstly at the flows, Figure 5.1 shows

Figure 5.1 Total inflows and non-Irish inflows, 1996–2005

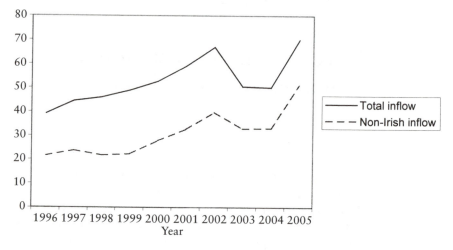

both the total inflow into Ireland and the non-Irish inflow since 1996 (the first year in recent times of uninterrupted positive inflows). Between 1996 and 2000 the non-Irish inflow averaged 23,400. This increased by over 40% to reach 33,000 in each of 2003 and 2004. In 2005 the non-Irish inflow jumped to 51,000 but it is difficult to say whether this is part of a trend or an exception, owing to the opening up of Ireland to the EU accession States on 1 May 2005.

Although we have information on the stock of immigrants in Ireland in 2002 (from the census) and also information on inflows (as just described), it is not possible to put a precise figure on the stock of immigrants currently in Ireland. This is because we do not have information on the national breakdown of population outflows from Ireland. The CSO does provide an aggregate figure for the outflow but not how this breaks down between Irish people leaving and immigrants exiting.

For this reason, we can provide an estimate only of the stock of non-Irish people living in Ireland in 2005. As of the 2002 census, non-Irish nationals represented 7% of the population (273,000 out of a total population of 3.86 million). Based on the gross inflow of non-nationals since 2003 and assuming half the outflow since then to have been non-Irish, we can estimate the net inflow of non-nationals since 2002 to have been about 90,000. This would imply a non-Irish total population of 363,000 in 2005, or 8.8% of the population.

Immigrant characteristics: all adults

We need to describe the data that are used in the analysis that follows, so we will begin this section with this description. The data used come from the 2004 (second quarter) Quarterly National Household Survey (QNHS), conducted by the Central Statistics Office (CSO).[4] The primary purpose of this survey is to collect employment-related information on the population and it is therefore used to provide information on the numbers employed and on participation and unemployment rates. The sampling procedure employed involves two stages. First, a sample of 2,600 small areas is selected where each bloc contains, on average, seventy-five dwellings. Second, within each small area, fifteen households are selected. This yields a quarterly sample of 39,000 households and around 100,000 individuals. The CSO publishes tabular information derived from each QNHS; however, it also makes a large proportion of the micro-data available to researchers, and it is this micro-data that we use below.

In addition to asking respondents about labour market variables, questions are also asked about place of birth and number of years of residence in Ireland. We use these questions to divide the sample into two components: 'Irish-born' and 'immigrant'. Immigrants are defined in the following way: they are people who were not born in Ireland and have lived there for ten years or less.[5] We define the Irish population as people who say they were born in Ireland. The data also allow us to look at some sub-categories of immigrants because the 'place of birth' variable is broken up into four categories: UK, US, rest of EU-15 and other. For our sample of all adults, we have almost 61,000 Irish-born and 2,000 immigrants. When we look at labour force participants the corresponding figures are about 35,000 Irish-born and 1,600 immigrants.

In using the QNHS, we would argue, we are getting as broad a view of the immigrant population as is possible, with the exception of the census 2002.[6] As every effort is made by the CSO to sample comprehensively from dwellings, the coverage of immigrants should be broad. However, a number of concerns do exist around the coverage of immigrants arising, for example, from difficulties imposed by language and the possibility of immigrants being housed in temporary dwellings such as in the case of construction workers.

In order to assess the degree to which this would be a problem, we compared the proportion of immigrants in the sample we use below with the proportion recorded in the 2002 census. This does appear to show underrepresentation by about 45% of immigrants from outside the UK, the US and the EU-15 combined. If this underrepresentation is selective along particular lines, the results we present below for immigrants in this 'other' category may be biased.[7] For this reason, we need to be careful in interpreting results for this group. In spite of these limitations, it is certainly the case that the use of the QNHS allows us to provide information on immigrants in Ireland that goes beyond looking at particular groups such as asylum seekers[8] and work permit holders.[9]

We can now begin our examination of the characteristics of all adult immigrants. Later, we will look specifically at labour market participants. The variables we concentrate on in this section are gender, age, region of residence and labour force status. We will discuss our interest in each variable in turn.

We look at gender because immigrant populations are often more heavily selected from one gender relative to the other. For example, in the case of Irish emigration the 1950s saw a higher number of men in the net outflow, whereas the 1960s saw a higher number of women.[10] Given the general finding of higher labour force participation rates among men relative to women, any significant imbalance in the gender mix of immigrants could have an impact on participation and hence the economic contribution of immigrants. From Table 5.1 we can see that there is no evidence of such selection in the case of immigrants into Ireland. Even though the 'other' group looks slightly more 'male' and the Americans look slightly more 'female', relative to the Irish population these differences are not statistically significant.

Turning next to region of residence, the data allow us to examine whether immigrants are more heavily concentrated in the Southern and Eastern (SE) region relative to the Border Midland and West (BMW) region. Our interest here is in assessing the degree to which immigrants are adding to the relatively stronger population growth in the SE region. While most writers accept that immigrants make a positive contribution to the economy of a host country in terms of output, some argue that the costs of immigrants in terms of increased congestion should be set against any output gains. From Table 5.2 it can be seen that the immigrant population in general shows the same regional distribution

Table 5.1 Gender distribution of immigrants and Irish-born (%)

Gender	Irish	UK	Rest of EU	Other	American	All immigrants
Male	49.1	50.6	45.9	52.2	44.8	50.1
Female	50.9	49.4	54.1	47.8	55.2	49.9
No.	60,893	1,037	462	925	116	2,540

*Denotes a proportion that is significantly different from the Irish proportion at the 5% level.
Source: figures calculated from CSO QNHS (q. 2).

Table 5.2 Regional distribution of immigrants and Irish-born (%)

Region	Irish	UK	Rest of EU	Other	American	All immigrants
BMW	26.5	38.5*	15.6*	18.1*	21.6	26.1
SE	73.5	61.5*	84.4*	81.9*	78.4	73.9
No.	60,893	1,037	462	925	116	2,540

*Denotes a proportion that is significantly different from the Irish proportion at the 5% level.
Source: figures calculated from CSO QNHS (q. 2).

as the Irish population. Hence the immigrant group do not appear to be adding to congestion in the more heavily populated SE region. There are, however, differences within the immigrant group. Both the 'rest of EU' and 'other' are more concentrated in the SE region, relative to the Irish; however, immigrants from the UK are more heavily concentrated in the BMW, again, relative to the Irish.

The next variable we consider is age. It is generally the case that recently arrived migrant populations are younger than either their home or host countries, partly because migration requires a degree of flexibility and also because migration can be viewed as an investment-like decision. By incurring the costs of migration, both financial and non-monetary, migrants expect a return in terms of a higher future stream of earnings. The longer the payback period the more profitable is the investment decision. It can be seen in Table 5.3 that the immigrant population very

Table 5.3 Age distribution of immigrants and Irish-born (%)

Age group	Irish	UK	Rest of EU	Other	American	All immigrants
15–19	10.4	10.2	6.1*	6.5*	9.5	8.1*
20–24	9.8	6.8*	25.8*	14.2*	10.3	13.1*
25–34	16.1	25.0*	43.5*	49.2*	30.2*	37.4*
35–44	17.5	29.2*	14.5	22.9*	27.6*	24.2*
45–54	17.2	12.7*	6.7*	5.6*	7.8	8.8*
55–59	7.5	6.0	0.9*	1.0*	4.3	3.1*
60–64	5.9	3.4*	0.9*	0.3*	5.2	1.9*
65+	15.6	6.8*	1.7*	0.3*	5.2*	3.4*
No.	60,893	1,037	462	925	116	2,540

*Denotes a proportion that is significantly different from the Irish proportion at the 5% level.
Source: figures calculated from CSO QNHS (q. 2).

much follow this expectation. Throughout the age distribution, the differences between the 'all immigrant' group and the Irish population are significant, with the immigrant population being concentrated in the twenty to forty-four age groups (70% versus 43%). Within each immigrant grouping there are also significant differences relative to the Irish population.

The final variable that we will look at for the full immigrant adult population is labour force status. As our later interest is in the economic contribution of immigrants, it is clearly of importance to assess the extent to which immigrants are (1) labour force participants and (2) employed. In Table 5.4 it can be seen that the proportion of Irish people that are 'not economically active' is higher (and significantly so) than that for all immigrants. As the inverse of this proportion is the participation rate, we can say that immigrants are more likely to be labour force participants. This finding is not generalised across each of the immigrant groups, however. The higher participation rate is seen only for immigrants from the UK and the 'rest of the EU' and is not found for Americans or others. All the proportions in the table are expressed as a proportion of the adult population and so the rates, for example, of unemployment shown in the table are not the usual measures where proportions are normally expressed relative to labour force participants. For this reason we will simply note here the higher rate of unemployment in the immigrant population but will discuss the issue more fully in the next section when we focus on labour force participants.

Table 5.4 Distribution of immigrants and Irish-born by ILO labour force status (%)

Status	Irish	UK	Rest of EU	Other	American	All immigrants
In employment full-time	45.7	48.4	60.4*	47.6	43.1	50.0*
In employment part-time, not underemployed	9.8	10.2	10.0	6.6*	12.1	8.9
In employment part-time, underemployed	0.1	0.1	0.0	0.1	0.0	0.1
Unemployed, seeking full-time work	2.1	3.9*	3.9	3.7*	3.4	3.8*
Unemployed, seeking part-time work	0.4	0.7	0.9	0.9	0.9	0.8*

*Denotes a proportion that is significantly different from the Irish proportion at the 5% level.
Source: figures calculated from CSO QNHS (q. 2).

Immigrant characteristics: labour market participants

We will begin our more focused look at labour force participants by looking again at ILO labour force status in Table 5.5. As noted above in the discussion of Table 5.4, the proportions are now of labour force participants and so the figures on unemployment can now be interpreted as standard unemployment rates. The unemployment rate for the Irish labour force is 4.6% (3.5 + 0.6 + 0.5); for the full immigrant population, the rate is higher, at 7.7% (5.9 + 1.2 + 0.6). The difference is statistically significant and is similar across the immigrant categories. Although the difference is statistically significant only for the UK and 'other' groups, it is the sample sizes for the American and 'rest of EU' rather than lower unemployment rates that lead to non-significance.

The finding of a higher rate of unemployment is important although difficult to interpret. If the unemployment is concentrated among recently arrived immigrants, it may simply be that they are looking for jobs and that there is no 'immigrant unemployment problem' as such. However, if the higher unemployment rate is a characteristic of the immigrant population in general, then this is a concern.

The next issue we want to consider is the sectoral distribution of immigrants relative to Irish employees. Our concern is that immigrants may experience a form of 'occupational segregation' whereby their labour

Table 5.5 Distribution of immigrants and Irish-born by ILO labour force status: labour force participants (%)

Status	Irish	UK	Rest of EU	Other	American	All immigrants
In employment full-time	78.3	75.8	79.9	80.6	72.5	78.2
In employment part-time, not underemployed	16.8	16.0	13.2	11.2	20.3*	14.0*
In employment part-time, underemployed	0.2	0.2	0.0	0.2	0.0	0.1
Unemployed, seeking full-time work	3.5	6.0*	5.2	6.2*	5.8	5.9*
Unemployed, seeking part-time work	0.6	1.1	1.1	1.5	1.4	1.2*
Marginally attached	0.5	0.9	0.6	0.4	0.0	0.6

*Denotes a proportion that is significantly different from the Irish proportion at the 5% level.
Figures calculated from CSO QNHS (q. 2).

Table 5.6 Distribution of immigrants and Irish-born by sector of employment: labour force participants (%)

Sector	Irish	UK	Rest of EU	Other	American	All immigrants
Agriculture forestry, fishing	6.9	0.8*	1.7*	2.7*	2.9	1.7*
Mining and quarrying	0.4	0.8	0.3	0.0	0.0	0.4
Manufacturing	15.0	14.5	16.9	15.4	24.6	15.7
Electricity, gas and water supply	0.8	0.2	0.0	0.9	0.0	0.4
Construction	11.5	11.2	7.2	6.6*	2.9	8.4*
Wholesale and retail	14.3	12.7	9.7	10.4	5.8	11.0*
Hotels and restaurants	5.2	6.5	17.2*	21.6*	8.7	14.0*
Transport, storage, communication	6.2	4.5	7.2	4.4	2.9	5.0*
Financial intermedia-tion	4.3	5.4	5.2	1.6*	2.9	4.0
Real estate, renting and business activities	7.9	13.4*	14.6*	9.7	8.7	12.2*
Public administration; defence; social security	5.0	2.4*	1.4*	1.1*	1.4	1.7*
Education	6.4	7.7	5.7	2.2*	17.4*	5.8

*Denotes a proportion that is significantly different from the Irish proportion at the 5% level.
Source: figures calculated from CSO QNHS (q. 2).

market opportunities are restricted. Looking first at the 'all immigrants' group, some clear differences exist relative to Irish employees (Table 5.6). The sector in which immigrants are most heavily represented is hotels and restaurants. The figure of 14% for all immigrants hides a large variation across the groups. For UK and American immigrants there is no difference in the proportion of employees in this sector relative to the Irish. However, immigrants from 'other' countries are almost four times more likely to be in this sector relative to Irish employees; for 'rest of EU' immigrants the ratio is over three times. One other sector in which immigrants are more heavily represented than Irish employees is real estate, renting and business activities. This is driven by immigrants from the UK and 'rest of EU'.

Sectors in which immigrants are underrepresented include agriculture, forestry and fishing, construction, wholesale and retail and public

Table 5.7 Distribution of immigrants and Irish-born by educational attainment: labour force participants (%)

Education	Irish	UK	Rest of EU	Other	American	All immigrants
No formal/ primary education	13.6	5.4*	1.1*	5.5*	5.8	4.6*
Lower secondary	18.8	17.2	3.7*	4.4*	7.2	9.6*
Upper secondary	28.1	20.8*	25.8	31.0	13.0	25.0*
Post-leaving	11.0	7.7	8.3	9.9	5.8	8.5*
Third level (non-degree)	10.9	13.4	17.8*	14.7	7.2	14.5*
Third level (degree)	17.5	35.3*	43.3*	34.6*	60.9*	37.9*
No.	35,547	662	349	546	69	1,626

*Denotes a proportion that is significantly different from the Irish proportion at the 5% level.
Source: figures calculated from CSO QNHS (q. 2).

administration, defence and social security. While most of these are unsurprising, the appearance of construction in the list may be considered a surprise. As a final note, although there is no significant difference between the proportion of Irish employees and immigrants in the health sector, there is a significantly higher representation among 'other immigrants'.

We turn next to consider the educational levels of immigrants relative to the Irish population. Our interest here is twofold. First, given that the primary focus of this chapter is on the economic contribution of immigrants, and that this contribution in turn will be partly determined by the human capital of the immigrants, education is a crucially important variable. Second, by looking at the education levels among immigrants we can get a sense of the types of employee that are attracted to Ireland.

The distributions of the immigrant populations and the Irish population by educational attainment are shown in Table 5.7 and there are some notable points to observe. Looking firstly at the lower end of the distribution, the proportion of immigrants with either no qualifications or only lower second-level qualifications is less than half that of the Irish population (14.2% versus 32.4%). Some of this difference would be removed if we controlled for age in the comparison, as the Irish population is older and the older generations in Ireland have lower education levels than the younger generation. However, our interest here is in assessing how the immigrant population compares with the total Irish population and not some sub-component, and for this reason we do not control for age.

Looking at the other end of the distribution, we see the notably high levels of education among immigrants. While 28.4% of the Irish population have third-level qualifications (both degree and non-degree), the corresponding figure for immigrants is 52.4%. This pattern of high educational attainment is seen across the immigrant groups, with the proportions for all groups in the highest category being significantly different from the Irish proportion.[11]

The high levels of educational attainment seen in Table 5.7 might lead us to assume that the immigrant population would be more heavily concentrated among the higher-level occupations relative to the Irish population. However, Barrett *et al.* (2005) have shown that this was not the case in the earlier data and so it is important to look at this again. In Table 5.8 we show the occupational distributions of the different groups.

If we begin by comparing the Irish and 'all immigrant' columns, the most immediate observation is a large number of significantly different proportions. In truth, this may lead us in a somewhat misleading direction, so it may be useful to aggregate some of the categories. In particular, if we combine the first three categories and the remaining six, we find the following: (1) 39.7% of immigrants are in the top-level occupations, compared with 36.5% of the Irish population; (2) 60.4% of immigrants are in the lower-level occupations, compared with 63.5% of the Irish population.

By focusing on these latter proportions, we can say that although the educational levels of immigrants exceed those of the Irish population, these levels of education do not seem to be fully reflected in the occupational attainment of immigrants. Barrett *et al.* (2005) show that this 'occupational gap' cannot be explained by the different age structures of the two populations and so other, more fundamental, explanations are required.

Indicators of employment quality

By combining the results from Tables 5.7 and 5.8 the suggestion arose that immigrants in Ireland, for whatever reason, are not accessing employment opportunities that are fully reflective of their skill levels. In this section we want to look further into the issue of employment quality to the extent that the QNHS data will allow. As the data set includes information on hours worked and the incidence of atypical working times, we can get some sense of how these differ across the Irish-born and immigrant populations.

Table 5.8 Distribution of immigrants and Irish-born by occupation: labour force participants (%)

Occupation	Irish	UK	Rest of EU	Other	American	All immigrants
Managers and admin-istrators	17.5	15.9	13.8	8.4*	15.9	12.9*
Professional	10.7	16.6*	14.3	12.3	21.7*	14.9*
Associate professional and technical	8.3	14.0*	10.9	8.8	20.3*	11.9*
Clerical and secretarial	12.2	8.9	10.6	6.6*	8.7	8.5*
Craft and related	13.5	11.5	10.6	9.3	8.7	10.5*
Personal and protective service	9.8	8.6	15.5*	19.2*	10.1	13.7*
Sales	8.3	9.8	9.5	6.6	4.3	8.4
Plant and machine operatives	8.8	6.2	3.4*	11.7	1.4	7.3*
Other (includes not stated)	10.9	8.5	11.5	17.0*	8.7	12.0
No.	35547	662	349	546	69	1626

*Denotes a proportion that is significantly different from the Irish proportion at the 5% level.
Source: figures calculated from CSO QNHS (q. 2).

Before looking at those variables, it is of interest to consider another variable that may be related to employment quality, namely union membership. In Table 5.9 the figures for union membership are presented and it is clear that immigrants are much less likely to be union members. This may be the result of the sectoral distribution of immigrants or of

Table 5.9 Distribution of immigrants and Irish-born by union membership (%)

	Irish	All immigrants
Union member	35.8	13.6*
Not a union member	64.2	86.4*
No.	7769	531

*Denotes a proportion that is significantly different from the Irish proportion at the 5% level.
Source: figures calculated from CSO QNHS (q. 2).

the fact that immigrants, as recent arrivals, may not have had a chance to join unions at the time of being surveyed. Whatever the reason, to the extent that non-union membership is an indicator of job quality, there is a clear distinction here.

In Table 5.10 we present the figures on atypical working hours and a number of significant differences emerge, all of which point to lower employment quality for immigrants. The proportions of Irish-born employees who never have to work in the evenings, on Saturdays or on Sundays are lower than for immigrants. Similarly, the proportion of the Irish-born who never do shift work is lower. While the differences are statistically significant, it should be noted that actual differences are not large and certainly do not lead to a picture of immigrant employment conditions being vastly different from those of Irish people. For example, it is the case that immigrants are more likely to do shift work but almost 80% of immigrants responding to this question said they never had to

Table 5.10 Incidence of atypical work times for immigrants and Irish-born (%)

Type of work	Incidence	Irish	All immigrants
Evening	Usually	8.4	10.9*
	Sometimes	24.1	26.2
	Never	67.4	62.8*
Night	Usually	4.8	5.6
	Sometimes	12.7	13.6
	Never	82.5	80.7
Saturday	Usually	20.7	19.9
	Sometimes	29.6	36.0*
	Never	49.7	44.1*
Sunday	Usually	12.2	12.4
	Sometimes	17.2	22.6*
	Never	70.7	65.0*
Shift	Usually	9.4	12.5*
	Sometimes	4.6	7.9*
	Never	86.0	79.5*
No.		27,452	1,246

*Denotes a proportion that is significantly different from the Irish proportion at the 5% level.
Source: figures calculated from CSO QNHS (q. 2).

do shift work. This is certainly lower than the corresponding Irish figure of 86% but not an indicator of a dramatic difference. In addition, part of the observed difference may be related to the younger age profile of immigrants.

The final indicator of employment conditions that the data provide is hours worked. Our analysis of responses to the question about the usual number of hours worked per week suggests little difference between immigrants and natives. The usual average number of hours worked is thirty-seven for both groups. When students are excluded from the analysis, the average figure barely changes. As a final route of analysis we looked at the group of people who said they usually worked over forty hours, in order to explore the possibility of there being a group of immigrants at the tail end of the hours distribution. The result of this analysis was to show long worker hours for the Irish-born and so again we are not finding evidence of poorer employment conditions for immigrants.

Search methods used by the unemployed

Before leaving our descriptive analysis of immigrants in Ireland we want to explore one more issue. The QNHS contains information on job search techniques used by individuals who are unemployed. Specifically, people who respond that they are not working but looking for work are asked if they engaged in a range of job search activities in the previous four weeks. As we have already noted a higher unemployment rate amongst immigrants, it is useful to see if their job searching is as intense as that of the Irish-born unemployed and also to see if similar approaches are used.

In Table 5.11 we show the proportions of both the Irish-born and immigrant unemployed using a variety of job search techniques. In four out of the six categories there is no difference in the immigrant and Irish-born proportions, suggesting a broadly similar approach to job search. The two categories where differences arise are in respect of private employment agencies and friends/relatives/trade unions. The finding that immigrants use friends, etc., less intensively may be explained by immigrants having less well developed networks of employment-related contacts than Irish-born people. It may also be the case that private employment agencies act as substitutes for informal contacts, thereby explaining the more intensive use by immigrants relative to the Irish-born.

Table 5.11 Job search methods used by Irish-born and immigrants who are unemployed

Method	Irish	All immigrants
Contacted public employment office		
%	55.1	53.4
No.	1,483	148
Contacted private employment agency		
%	32.3	41.2*
No.	1,488	148
Applied to employers direct		
%	78.6	75.0
No.	1,490	148
Asked friends, relatives, trade unions, etc.		
%	82.3	73.0*
No.	1,492	148
Inserted or answered advertisements in newspapers or journals		
%	28.6	30.4
No.	1,492	148
Studied advertisements in newspapers		
%	91.8	89.9
No.	1,493	148

*Denotes a proportion that is significantly different from the Irish proportion at the 5% level.
Source: figures calculated from CSO QNHS (q. 2).

Estimating the economic contribution of immigrants

In the earlier sections we have provided information on the number of immigrants in Ireland and also on their characteristics. In this section we take this information and try to estimate the economic impact of immigrants in Ireland, including their contribution in terms of increased GNP. Exercises such as these are not without controversy, so it is important for us to set out how we go about the task of estimating impact. If we are explicit on our methodology the reader can at least see where the results come from and can assess them accordingly.

The first broad point that should be made about estimating immigrant impact concerns a simple methodological difficulty. If researchers attempt to apply a simplistic regression approach and look at the relationship between, for example, wages and immigrant inflows at a national level, misleading results will emerge. A simple regression of this type will almost certainly show a positive relation between wages and immigration. However, the direction of causation is also almost certain to run from wages to immigration and so the question of how immigration impacts upon wages remains.

There have been three broad approaches used in the economics literature to estimating the impact of immigrants and to overcoming the difficulty described in the preceding paragraph. We will briefly outline each, partly by way of explaining why we employ one of the three approaches rather than either of the others. The three approaches can be labelled as follows: (1) the geographical approach; (2) natural experiments; (3) simulation.[12]

The geographical approach to estimating immigrant impacts has mainly been used in the United States. Under this approach, changes in the ratio of immigrants and domestic residents across a large number of metropolitan areas in the United States are correlated with changes in the ratio of immigrant and domestic wages. By exploiting regional variation in labour market performance, this approach reduces the influence of the sort of reverse causality described above. The outcome from most of these studies is to suggest that immigration has, at most, a very marginal impact on domestic wages.[13]

The natural experiment approach seeks to overcome the problem that immigration is endogenously determined in a system including wages and national output by looking for exogenous inflows. By this we mean that an immigrant inflow that can be considered unrelated to economic conditions in the receiving country. One such example was the Mariel Boatlift, when Fidel Castro allowed an outflow of Cubans to Miami. The effects of this on the Miami labour market were examined and the conclusion was that the impact was minimal.[14]

In order to explain the reasoning behind the third approach (simulation), it is necessary to point out the failings that were identified in the two approaches just outlined. According to Borjas *et al.* (1997),[15] the results from geographical and natural experiment approaches could be explained if domestic workers left the cities into which immigrants were arriving, or if domestic workers postponed migration into those same cities. If this were the case, the finding that immigrants had little impact on wages may simply have arisen because the labour supply increase from immigration was offset by a labour supply loss from outward migration. Based on this difficulty with either the geographical or natural experiment approaches, Borjas *et al.* argued that the 'correct' approach to estimating immigrant impacts was to construct a model of the labour market and to simulate the impact of immigration.

Leaving aside for the moment the Borjas *et al.* critique of the other methods, it is clear that the geographical and natural experiment approaches could not be used in the Irish context. The country is too small to think in terms of regional variation in labour market perform-ance and there has been no natural experiment as regards population inflows. For this reason we would have to use the simulation approach in estimating the impact of immigrants. However, the arguments put forward by Borjas *et al.* suggest that this should be the preferred approach anyway.

The starting point for our simulation approach is the econometric estimation of a model of the Irish labour market. We will provide here a brief outline of the model; a fuller presentation is provided in Barrett *et al.* (2005) and Bergin and Kearney (2004).[16] There are five strands to the model: high-skilled labour demand and labour supply; low-skilled labour demand and labour supply; a production function translating labour used into output. Parameters on the equations in the model are either estimated using time series data from 1966 to the present or are imposed on the model, using parameter estimates from other sources. Through jointly modelling all elements, we are able to simulate how changes in variables impact on a set of variables of interest.

The fact that we model both the high-skilled and low-skilled labour market is both important and useful.[17] As domestic production has become more technologically advanced and the educational levels of the work force have improved, high-skilled and low-skilled workers have become less substitutable. Our estimates suggest that by the mid to late 1990s there is essentially zero elasticity of substitution between high-skilled and low-skilled labour. High-skilled labour supply is very elastic because of the ready availability of migration flows, and those with high levels of education are typically more mobile. It also reflects the relatively high-skilled female labour supply elasticity.[18] High and low-skilled labour are assumed to be complements at the level of the economy, as a rise in the cost of either will serve to reduce Ireland's competitiveness and therefore output and employment of both types of labour. We include two possible mechanisms for adjustment within the low-skilled labour market. In one case, low-skilled wages are assumed to be a fixed mark-up on social welfare payments; this places a floor on low-skilled wages and so adjustment is through changes in unemployment. In the other case, market clearing operates and adjustment is through wages.

The details of the simulation are as follows. We have chosen to estimate the impact of the immigrant inflow for the three years up to 2005. As shown in Figure 5.1, the gross non-Irish inflows from 2003 to 2005 total 117,000 people. We need to adjust this figure to take account of the outflow and the fact that a proportion of the inflow was of children. Adjusting for these leaves a net inflow of non-Irish adults of 90,000. Based on Table 5.4 above, we can assume that about two-thirds are labour force participants. From Table 5.7 we can assume that 15% of the immigrants are low-skilled (having no qualifications or only lower secondary schooling), hence we define the remaining 85% as being high-skilled.

Table 5.8 suggested, on the basis of the distribution of occupations, that immigrants were not being employed to their fullest degree relative to their education levels. Given this, we will take the first set of estimated

Table 5.12 Results of simulation with immigrant 'fully employed'

Variable	Low-skilled unemploy-ment adjusts	Low-skilled wages adjust
	% change	
GNP		
Per head	0.9	0.8
Per worker	0.8	0.8
Total	3.0	2.8
Employment rate		
Total	2.2	2.0
High-skilled	2.3	2.1
Low-skilled	1.9	1.9
Labour supply		
Total	1.7	2.0
High-skilled	2.3	2.1
Low-skilled	0.8	1.9
Average wage		
Overall	−3.9	−3.7
High-skilled	−5.0	−4.8
Low-skilled	0.0	0.8
	As % of labour force	
Unemployment rate		
Total	−0.4	0.0
Low-skilled	−1.0	0.0

Table 5.13 Results of simulation, adjusting for 'immigrant occupation gap'

Variable	Low-skilled unemploy-ment adjustments	Low-skilled wages adjustments
	% change	
GNP		
Per head	0.4	0.3
Per worker	0.7	0.6
Total	2.4	2.3
Employment rate		
Total	1.7	1.6
High-skilled	1.8	1.7
Low-skilled	1.5	1.5
Labour supply		
Total	1.8	1.6
High-skilled	1.8	1.7
Low-skilled	1.7	1.5
Average wage		
Total	-3.1	-3.0
High-skilled	-3.9	-3.7
Low-skilled	0.0	-0.2
	As % of labour force	
Unemployment rate		
Total	0.1	0.0

impacts as being a set of upper-bound estimates. We then perform the simulation again, this time assuming the immigrants and the Irish-born have the same educational attainment. This is a somewhat blunt method of discounting immigrant skills and of accounting for the occupational gap. It probably results in an underestimate of immigrant impact, and for this reason we consider the results in this simulation as being a lower-bound estimate.

The results of the first simulation are presented in Table 5.12. Recall that what is being modelled is the impact of adding 90,000 adult immigrants to the population and hence about 60,000 labour force participants. The results can be explained as follows. As the immigrants are mainly skilled, there is an increase in the supply of skilled labour. This tends to reduce high-skilled wages, and high-skilled employment rises. An increase in the employment of high-skilled labour results in an increase in the demand for low-skilled labour, since these are complements in production. Overall, employment increases (by between 2% and 2.2%) and national output, or GNP, increases too (by between 2.8% and 3%). Hence the immigrant group that arrived between 2003 and 2005, according to our simulation, increased GNP and low-skilled wages. However, they tended to put downward pressure on high-skilled wages. In reality, high-skilled wages did not actually fall in Ireland but what this analysis suggests is that high-skill wages would have been higher in the absence of immigration.

In Table 5.13 we repeat the analysis but with the impact of immigrants diluted to account for the fact that they are not employed to the level suggested by their education levels. As can be seen, the pattern of results is similar but the sizes are smaller. For example, the impact on GNP is now estimated to be between 2.3% and 2.4%.

Conclusion

One objective of this chapter has been to provide information on the characteristics of Ireland's immigrant population with a particular focus on labour market characteristics. A second objective has been to quantify the economic impact of the immigrant inflow.

Similar to earlier studies by Barrett and Trace (1998) and Barrett *et al.* (2005) we have found that immigrants in Ireland continue to have, on average, notably high levels of educational attainment, relative to the Irish-born population and relative to immigrant populations elsewhere. This raises an interesting question about what it is that makes Ireland attractive to high-skilled immigrants. One theory that may have relevance here is that of Borjas (1987).[19] According to this theory, high-skilled immigrants (and hence high-earning immigrants) will be attracted to destinations where earnings are relatively unequally distributed. This is because high earners will benefit from a wide dispersal of earnings but low earners lose in such a setting. To the extent that Ireland exhibits a relatively high degree of earnings inequality, this may partly explain the presence of high-skilled immigrants. In addition, if economic developments in Ireland in recent years have been biased in favour of high-skilled labour (as suggested by Bergin and Kearney, 2004), this also may have acted to attract the high-skilled.

While immigrants are more highly educated than the Irish-born population, their representation across occupations is not dissimilar to the Irish-born. This suggests underutilisation of immigrant skills. Without data on the precise length of time each immigrant has been in Ireland it is not possible to say if this underutilisation is related to a short-term problem as immigrants adjust or a more fundamental problem.

The other dimensions of the labour market experience of immigrants in Ireland that we looked at suggested that immigrants were not more likely to be in jobs with undesirable characteristics such as atypical hours or long hours. Also, unemployed immigrants seem to use the same types of job search techniques as unemployed Irish people. While the success of those methods might differ between immigrants and the Irish-born, no evidence of marginalisation arose from the data on job search methods.

Finally, our estimates of the economic impact of immigrants suggest the following. The net immigrant inflow between 2003 and 2005 is estimated to have added between 2.3% and 3% to GNP. The route through which this was achieved was to lower high-skilled wages relative to where they otherwise would have been and to facilitate the increased employment of high-skilled labour. The effect of this was then to increase the demand for low-skilled labour and hence low-skilled wages (or to reduce low-skilled unemployment, depending on how this is modelled). Either way, immigration into Ireland has been positive in terms of both increasing GNP and reducing earnings inequality.

Notes

1 A. Barrett and F. Trace, 'Who is coming back? The Educational Profile of Returning Migrants in the 1990s', *Irish Banking Review,* summer 1998.

2 A. Barrett, J. FitzGerald and B. Nolan, 'Earnings Inequality, Returns to Education and Immigration into Ireland', *Labour Economics,* 9: 5 (2002).

3 A. Barrett, A. Bergin and D. Duffy, *The Labour Market Characteristics and Labour Market Impacts of Immigrants in Ireland,* IZA Discussion Paper No. 1553 (Bonn: Institute for the Study of Labour (IZA), 2005).

4 For a fuller description of the methodology of the survey see Central Statistics Office, *Quarterly National Household Survey, Quarter 2* (Dublin: CSO, 2004).

5 The 'ten years or less' residence condition is imposed by the manner in which the micro-data are provided. Ideally we would have wanted year-by-year information on residence. However, as we can identify people who were not born in Ireland but who have lived there since 1994 and later, we are essentially capturing arrivals in the Celtic Tiger era and beyond.

6 Micro-data from the census are available, but it provides fewer labour-related data and is also less timely than the 2004 QNHS.

7 For a related discussion on how well sample surveys capture Ireland's ethnic composition see B. Fanning and M. Pierce, 'Ethnic Data and Social Policy in Ireland', *Administration,* 52: 3 (2004).

8 See, for example, B. Fanning, S. Loyal and C. Staunton, *Asylum Seekers and the Right to Work in Ireland* (Dublin: Irish Refugee Council, 2000).

9 See, for example, M. Ruhs, *Managing the Immigration and Employment of*

non-EU Nationals in Ireland, Policy Institute Blue Paper No. 19 (Dublin: Trinity College, 2005).

10 See A. Barrett, 'Irish Migration: Causes, Characteristics and Consequences', in K. Zimmermann (ed.), *European Migration: What do we Know?* (Oxford: Oxford University Press, 2005).

11 As we noted above an underrepresentation among certain immigrants, it is useful to note that this finding on education was also present in C. Minns, 'How Skilled are Irish Immigrants? Evidence and Implications', paper delivered to the Statistical and Social Inquiry Society of Ireland, 24 February 2005, where the data used come from the census 2002 (Dublin: Statistical and Social Inquiry Society of Ireland, 2005).

12 A good overview of these approaches is provided by R. Friedberg and J. Hunt, 'The Impact of Immigration on Host Country Wages, Employment and Growth', *Journal of Economic Perspectives*, 9 (1995).

13 For an early example see J. B. Grossman, 'The Substitutability of Natives and Immigrants in Production', *Review of Economics and Statistics*, 54 (1982).

14 C. David, 'The Impact of the Mariel Boatlift on the Miami Labour Market', *Industrial and Labor Relations Review*, 43 (1990).

15 G. J. Borjas, R. B. Freeman and L. F. Katz, 'How much do Immigration and Trade affect Labor Market Outcomes?', *Brookings Papers on Economic Activity*, 1 (1997).

16 A. Bergin and I. Kearney, 'Human Capital, the Labour Market and Productivity Growth in Ireland', ESRI Working Paper No. 158 (Dublin: ESRI, 2004).

17 We define high-skilled as those who have at least a higher secondary qualification and low-skilled as those with at most a lower secondary qualification.

18 See A. Doris, 'Labour Supply Elasticity Changes during the 1990s', *Quarterly Economic Commentary, December* (Dublin: ESRI, 2001), for a discussion of the difference between male and female participation elasticities.

19 G. J. Borjas, 'Self-selection and the Earnings of Immigrants', *American Economic Review*, 77: 14 (1987).

6

Neo-liberalism and immigration

Kieran Allen

There is a deep paradox at the heart of Ireland's political economy. The dominant economic philosophy suggests that the market must be allowed to function with minimal state intervention. Yet, when it comes to human labour, Soviet-style planning and command and control mechanisms prevail. Labour is treated as a mere commodity that has to adjust to the laws of supply and demand, but, prior to its entry on to the market, state mechanisms have been designed to ensure an outcome favourable to the corporations. It is a paradox worth exploring a little further.

For three years in a row Ireland topped the A. T. Kearney/Foreign Policy Globalization Index, making it a model of neo-liberal economics.[1] If confirmation was required, one need only look at its ranking in the Heritage Foundation 'economic freedom' index. The Heritage Foundation is a right-wing US think tank that is funded by forty-five large corporations such as Exxon Mobil, Chevron Texaco and Merrill Lynch. It benchmarks countries for their adherence to neo-liberal measures and awarded Ireland fifth place in its 'freedom' index – significantly higher than the United States itself.[2] Echoing these ratings, the National Competitiveness Council has produced detailed charts to show how Ireland comes near the top of the world league for cutting business taxes and for light regulation.[3]

The latter point deserves a little more focus, as it often slips into the background compared with the tax advantages that Ireland offers corporations. In fact Ireland is regarded as one of the strongest advocates in the European Union of reducing 'uncompetitive' regulation of business. The Minister for Enterprise Trade and Employment summed up the approach when he stated, 'I am conscious that when you go the foreign investment route in the US, what companies say is that they like the government's ability to get things done in Ireland and that they are not over-regulated like in mainland Europe.'[4] The financial services sector provides an important example of the 'regulation-lite' approach. The IDA, for example, explicitly markets the International Financial Services

Centre on the grounds that there is 'no transfer pricing legislation' or 'thin capitalisation rules' and that 'Ireland uses an Anglo/Saxon business model'.[5] More recently Ireland has introduced a Regulatory Impact Analysis, whose aim is to reduce 'unnecessary' regulation of businesses, in all government departments.

Irish economic policy is often based on the assumption that the market naturally reaches a state of equilibrium – provided it is not subject to 'rigidities' imposed by the state. This neo-liberal dogma, however, has a strangely utopian quality. It purports to describe a world where 'perfect competition' prevails – even though this is only an analytical construct. The discrepancy between the model and 'real existing capitalism' leads to incessant demands for more 'economic freedom'. But this in turn brings an important dialectic into play as 'freedom' for corporations means greater tyranny at the level of the workplace. The more companies demand 'flexibility' in responding to markets the more they attack trade unions, develop a bullying managerial style and threaten workers who do not conform to 'reality' with the sack. Far from neo-liberalism bringing 'freedom', it usually creates more pressure, stress and control.

These same contradictions between freedom and control also operate at the level of the Irish political economy. While every effort is made to reduce the regulatory burden on business, the state has expanded its efforts to plan and shape the labour market. Soviet-style planning has become the reverse side of the market freedom demanded by business. The principal target of this planning is migrant labour.

Organising the corporate agenda

Ireland's migrant labour system initially developed in an *ad hoc* fashion. The first wave of migrants who came to Ireland in the 1990s were the asylum seekers, and the main debate was whether they should be allowed to obtain a right to work. For a brief period a humanitarian ethos coincided with economic logic, and asylum seekers who arrived before 26 July 1999 were allowed to work. This provision survived for less than a year as the state bureaucracy became frightened that it would become too attractive a 'pull' factor, particularly for asylum seekers from Africa. In a sharp about-turn, asylum seekers who came after 10 April 2000 were subject to a more punitive policy. No only were they denied a right to work but they were also forcibly dispersed throughout the country and made subject to direct provision.[6]

As the economy boomed, however, labour shortages grew, and very rapidly, and without much publicity, a work permit system developed on an extensive basis after 1999. In the early years of the Celtic Tiger boom fewer than 6,000 work permits were issued each year from 1995 and 1999. The previous decades of underdevelopment had created considerable reserves of labour and returned emigrants and women who might previously have stayed in the home filled the gaps. From 1999 to 2003, however, the number of work permits jumped by 700%, with 47,707 permits being used in the latter year alone.[7]

The work permit system was modelled on the guest worker system which was devised by the major industrial powers after World War II. The system assumed that immigration is temporary and that the individual worker should be treated as a guest who would eventually leave. Guests, of course, need particular hosts to invite them, and for workers this meant an employer on whom they were dependent. Hosts, of course, can only look after guests in times of plenty and in leaner periods they may have to ask guests to leave. This elaborate official fiction was organised though practices such as the 'rotation principle' whereby migrant workers had to leave their host country before applying for new permits or through bans on family reunification, which suggested that the worker had only an instrumental and temporary relation with their host society.

By 1999, when the Irish economy embraced the guest worker system, there was an abundance of evidence that the official fiction about guest workers had broken down. The Turkish guest workers who came to Germany in the 1960s were having children and even grandchildren who claimed a dual cultural allegiance.[8] The Mexican population who arrived on the *bracero* programme in the 1950s in the United States had exploded into millions. Even the threats to deport guest workers from the South East Asian economies after the 1997 crash did not materialise as countries found that migrants had become structurally embedded.[9] Nevertheless, the Irish state carried on with the official fiction regardless – migrants were only guests and had to be legally treated as such. There was no provision for permanent residence, no automatic assumption of family reunification, and permits could be applied for only from outside Ireland.

The primary mechanism by which this legal fiction was enforced was by assigning the work permit to the employer rather than the employee. Employers had to pass a formal labour market test by advertising jobs on the Irish market for four weeks before applying for a permit. But once they did this very few applications for permits were refused. Once the permit was granted, employers had in effect a system of bonded labour – as the worker could not leave for another job and was dependent on the employer to renew the work permit.

The flexibility of the employers was further increased through the use of recruitment agencies. In 1997 there were 272 recruitment agencies in

Ireland but by 1999 the number had jumped to 447. The Department of Enterprise Trade and Employment claims that the practice of collecting data on the number of workers registered with temporary agencies was discontinued after 1995 and only fragmentary figures exist.[10] This is an extraordinary claim, as recruitment agencies are legally obliged to make these returns and it is the function of the department to enforce the law. It has become a routine matter for departments to lose embarrassing files, and it seems this practice has now emerged in the gathering of official statistics. By contrast, even in the United States, the Bureau of Labor Statistics can provide detailed figures on very specific categories of contingent workers through regular supplements to the Current Population Survey.[11] One study, however, using data from the European Foundation's Third European Survey on Working Conditions by Conroy and Pierce in 2002, suggested that Ireland had the highest percentage of workers employed on a temporary agency contract (5.2%) in the European Union, whereas the average across the then fifteen States was 2.2%.[12] Legally there is insufficient regulation of recruitment agencies – they merely have to be set up by people of good character, to pay an initial licence fee and then to submit returns on placements.

The neo-liberal injunction that companies must attain the maximum freedom to adjust to labour market conditions, however, created an extraordinary regime of fear and tyranny for many migrants. The Irish state masked this economic terror by claiming that migrant workers were protected by the same labour legislation that applies to other workers. Yet this defence does not hold both on the grounds of enforcement procedure and scope of legislation.

Ireland has presently thirty-one labour inspectors to cover a work force of nearly 2 million – and this represents a recent increase of ten. To put matters into perspective, there are fifty dog wardens to cover a canine population of 150,000. There are also forty-one inspectors whose sole function is to enforce the smoking ban in pubs. A leaked report to the *Irish Times* indicated that morale within the labour inspectorate was extremely low. Training for the post was deemed to be haphazard and, bizarrely, knowledge of labour legislation was not deemed to be a necessary requirement for recruitment. Turnover was high and most staff felt fully confident to carry out duties only after a twelve to eighteen-month period.[13] Despite anecdotal reports of abuses, the number of inspections carried out has actually fallen from 8,323 in 2002 to 5,160 in 2004. In that year a mere fourteen successful prosecutions were carried out, with typical fines ranging from €500 to €2,000. The assumption that the labour inspectorate could protect migrant workers within the system of bonded labour is therefore absurd.

Moreover, even if the labour inspectorate was increased, that would still not fully solve the problem. The powers of the inspectorate are extremely limited and reflect the wider ethos of the Irish state that regulation of business should not be over-'burdensome'. Inspectors cannot compel employers to pay overtime rates, Sunday rates or bank holiday rates. Under the Organisation of Working Time Act they are able to ensure only that employers keep records but they cannot carry out direct investigations to gather evidence. Inspectors cannot prevent overworking, stress or the daily verbal abuse which has become the norm for many migrants. Even if they are able to enforce the Minimum Wage Act, they are unable do anything about the loopholes that allow employers to pay below the rate while an employee is in 'training'.

There is ample evidence that the work permit system has created an institutionalised form of abuse that cannot be explained by the actions of a few 'unscrupulous' employers. In its report *Labour Migration into Ireland* the Immigrant Council of Ireland has highlighted through various cameo pictures the scale of the abuse which migrants face. One such cameo illustrates the fundamental imbalance in migrant–employer relations

> Sergei is a Latvian national who came to Ireland at the height of the Celtic Tiger boom. He has been living in Ireland for three years. Sergei is employed as a shop manager and is on his third employment permit. Sergei is the only person who is not Irish in his workplace. He has got to know his workmates very well over the past three years and likes his job, his colleagues and the craic.
>
> Two months ago, Sergei discovered that his Irish colleagues were paid more than he was for the same job. The other shop managers were paid €9.75 an hour while Sergei is paid the minimum wage. His employer has never paid overtime, and told Sergei that in Ireland people are paid the same wage every week. Most weeks Sergei has worked in excess of fifty hours. Sergei was also told that in Ireland all holidays are unpaid. He was unable to afford to take a holiday in the past three years. When Sergei confronted his employer with this information, he was sacked. He has been looking for another job but is having difficulty explaining why he is out of work. His former workmates have been trying to help him but he cannot get a reference from his old job.[14]

The most damning indictment of the guest worker system comes, however, from a study commissioned by the Labour Relations Commission. After analysing the experiences of migrant workers taking their cases to the Rights Commissioner, they found that:

> The main issue was underpayment of wages, including payment below the minimum wage; followed by non-payment of overtime (including

non-payment of Sunday and public holiday premiums), excess hours and non-payment of holiday pay. Other issues were those of unfair dismissal, unlawful deductions, bullying and non-issuing of pay slips. What was particularly remarkable about the issues raised is that, in almost all cases, the claimant listed more than one and, in many cases, listed all of the above complaints'.[15]

The report noted that 80% of migrant workers' claims were successful in 2002, with this figures rising to 85% in 2003.[16] More remarkably, the report detailed the structural obstacles that migrants have to go through to gain access to this system of redress.

Almost all cases (99% according to SIPTU) were brought by workers who had already left their employer because, as the report indicated, 'their greatest and overriding fear is that of losing their work permit and being deported'.[17] To process complaints to the Rights Commissioner a worker must fill in a complaint form which is copied to the employer. This same employer, it should be remembered, holds the work permit. If he refuses to renew it, the worker must first return home to reapply for another. Often there can be a delay in hearing the complaint and workers may have had to leave the country before their case comes up for hearing. They must, however, appear in person for the case to be processed – even though this is beyond the means of most migrants who have left the country. Only one migrant returned to appear at their case in 2002/2003.[18] An employee who has become undocumented has no legal right to process a complaint, even though employees frequently become 'undocumented' because the employer fails to renew the work permit. To renew a permit, employers must show that they are tax-compliant and must produce six random pay slips to demonstrate that the employee was paid in accordance with the original contract. If employers cannot meet these conditions they often do not apply for renewal of the permit.

This is the institutional background against which the celebrated GAMA case occurred. In this case Turkish workers were forced to work for more than eighty hours a week for rates of about €2.20 an hour.[19] The Registered Employment Agreement for the construction industry set wages at €12.95 an hour but the workers had to stage a seven-week strike and face threats of physical violence before they finally reached settlement of €8,000 each in back money. According to government Ministers, this was another unusual case of an 'unscrupulous' employer who was flouting the Irish system. This, however, barely stands up to scrutiny, as Gama was a major construction company which specialised in state projects. It came to Ireland after the Minister for Enterprise Trade and Employment, Mary Harney, travelled to Turkey to invite it there. No one appeared to raise an eyebrow when it was able to tender far below its rivals – in the case of a project for Clare County Council, its tender was €14 million cheaper than the original price.[20] In 2003 Harney was informed by the Bricklayers' Union that GAMA was engaged in such practices but she claimed that a senior official in the Department of Enterprise Trade and Employment had found the charges to be 'without substance'.[21] A few months after the Gama scandal broke, the Transport Minister, Martin Cullen, performed the opening ceremony on the new Clontibret–Castleblayney bypass, the contract for which had been awarded to Gama even after the revelations about underpayment of staff.[22] It was an apt symbol of official connivance with a company which had become synonymous for abusing its migrant staff.

After 2000 the Irish state developed a more elaborate categorisation system to indicate a more precise connection between social rights and marketable skills. A work authorisation or visa system was introduced for more skilled employees. As certain skills were in short supply in the global economy, the state offered extra attractions to such workers. Work visas/authorisations were issued to the worker rather than the employer and so workers were able to change jobs as long as they stayed within the same skill category. The visas could also be held for two years rather than one and could be renewed for a further two years. Despite these minor advantages, holders of work visas also faced significant restrictions. The most significant was the failure to grant such workers an automatic right to be reunited with their families. One of the overriding assumptions behind state policy was that migrants should not become a burden on the Irish exchequer, and this led to restrictions on the entry of 'dependants'. Filipino nurses mounted a strong campaign to get these restrictions reversed and were partially successful in February 2004 when the Minister for Enterprise Trade and Employment made concessions but then discovered that most of their spouses were put on the work permit schemes and so limited in their employment prospects.[23] The number of migrants who held work visas remained comparatively small, with only 10,300 visas being issued between 2000 and 2004.[24]

This was the basic structure of Ireland migrant labour scheme up to 2003. It had developed in a crude *ad hoc* manner to serve employer interests by defining workers primarily as a marketable commodity. They had arrived solely to sell their labour – their wider social being as a member of a family or as an active participant in the host society was neglected. Their relation to the wider Irish society was defined as temporary and it was assumed that they would leave once the boom ended. A nod and a wink culture was an intrinsic part of state policy. Despite the fact that many employers did not renew work permits, there were few if any prosecution cases. An interesting example of the officially sanctioned nod and wink culture is the case of domestic workers. Officially, work permits for domestic-based workers were issued only after an employee had worked abroad with the family for at least one year prior to the date of application. Yet the Philippine Overseas Employment Administration – the state-run recruitment agency with which the Irish state has developed close links – could tell applicants that 'it has been observed that the Department [of Enterprise of Ireland, *sic*] does not adhere strictly to the policy and continues to issue work permits. It regards domestic staff as a different category from other household help, like caretakers of children, and has no prohibition for the issuance of work permits'.[25]

Soviet-style modernisation

Ruhs has argued, correctly, that after April 2003 the Irish state adopted a more interventionist approach to the labour migration. Henceforth government policy assumed that most or all vacancies in the Irish labour market would be filled from EU accession countries. In line with this, Ireland adopted one of the most liberal positions on the entry of workers from Eastern Europe and in the Employment Permits Act of 2003 allowed workers from the ten accession states to take up employment without a work permit. Simultaneously the issuing of work permits to workers from non-EU member states was scaled back.

Ruhs's argument is correct in so far as it goes but it tends to analyse the labour market on a purely formal level and avoids any discussion of the class interests behind the policy. It also contains also an implicit notion of progress as the state shifts from an *ad hoc* to a more 'managed' approach. One might also draw the conclusion that Ireland's policy towards the accession states was motivated by a more liberal and enlightened position. What this leaves out is the manner in which business interests dictated how the modernisation of the migrant labour system was carried out.

A key mechanism in this regard was the formation of the Expert Group on Future Skills Needs in 1997 out of the social partnership process. Although formally an advisory body, it developed close institutional links with FÁS, the national manpower service. By 2001 a Skills and Research Market Research Unit was set up in FÁS to serve the planning needs of both its parent organisation and the EGFSN. What is striking about the development was the role that the key corporate leaders played in both agencies. On 21 November 2001 Brian Geoghegan, the former director of the employers' organisation IBEC was appointed the Director of FÁS. Nine days later he married the Minister who appointed him, Mary Harney, the leader of the avidly pro-business Progressive Democrats.

Within the EGFSN corporate leaders were overrepresented compared with the unions and took the driving seat. The present chairperson of the EGFSN is Anne Heraty, the Chief Executive Officer of Computer Placements. Of the nine ordinary members, one is the direct representative of IBEC and four others directly represent business interests. They include Jack Golden, the Human Resources Director of Cement Roadstone; Una Halligan, a member of the board of the American Chamber of Commerce and the Hewlett Packard manager responsible for the Government and Public in Ireland Affairs; Senan Cooke, the Training and Communications Officer of Waterford Crystal; Joe McCarthy, the Managing Director of Arkaon.

The EGFSN has been given full access to databases for projections on the Irish labour market. Its approach has been to construct the most detailed tables of future supply and demand for particular industrial sectors and then to promote policies which overcome labour and skill shortages. The implicit aim is to prevent wages rising by ensuring that there is an alignment of supply and demand. In 2000, for example, the second report of the EGFSN noted that there were skill shortages in the seven main craft areas in construction and noted that this was evident in the statistics for wage inflation in the sector. However, instead of tackling the reluctance of employers to take on apprentices it looked to migration primarily as the way to reduce wage pressures. It assumed (wrongly, as it turned out) that the skill shortages would peak at almost 5,000 in the year 2000 and persist at a reducing level until 2004.[26] The role of the EGFSN continued to grow, and by 2001 Mary Harney, the Minister for Enterprise Trade and Employment, described it as 'the central resource' for advising on skills needs.[27]

The most recent report of the EGFSN, *Skills Needs in the Irish Economy: The Role of Migration*, provides an interesting example of the general approach of the group. Formally, there is adherence to the norms of free-market economics, which treats labour as a commodity like any other and suggests that labour shortages are primarily overcome through rising wages levels:

> labour shortages generally only occur in situations where wages do not react to market forces. In such scenarios, immigration can be used as a tool to suppress real wage growth. The suppression of real wages can then dis-incentivise the resident work force from upskilling themselves as wage differentials are narrowed....
>
> Thus, a policy that attempts to address labour shortages through inward migration will result in a constant spiral, with immigration being used to address existing labour shortages, followed by an increase in consumer demand, finally resulting in new calls for even more emigration ...[28]

Yet at no point does the group recommend that restrictions on wage increases be removed and workers be allowed to gain more than the terms of social partnership agreements.

Instead skill and labour shortages in 'enterprise sectors' that were categorised as being of economic importance to the economy as a whole are identified. The level of detail and the certainty by which predictions are made is truly awesome. So one learns that the shortfall of computing graduates in 2006 will be 606, in 2007 it will be 969 and in 2010 it will be 1,217.[29] By 2008, it is suggested, Ireland will need an extra 600 mushroom pickers; thirty propagation workers for plant nurseries and fifty food technology agronomists.[30] In the financial sector a 'low skill' shortage is detected in areas such as fund administration due to a 'retention problem'.[31] In tourism it is noted that, owing to poor staff retention rates, there will be a shortage of 35,200 workers in 2010.[32] Precise figures are also given for different trades in construction but once again there is little examination of why more apprentices were not coming on stream. Instead it is baldly stated that 'it is important that construction price inflation should not be fuelled by a shortage of skilled workers as occurred in the period 1997–2001'.[33]

After this detailed analysis, the EGFSN report turns to a set of detailed charts on the labour supply of Eastern European countries. The focus was on their educational attainment levels, literacy scores and on precise figures for how their wages levels fare *vis-à-vis* Ireland. It was noted, for example, that there are eight EU countries where average earnings are less than 60% of the average in Ireland. These are Slovenia (56%), the Czech Republic (48%), Poland (46%), Slovakia (44%), Hungary (42%), Estonia (32%), Lithuania (28%) and Latvia (25%). However, a further analysis of graduate wages was made and here a more surprising result emerged. Irish graduates receive much lower wages compared with their counterparts in the 'old' European Union and do not receive much higher earnings than counterparts in the 'new' accession states.

This discrepancy between wages in Ireland for relatively unskilled labour and those of Eastern European countries meant that Ireland exerted a considerable 'pull' for their workers. The EGFSN therefore concluded that 'Ireland's demand for low-skilled and unskilled labour over the period to 2010 is likely to be met from the labour supply available from the expanded EU states'[34] It was further noted that the labour pool of those with upper secondary education was in the order of 25 million.. These figures provided the justification for closing off the work permit system for non-EU unskilled workers.

However, even as the older work permit system was being restricted, the Irish state did not give up on the idea of bonded labour. It merely

Table 6.1 Average industrial and services earnings (excluding public administration) for those with tertiary education in 2002

Country	Average earnings (PPP) of those with tertiary education	Average earnings of those with tertiary education relative to Ireland (%)	Rank
Germany	59,461	179	1
Luxembourg	57,199	172	2
Austria	54,393	164	3
Netherlands	49,420	149	4
UK	47,862	144	5
Belgium	45,015	136	6
Italy	43,991	133	7
France	42,617	128	8
Denmark	42,278	127	9
Portugal	41,062	124	10
Spain	35,193	106	11
Sweden	34,832	105	12
Greece	34,612	104	13
Ireland	33,200	100	14
Slovenia	33,128	100	15

Source: Eurostat, Structure of Earnings Survey, 2002.

modified it by introducing a 'habitual residence condition' for foreign
workers who came in after 2003. These workers were not entitled to
claim social welfare – including child benefit, unemployment benefit,
disability benefit – for at least two years. Even then they had to prove
that they intended to make Ireland their permanent home and that their
family resided here. By denying workers the right to claim unemployment benefit the Irish state ensured that a huge obstacle was put in their
way of leaving employers. They became in effect a vulnerable group open
to super-exploitation.

The EGFSN drew different conclusions when it came to graduate labour.
Noting that 'as Ireland had only the fourteenth highest graduate earnings
in real terms across the EU countries ... [and] the financial incentive to
move to Ireland is limited ... Given the above it seems highly appropriate to facilitate the in-migration of high-skilled labour from countries
outside the EU'.[35] The group therefore favoured a 'green card' system
for these workers. Ireland needed a more flexible policy – but one which
also ensured that workers were still reduced primarily to an economic

category. The 'green card' as proposed by the EGFSN would be available to non-EU workers but it contained an important number of restrictions. Family reunification could take place only when the migrants had sufficient earning capacity. It was also suggested that skilled migrants should enter Ireland only if they were in receipt of a job offer and so 'immediate job mobility may ... not be practical'. It was further suggested that 'the duration of the period during which the migrant remains tied to their initial employer ought to take account of the time it would take an employer to recoup their investment in that migrant' and this would normally take one year.[36] The EGFSN also wanted the state to carefully control the flow of skilled migrants and claimed it was necessary to 'be able to amend eligible sectors, occupations, salary levels or qualifications on a regular basis, in accordance with the changing needs of the enterprise sector'.[37] To do this, it advocated a system where decisions could be made on an 'administrative' basis rather than specifying conditions for the green card system in actual legislation. Despite agreeing in principle that skilled migrants ought to be able to obtain permanent residence, the EGFSN also recommended that 'The Minister should retain discretionary powers to either refuse or cancel permanent residence'.[38]

This 'flexible' strategy whereby the Irish state could respond to immediate labour market conditions is at the heart of the government's latest Employment Permits Bill. This gives legal foundation to the concept of ministerial discretion to regulate the supply of skilled migrant labour by 'administrative' means. The original concept of a green card system implied a right of migrants to become citizens of the country where they work. However, the new Bill does not contain any provision for permanence. Instead the Minister is given discretion to lengthen the duration of skilled worker permits in the future. People will have to earn over €55,000 per year in order to be eligible for the scheme but, again, this figure is not contained in the law itself – but can be altered by regulation by the Minister. The new Bill gives no automatic right of reunification – even in the case of skilled migrants. There is a minor modification of the system of work permits so that the permit is formally held by the worker. But, in a Catch 22-style situation, the permit is operable only if an employer applies for it on his or her behalf. So, if workers believe they are exploited, they cannot automatically look for a new job but must wait until another employer goes through the process of applying on their behalf – and meanwhile they will have to survive without access to social welfare.

Information is power, according to the old cliché, and it certainly is when one engages in Soviet-style planning. What is striking about the EGFSN reports is the level of detail that has been provided to corporate interests to plan how they can manipulate the labour market to prevent wage inflation. In effect a crude form of geography was developed. The ten new accession states were to become the main suppliers of cheap, unskilled labour. Workers from these countries would enter the meat-packing plants, work as labourers on building sites, become the backbone of Ireland's tourist industry, gradually displacing former holders of work permits from non-EU countries. Deprived of social welfare, they would be the nearest equivalent to the Workfare victims of the United States – forced to work for relatively low wages and poor conditions. For skilled workers, however, Ireland was encouraged to raid the resources of non-EU countries such as India or the Philippines. Concessions had to be made because of the competition at global level for these workers – but concessions were to be kept to a minimum.

Conclusion

Soviet-style planning was far from perfect even in terms of serving the state, not to mention the needs of the vast majority of the people. Targets were often fictitious; predictions turned out to be wrong; information on key activities was lacking. No doubt the same problems apply to the EGFSN's work but what is interesting is the conscious attempt to manipulate the labour market through state intervention. Ironically, the neo-liberal doctrine that state intervention must be kept to the minimum is casually discarded when it comes to labour supply. Rather the national manpower agency FÁS is encouraged to focus actively on key countries in Eastern Europe to help Irish employers at home. The EFGSN called for a strengthening of the resources given to FÁS to step up its recruitment activities in this area –coyly noting that 'while recognising the role of enterprise, there is a role for the state in providing information and contacts for employers'.[39]

Corporate manipulation of the labour market relies on keeping migrant labour in a subservient role. At the level of rhetoric and symbol, employer organisations have embraced anti-racism. Each year they join other social partners and organise an Anti-Racist Workplace Week but in line with the ethos of social partnership 'divisive' issues are barely mentioned. Instead the focus is on 'managing cultural diversity' and celebrating good practice. Typically employer leaders issue a set of platitudes that avoid all reference to cases like Gama or Irish Ferries. Yet even while expressing such formal anti-racist sentiments, employers gain considerably from the migrant labour system which the EGFSN has played such an important role in devising. Migrants who are deprived of social welfare, who are effectively forced to stay with one employer for up to a year, who can apply for permits to remain in Ireland only on the say-so of employers – these are all ideal candidates for cheap labour. Institutionalised racism is not based on crude insults at street level but rather works through a system which creates state categories which deeply affect lives.

If the state strategy is based on undercutting the social rights of migrants in order to lower wages, an anti-racist strategy must champion these rights. Here important steps have been taken by Ireland's main union, SIPTU. The manner in which it both challenged Irish Ferries for displacing Irish workers *and* extended a hearty welcome to migrants to join its ranks is welcome. So too is its opposition to the habitual residence conditions which reduce workers to labour conscripts. These moves need to be supplemented by a vigorous organising drive which is inspired by a union vision to fight all aspects of the oppression of migrants. Employers will still pretend that they give migrants 'opportunities' for advancement. Unions must show that they take seriously the many expressions of suppressed anger that exist in migrant communities about their treatment by Irish society. Ultimately this will mean challenging the very basis of social partnership that encourages the type of tokenistic platitudes which the Irish state uses to cover its neo-liberal tracks. Only by doing so will the unions undermine a strategy designed to pit one worker against another. If they fail, Ireland will have the unenviable record of joining the top ranks in the race to the bottom.

Notes

1 A. T. Kearney, 'Measuring Globalization: Economic Reversals, Forward Momentum', *Foreign Policy,* March–April 2004, pp. 52–62.
2 A. Eiras, 'The United States is no longer the Champion of Economic Freedom', Heritage Foundation Web site www.heritage.org/research/trade-andforeignaid/bg1781.cfm.
3 National Competitiveness Council, *Annual Competitiveness Report,* chapter 4 (Dublin: Forfas, 2005).
4 'ISE Review likely after Fyffe's case', *Irish Times,* 21 June 2003.
5 IDA publicity material sent to author.
6 See S. Loyal, 'Welcome to the Celtic Tiger: Racism, Immigration and the State', in S. Coulter and S. Coleman (eds), *The End of Irish History: Critical Reflections on the Celtic Tiger* (Manchester: Manchester University Press, 2003), pp. 74–95.
7 M. Ruhs, *Managing the Immigration and Employment of non-EU Nationals in Ireland* (Dublin: Policy Institute, 2005), p. 15.
8 See K. Schonwalder, 'Migration, Refugees and Ethnic Plurality as Issues of Public and Political Debates in (West) Germany', in D. Cesarani and M. Fulbrook (eds), *Citizenship, Nationality and Migration in Europe* (London: Routledge, 1996), pp. 159–79.

9 P. Stalker, *Workers without Frontier: The Impact of Globalization on International Migration* (Boulder, CO: Lynne Rienner, 2000), p. 31.

10 Correspondence from Employment Agency section of DETE to author, 7 December 2005.

11 See S. Hipple, 'Contingent Work in the late 1990s', *Monthly Labour Review*, 124: 3 (2001), pp. 1–25.

12 P. Conroy and M. Pierce, *Temporary Agency Work: National Reports Ireland* (Dublin: European Foundation for Improvement of Living and Working Conditions, 2002), p. 16.

13 'Labour Inspectors condemn lack of resources', *Irish Times*, 8 April 2005.

14 Immigration Council of Ireland, *Labour Migration into Ireland* (Dublin: ICI, 2003), p. 29.

15 Labour Relations Commission, *Migrant Workers and Access to the Statutory Dispute Resolution Agencies* (Dublin: LRC, 2005), p. 15.

16 Ibid., p. 15.

17 Ibid., p. 20.

18 Ibid., p. 24.

19 'More inspectors to protect migrants', *Irish Times*, 13 April 2005.

20 'Clare council accused over Gama contract', *Irish Times*, 10 May 2005.

21 'Gama blame game begins', *Irish Examiner*, 15 April 2005.

22 'A dirty fight', *Irish Times*, 3 December 2005.

23 'Work-permits for spouses of 10,000 non-nationals', *Irish Times*, 18 February 2004.

24 Ruhs, *Managing the Immigration and Employment of non-EU Nationals in Ireland*, p. 17.

25 Philippine Overseas Employment Administration, Market Update series 2002, www.poea.ph/html/mu2002.html.

26 *Second Report of the EGFSN* (Dublin: EGFSN, 2000), pp. 41–2.

27 Press release, 'Tanaiste welcomes Third Report of Skills Group', 31 July 2001.

28 EGFSN, *Skill Needs in the Irish Economy: The Role of Migration* (Dublin: Forfas, 2005), p. 31.

29 Ibid., p. 63.

30 Ibid., p. 91.

31 Ibid., p. 69.

32 Ibid., p. 86.

33 Ibid., p. 88.

34 Ibid., p. 108.

35 Ibid., pp. 114–15.

36 Ibid., p. 142.

37 Ibid., p. 144.

38 Ibid., p. 141

39 Ibid., p. 131.

7

Between 'here' and 'there': Nigerian lone mothers in Ireland

Insa Lichtsinn and Angela Veale

This chapter examines the acculturation experiences of Nigerian asylum-seeker lone mothers as they negotiate new lives for themselves and their children in Ireland. It is based on research undertaken in Cork throughout 2005. At the time the research was undertaken Nigerians comprised the largest single group of asylum seekers in the Republic of Ireland. Many, like the women who were interviewed for this study, are parents. As of March 2005 a quarter of those living in direct provision asylum-seeker centres were young children under the age of four.[1] Of the five women interviewed for this study all were lone mothers living initially in direct provision with one young Irish-born child. Four identified a husband who was living in Nigeria. Two women had other children who had remained with family members in Nigeria. Interviews took place in January 2005 and again with the same participants in November 2005. The title reference to being between 'here and there' refers to the accounts of acculturation presented by the women. In each case the contact zone between Irish and Nigerian culture was experienced differently not least because the women had different experiences in their communities of origin that affected their experiences of living in Ireland. Experiences of immigrant acculturation are by no means homogeneous even amongst those who at face value share similar characteristics and experiences.

Immigration and acculturation

One of the most influential theories on the subject of acculturation in psychology has been the model outlined by Berry.[2] This model refers to four distinct strategies that immigrants can use in a new cultural context. *Assimilation* describes individuals who adapt to the dominant group whilst not maintaining their own cultural identity. *Separation* relates to immigrants who preserve their cultural identity without seeking to make contact with the host group. *Integration* is said to happen when an individual tries to keep contact with both cultures, therefore favouring both maintenance of their own culture and adaptation to the host culture. *Marginalisation* relates to those individuals who loose ties with both their own and the host culture. According to Berry's model, the optimal strategy is integration, which predicts consistently more positive outcomes than the alternative strategies.[3] In Berry's model, immigrant status is conceptualised as based on psychological identifications and attitudes that are relatively stable, individualised, internal dispositions.

Berry adopts a *universalist* perspective on acculturation, which assumes that, despite 'substantial variations in the life circumstances of cultural groups that experience acculturation, the psychological processes that operate during acculturation are essentially the same for all the groups'.[4] This implies the notion of a core independent self, with some natural properties, that are assumed to be there prior to culture or separately from a cultural context.[5] In Berry's acculturation model, culture and history are best understood as broad classes of variables that are different and separate from psychological-individual level variables, that is, it understands the role of culture as shaping 'underlying psychological operations' rather than mutually constituting them or being inextricably interwoven with them.[6] As a result, historical, social and political aspects rarely enter the discussion of psychological research on acculturation, and when they do they are mostly only classified as group variables. This fails to 'capture how issues of power and race are deeply interconnected with the development of an immigrant's identity'.[7] In contrast, it might be more useful to adopt an approach within the field of cultural psychology that acknowledges that culture and self are not mutually exclusive variables, but rather inextricably intertwined with each other.

Immigration and cultural psychology

Theories within the field of cultural psychology understand identity and the self not as a bounded or stable entity, but understand meanings about self and identity as closely mediated and organised through everyday socio-cultural practices. Culture is not an abstract independent concept that influences the self as a variable, but rather is understood as formed through selves in interaction. Culture is seen as a connected complex structure that is socially organised and re-created by engaging in activities with others. In the present era of globalisation culture is ever more detached from geography.[8] Bathia and Ram suggest that instead of perceiving culture as geographically located the focus of study should be on *cultural processes,* the meeting point between different cultures, where boundaries become increasingly permeable. Here the metaphor of travel helps to decentralise understandings of culture, 'in that cultural action and the making and remaking of identities take place not in the middle of dwelling but in the *contact zone* along the intercultural frontiers of nations, people and locales'. This implies looking at cultural changes in the meanings and practices of people who meet other cultural groups, and looking at understandings, misunderstandings, conflict and power differences in these contact zones.

Bathia and Ram argue that the constant struggle of negotiation with multiple cultural sides can be understood only in connection with larger sets of political and historical practices. Their contribution lies in highlighting the political aspects of migration, a side that psychology generally tends to neglect. They describe asylum seekers in their host country as being in constant struggle, negotiation, intervention and mediation, all of which are connected with a larger set of political and historical practices that are in turn shaped by issues of gender, race and power. According to Bathia and Ram, we undervalue the asymmetrical relations of power and the inequities and injustices faced by certain immigrant groups as a result of their nationality, race and gender. Especially, non-white immigrants are more likely to be positioned as the 'other' and face exclusion and discrimination, experiences that are tightly knitted to the evolving conception of selfhood. These considerations show how important it is to consider the individuality of refugees and asylum seekers, in that they occupy different social positions and are differently influenced by socio-political structures. As Galvin explains, 'the categorisation of people as refugees is both simplistic and problematic and ... serves to obscure the complex reality of forced migration. Refugee populations are diverse in nature'. [9]

Any failure to consider the diversity of refugees especially concerns women, who have been described as a 'forgotten majority'.[10] Even though the UNHCR estimates that 75–90% of the world's refugee population are women and their dependent children,[11] prior to the 1980s they have been a 'muted group whose specific needs are too often neglected and whose marginalisation in resettlement societies tends to be exacerbated by disproportionate influence of men over aid and resettlement policies'.[12] It has become increasingly recognised that asylum processes affect women differently from men.[13] Nevertheless, research that places emphasis upon gender usually treats it as a variable that is uniform across all cultures.[14] This overlooks the fact that cultural norms, practices and ways of gendering might be distinct for different cultures and therefore lead to varying forms of womanhood and motherhood. All this points up the importance, when conducting research amongst asylum-seeking women or other migrants, of gathering personal narratives.

There have been some changes to immigration policy in Ireland that have had implications for asylum-seeker parents of Irish-born children, many of whom are lone mothers. The Irish Nationality and Citizenship Bill 2004 effectively removed the entitlement to citizenship in respect of a person born in Ireland to non-national parents. Non-national parents of Irish-born children who were in the state before the legislative changes were introduced were offered residence for the parents and their Irish-born child. Those granted residence on this basis had to sign a declaration affirming that they have no entitlement to family reunification. In addition, non-Irish-born siblings of the Irish-born child living in Ireland were not granted residence but have had to apply in their own right. The right to family reunification for those with refugee status is recognised but limited. Section 5.3c of the Immigrant Bill 2004 notes family reunification for family members of a refugee applies to a spouse and children under eighteen years of age. It does not recognise the family unit and dependent family members as delineated in Section 18.4b of the Refugee Act 1996 which states that dependent family members can include grandparents, parents, brothers, sisters, children over eighteen and dependent family members suffering from a mental or physical disability. These legislative developments form part of the political context in which Nigerian lone mothers negotiate their new lives in Ireland.

The women who contributed to this study – Joelle, Hope, Georgina, Noeline and Amina – were aged from their early twenties to late thirties; to ensure anonymity, all names have been changed. The interviews were conducted in January 2005 and participants were again interviewed in November 2005. During the first investigation period four of the five interviewees were residing in direct provision. All these women had lived in Ireland for periods ranging between one and four years. The children residing with these women in Ireland were all Irish-born children ranging in age from eleven months to three years and four months. A process-oriented research approach was employed.[15] Interviews examined transitions, conflicts and negotiations experienced by women in their movement from Nigeria to Ireland.[16] Given that mothers have a specific role in passing on cultural heritage to their children, interviews explored child-rearing practices as a cultural contact zone and explored cultural practices and change and their relation to social and political forces in the host country.

Negotiating identity in Ireland

Joelle and Hope offered contrasting perspectives about their experiences of tolerance and intolerance since arriving in the Republic of Ireland. These perspectives were informed by their very different experiences of life in Nigeria. Joelle came from an Islamic-dominated area in Nigeria where being a single parent was viewed as a crime of adultery and single women were viewed as deviant. Her experience in Ireland was that Irish people did not look down on a fatherless child or on her as a single mother:

> They don't really ask you who you are, you know? ... They just take you for who you are, what you can give, you know? So I think, I like that about Ireland. ... And I don't think nobody would really look down at your child, like, Oh! Your mother is not married, Oh, you don't have a daddy. But meanwhile in Nigeria that would happen. (Joelle)

Hope described how she was educated by her Christian mother to be considerate and non-judgemental. Hope's life in Nigeria was socially organised around being a married working mother supported by her extended family. She was afforded a social position where she felt accepted and had status. She contrasted this with the prejudice and discrimination she now faced in Ireland:

> They have a particular stereotype against Nigerians. ... The way they look at you on the street, you know that feeling. It's just the way, they feel, that you are not wanted. ... Like, if you have a prejudice that means, you have already pre-judged a person. ... So you cannot just generalise, that all Nigerians are bad. ... We are open, any time, if they want to come and listen. But most of the time they are waiting and they just look at you. ... If they were willing to have interaction with us, they would know us better and be able to appreciate us more. (Hope)

For two other women, Georgina and Noelle, their experiences of economic integration in Ireland were also influenced by their pre-migratory history. Georgina came from a very poor economic background where she found it difficult to access education and to find a job. Coming from this background, Ireland constituted a social field of possibility and hope for herself and her child:

> In Ireland, there is hope and there is future. ... You can do anything you want to do, any what you want to learn, in so far as you have your money, you will learn in Ireland and find yourself, where you can fend on your own. But where I'm coming from there is no hope and there is no future. ... Being a Nigerian mother here in Ireland, I think it is OK, because I can train my little baby. I can train her to any level God can help me to train her. ... I don't find it difficult on my own because I can work. (Georgina)

That said, she identified problems with her life in Ireland resulting from insufficient money, not having been allowed to work and not having the opportunity to pursue her education.

Noeline was more pessimistic about life in Ireland. Three of her children still lived in Nigeria. There she had been able to go to work while family relatives would help her with child minding. She recalled being loved, respected and supported by her extended family. Her life in Ireland was, by contrast, isolated and it was harder for her to construct a positive meaning from her experiences:

> Being a lone mother, it's not easy, because, you know, everything, you will be the person that will do it. You are responsible to everything about your child. Even my child doesn't even know that she has a father. ... I'm not doing the things I'm used to doing. I find myself ... in a land where I am idle, I'm not doing the things I like doing, the things I'm used to doing. I am not staying with my family. You know, it's not easy. ... In fact that I'm not with them, I don't know how they are faring, I don't know their condition. You know? In fact most times I feel depressed. (Noeline)

Joelle was not married and, as such, she was sensitive to how cultural stigmatisation of unmarried mothers in Nigeria was being replicated and reproduced in her relations with fellow Nigerians. In Nigeria, Joelle explained, single mothers were extremely uncommon and generally seen as irresponsible. They were often disrespected and faced isolation. She believed most Nigerian lone mothers in Ireland were physically separated from their husbands. Joelle felt that disclosure to other Nigerian mothers in Ireland that she was a lone mother 'out of wedlock' would reduce her status and result in social marginalisation:

> Over here nobody knows I am a lone parent. ... And I wouldn't go and tell them I'm not married because they don't expect me not to be married basically ... once I do that, that's the end of a friendship. They would say. 'Oh she's single, she's not married, she must be wayward.' You know the same thing you would hear from Nigeria, that's happening here again. ... It's like living in isolation ... Even my closest Nigerian friends, I can't tell them ... and once the child starts talking it's going to be more difficult. The child is going to say, 'Where's my dad? Why don't I have a dad?' ... I can't imagine myself telling him, there is no dad. (Joelle)

Pre-migration positions of power and status were deeply infused in the developing relationship between these mothers and the new host society, and in their self-understanding and identities. These were brought into the cultural contact zone in which these women understood and responded to in their own ways the challenges they faced.

Child-rearing practices as a cultural contact zone

A lone mother seeking refuge with her child in a culture different from her own inevitably faces conflicts on whether to rear her child in the traditions of her own or those of the host culture. Every culture has parental ethnotheories that can be defined as 'cultural models that parents hold regarding children, families themselves as parents, an organised set of ideas that are shared by members of a cultural group'.[17] These are culturally regulated customs of child care that reflect cultural values about what behaviours are important in becoming a competent member of the community. Parental ethnotheories are often implicit or taken for granted ideas about the 'natural' way to act, but immigration brings practices and belief systems from different cultures into contact with each other. The participants of this study made differing choices, accompanied with feelings of uncertainty, about maintaining ideas and practices of parenting from Nigeria or explicitly adopting practices from the host culture. Noeline hoped to return with her child to Nigeria one day so maintaining cultural traditions in child-rearing was important to her.

> I would try to bring her up in a way, that she maintains my culture. Because definitely in the end of the day we still go back to our culture. And when you bring up your child in such a way, that your child will not have your culture. When you go home, they will abuse you. Why did you bring up your child in a Western culture? Don't you know she has an origin? She has that culture. It will be very difficult, because she is not in Nigeria. It will not be the easy way. I still try my best, but it will not look like when you are in Nigeria. (Noeline)

Georgina wanted to raise her daughter as Irish while maintaining what she values from Nigerian culture.

> I am out of that culture. I just want to bring her up here to know everything about Irish and everybody. She born here, she will claim Ireland. No other culture that's come to her mind. She has to know everything about Irish culture. She has to learn the language, and when they are doing something on the television I have to put on the television when they are speaking Irish. She didn't understand but she will be learning both, I would just tell her that in Nigeria they usually respect their elders ... She must learn how to respect. I will teach her, that she knows how to respect elders. (Georgina)

The cultural practices that resulted in the most signification tension between Nigerian and Irish practices were with respect to breast-feeding, child discipline and Nigerian values of respect for elders.

In Nigeria, participants noted that breast-feeding is commonly practised until the child is two years of age. It is widely held that breast-feeding is natural and good for the child. Mothers breast-feed their babies naturally in public places. For the mothers in this study, their wish to keep this practice up in Ireland faced many obstacles. Some obstacles were due to their situation as asylum seeker when they lived in a direct provision hostel. Participants complained that the food in the hostel was not nutritious enough to keep breast-feeding; this has been a recurring issue in the direct provision system.[18]

Noeline talked about the differences she experienced in breast-feeding her children when she was in Nigeria compared with her experiences in Ireland.

> Yeah, when I had my children in Nigeria ... they encourage breast-feeding a lot. They are very strict on it ... If they see you with bottle, feeding, they would collect it and throw it away in the hospital or in a public place. Yes, they don't like it. You just feed your baby with your breast. So my children in Nigeria, I breast-fed them exclusively without anything for four months. (Noeline)

Her Irish-born child was born while she was in a direct provision centre. She tried breast-feeding but stopped, as she could not express and store milk, as fridges were communal, so the environment was not appropriate. Other mothers said they experienced conflict about breast-feeding, as their experience was that it is difficult in Ireland to breast-feed in public. This caused some mothers to hide while they were breast-feeding or even to give up.

> When I just had my baby, I was in the shopping centre at ——, I was feeding him and the woman passed by, she was pushed, she was in the wheelchair and she saw me and she passed by and she told the person to turn back and she came back to me and she said can you put that thing back in, we don't do that here, put it in. I said, 'All right. Sorry. Thank you.' But I kept feeding my baby. And she said, 'Would you put it in!' She was upset. I am sorry I am feeding him. ... I stopped it, anyway. I just put my breast back in. And then she went away ... Sometimes, when I want to feed him, they told me there is a mother room. (Amina)

Joelle felt a conflict between her desire to breast-feed and the considerable pressure to become 'economically viable', as this is one of the criteria that is needed for the renewal of residence status. She was attending a course to get a recognised qualification to improve her changes of working and felt she should give up breast-feeding.

> When you are breast-feeding they are so attached to you, you know? When I leave him for the minder he is crying and crying and the minder is telling me you have to stop breast-feeding, the reason he is crying is because he wants the breast. So, if I give him breast he stops crying. It's important we breast-feed, we believe they are more brilliant than if they are not breast-fed. (Joelle)

A second practice that resulted in conflict in the cultural zone between Nigerian and Irish social practices was around child discipline. Child discipline in Nigerian parental ethnotheories is implicitly tied to understandings of social intelligence in children; that a competent and well behaved child is one that is obedient and respects his or her elders. Smacking is tolerated and seen as part of responsible parenting to train children to be competent social actors.

> Here is different from the way how they train her in Nigeria. In Nigeria … now maybe as she small she have to do things in the house. Every day we say I just go and bring. You have to learn how to sweep. You have to learn how to do this, but she is in Ireland I cannot. Even when I smacking, she asking, 'Why are you smacking me?' In Nigeria you cannot ask your parents. 'Why are you smacking me?'
>
> Mmm, the way they are treating their children here is different. This girl is standing now, as I am talking to her she will refuse to sit down, you use this thing on her and then she will not stand up from that place. If you talk to them they will refuse to hear you. They will not listen to you. No, it's not like that and immediately I use my eyes to talk to her. I will use eye contact, I would just look at her like this and she will understand what I mean. But over here you cannot use eye contact to talk to them. It's not possible. But in Nigeria they will teach you how to use eye contact to talk, even say I am sitting here like this. I am talking to my baby, she is from Nigeria, with eye contact, she will understand what I am saying. (Georgina)

However, in Ireland child discipline practices of physical punishment are often considered abusive of children and not tolerated. Amina notes:

> In Nigeria we smack our own children if they misbehave. But in Ireland you cannot smack children. The children overrule the parents. But it is not like that in Nigeria, you have the authority over your children. Not the children have authority over you. You will have to talk to them and they will listen. You tell them to sit and if they refuse to sit you smack the child. Its not like that in Ireland. The parent is talking to the child and the child will say, 'No! I don't!' and they cannot, they will not say anything again. But in Nigeria you don't have the right to do that to your parents. They will smack you to understand what they are saying. (Amina)

Georgina's experience also highlighted the conflict between Irish and Nigerian customs towards child discipline.

> In Ireland I cannot smack her like this. Why? I should just tell her the reason. Why did I smack her? But in Nigeria you cannot ask your parents, 'Why did you smack me?' That person would not ask for tragedy because you disobey your parents. But in Ireland I cannot smack her. When you came here now she was disturbing, but I cannot smack her. I would have to give her drinks, like, give her juice to better. That is the difference in the way we train between Nigeria and this place. (Georgina)

In Nigeria child rearing is often seen as a collective responsibility where every adult feels responsible for the education of every child. Working mothers are often supported by extended families. From this perspective, being an isolated single mother in Ireland without any support in child minding or anybody to share the responsibility came as a culture shock:

> In Africa, like, when I had my first child, my mother-in-law was there, my mother too, aunties taking care of the child, bathing him; it is only when I breast-fed the child they will bring him to me. They change nappies for him, they cook for me and everything. Since I had my child here, I've been doing everything myself. (Hope)

> I was alone, it's not easy to be a lone parent. As a lone parent that you don't have relation, as an asylum seeker. There are some Irish people that are lone parents, they have relations. You know? ... But here, nobody. I was alone in the hospital even when I had her. (Amina)

> In Nigeria ... that child is not just for you. It's for the whole extended family, they would be happy to take him without even taking a penny for him ... Your mind would be better too, so ... the extended family is something really missing. The Nigerian women are really supportive ... There are some of my friends around here that, she is the one taking care of every child. ... Without her I couldn't find someone to take care of my son ... It's only emergencies. (Hope)

Respondents described the absence of such support in Ireland. They described trying to give and receive mutual support from other mothers in similar circumstances. However, the pressures upon them to pursue education and become economically active undermine the opportunities for mutual support:

> If you are sitting at home they are not going to renew your document. So everybody is looking for work so that they can renew their documents, but nobody is going to assist you to look after the care for the baby. Also to look after the baby, that's the problem. .... Nobody is willing to take her because all of them have their own children. ... I am looking for the person that will take care of my baby. I am looking for her more than three month now. For the person that will take her to school and bring her back home. I didn't see her. (Georgina)

Motherhood, then, is negotiated within a political context where women will need to demonstrate their ability to be economically self-sufficient and in a social context of isolation. Child care is a problem for many Irish women. The subjective experience of isolation for Nigerian lone mothers is enhanced by contrast to the culture of collective responsibility for children that they have left behind.

Moving from enforced dependence to independence

The attainment of residence status was experienced as liberating for the women interviewed here. They described it as 'freedom' and a chance to settle down. Each of the women participants was now struggling to find work. Also, they need to demonstrate that they are economically viable within two years as a condition of having their residence status extended. Some, like Joelle, discussed the consequences of not having rights to work and education whilst in direct provision:

> The greatest thing that happened was me going to college, because now I can work with my certificate, which is very good for me. And that's another thing most people are finding difficult now, because they have been in the hostel for so long and they have no job to do, they have no references to give out. They won't take you without the reference. ... So it's quite difficult, it's quite a difficult transition for them, coming out of the hostel and getting a job ... They have nothing to show that they can do this job. (Joelle)

All the women emphasised the struggles they faced in this regard. For example:

> They have done the system in such a way that if you are doing a part time job you would be poorer than being under the social welfare ... When I was doing the part-time job ... I was paying child care, I was paying for my transport, and the tax was killing a bit, but you know they didn't calculate that I was paying child care, they took everything out of my money and they left me with nothing ... I just want to be out of the social ... I don't like their money because it's like I'm still in the hostel. ... I spend as much time with [my son] as possible. When I was doing the agency work I went to work from eight o'clock in the morning ... and I came home around nine in the night. ... I didn't see him for that day. ... But I am getting used to it now. It's something I have to do for both of us; ... I think I need to work for myself to bring back my self-image, I need to work for him as well. ... Although it will take a lot of courage and time. (Joelle)

On top of such difficulties the women recounted experiences of racism and discrimination in accessing private-sector accommodation. They also discussed difficulties in obtaining employment:

> Getting accommodation is hugely difficult, because most people would tell you they don't want rent allowance, some don't even want babies in the house, you know? They tell you straight away, they don't want children in the house, some don't want blacks at all, you know. It's difficult, but they just don't want black, you know?... You need a lot of confidence, you need a lot of hope, you know. ... Because if you are not confident to yourself, you know, the way they ask you questions, will even kill the spirit, the spirit, the eagerness you have in you, to look for a job. ... And some people will ask

you, are you sure you have the right to work in this country? Are you sure you have residence in this country? (Joelle)

The participants in this study were tackling the challenge of returning to education and looking for work in a constructive manner. A sadness that tinged this effort was the lack of possibility of family reunification with partners or dependent children.

OK, they give you residence [although] this child, siblings, the child is Irish, so they give you the residence on the basis of that child, so, like my child now, the father he has not set eyes on him, the child has other brothers and sisters, the child is an Irish citizen and it's on the basis of being an Irish citizen that they give us the residence, so that we can be here to take care of that child, but psychologically and emotionally they are denying this child of the father, they are denying this child of the siblings, the love and everything of the [family] ... What I know is that under international law the respect the right of the family unit, that family should be together, so ... , we are happy about that, but it's not fully, you know? (Hope)

Conclusion

Examination of the contact zone of the Nigerian mothers who contributed to this chapter reveals that much of their negotiations were influenced by broader societal and political structures. Lesser entitlements, experiences of prejudice and lack of support have impacted on how these women experience their transition from Nigeria to Ireland. Under direct provision the women were in a position of enforced dependence had only limited opportunities to participate in Irish society. Enforced passivity made difficult the transition from direct provision accommodation to independent living. Inevitably such experiences of disempowerment affected the possibilities they identified for acculturation and integration. Yet the women actively pursued opportunities to work, to reduce their social isolation themselves and to rear their children with an awareness of both Irish and Nigerian cultural traditions. However, negotiation of identity and acculturation in Ireland remains caught between 'here' and 'there' in daily negotiation of child-rearing practices and in self-identity as a lone mother. Political factors such as no right to family reunification means that families are separated and have to conduct their lives at a distance from each other. Political, economic and cultural aspects of women's lives are inextricably interwoven in psychological acculturation processes. It is not possible to understand the psychological correlates of migration for these women without an understanding of larger political and recent historical practices.

Notes

1 www.irishrefugeecouncil.ie, December 2005.
2 J. W. Berry, 'Acculturation as Varieties of Adaptation', in A. Padilla (ed.), *Acculturation: Theory, Models and some new Findings* (Boulder, CO: Westview, 1980); J. W. Berry, 'Cultural Variations in Cognitive Style', in S. Wapner (ed.), *Bio-psycho-social Factors in Cognitive Style* (Hillsdale, NJ: Erlbaum, 1990); J. W. Berry, 'Immigration, Acculturation and Adaptation', *Applied Psychology*, 46 (1997), pp. 5–68; J. W. Berry, U. Kim, S. Power, M. Young and M. Bujaki, 'Acculturation Attitudes in Plural Societies', *Applied Psychology*, 38 (1989), pp. 185–206.
3 J. W. Berry and D. Sam, 'Acculturation and Adaptation', in J. W. Berry, M. H. Seagull and C. Kagitcibasi (eds), *Handbook of Cross-cultural Psychology: Social Behavior and Applications* III (1997).
4 Ibid., p. 296.
5 S. Bathia and A. Ram, 'Rethinking "Acculturation" in relation to Diasporic Cultures and Postcolonial Identities', *Human Development*, 4 (2001), pp. 1–18.
6 Berry and Sam, 'Acculturation and Adaptation', p. 296.
7 H. J. M. Hermans, 'Mixing and Moving Cultures require a Dialogical Self', *Human Development*, 44 (2001), pp. 24–8.
8 H. J. M. Hermans and H. J. G. Kempen, 'Moving Cultures: the Perilous Problems of Cultural Dichotomies in a Globalising Society', *American Psychologist*, 5: 10 (1989), pp. 1111–20.
9 T. Galvin, 'Preface', in C. Debilius, *Lone but not Alone: A Case Study of the Social Network of African Refugee Women in Ireland* (Dublin: Department of Sociology, Trinity College, 2001).
10 G. Camus-Jacques, 'Refugee Women: the Forgotten Majority', in G. Loescher and L. Monahan (eds), *Refugees and International Relations* (Oxford: Oxford University Press, 1989).
11 Irish Council for Civil Liberties Women's Committee, *Women and the Refugee Experience: Towards a Statement of Best Practice*.(Dublin: ICCL, 2000).
12 B. E. Harrell-Bond, *Imposing Aid: Emergency Assistance to Refugees* (Oxford: Oxford University Press, 1986).
13 Dibelius, *Lone but not Alone*.
14 Bathia and Ram, 'Rethinking "Acculturation"'.
15 Interpretative Phenomenological Analysis (IPA) was employed. IPA explores the participants' personal perception and meanings as opposed to producing objective statements. IPA undertakes an idiographic case-study approach, focusing very much upon unique personal experiences and working slowly from the readings of particular cases up to more general categorisations or theories. See J. A. Smith and F. Dunworth, 'Qualitative Methods in the Study of Development', in K. Connolly and J. Valsinger (eds), *The Handbook of Developmental Psychology* (London: Sage, 2003), and J. A. Smith, 'Towards a Relational Self: Social Engagement during Pregnancy and Psychological

Preparation for Motherhood', *British Journal of Social Psychology*, 38 (1999), pp. 409–26

16 Individual interviews lasted from sixty minutes to 110 minutes. They were conducted in the community rooms of a direct provision centre, in the homes of the participants and in an immigrant support voluntary in Cork. Interviews explored family networks and life in Nigeria, social support networks and life in Ireland, experiences as a mother and child-rearing practices, role and identity as a mother in Nigeria and Ireland and social relations in Ireland.

17 S. Harkness and C. Super, 'Themes and Variations: Parental Ethnomethodologies in Western Cultures', in K. Rubin and O. Chung (eds), *Parental Beliefs, Parenting and Child Development in Cross-cultural Perspective* (New York: Psychology Press, 2004).

18 B. Fanning, A. Veale and D. O'Connor, *Beyond the Pale: Asylum-seeking children and Social Exclusion in Ireland* (Dublin: Irish Refugee Council, 2001), p. 35.

8

Forced migration and psychological stress

Dermot Ryan, Ciarán Benson and Barbara Dooley

There has been much debate in recent years about the impact of forced migrants on Western societies but relatively little about the impact of these societies on forced migrants. Persons who seek asylum face a range of restrictions on their personal freedoms that are not experienced by resident populations. For example, in Ireland they are not allowed to work and are not entitled to regular social welfare benefits. They can experience prolonged periods of legal status insecurity and the constant threat of deportation that goes with it. The policy of dispersal means they have little or no say over where they live. Their personal control is eroded further through the institutional demands of hostel life. Along with the demands of asylum, forced migrants often have to contend with huge personal losses rooted in the conditions that led up to their flight or in the actual act of leaving their home country. Life in exile invariably involves separation from family or friends for those who still have some left. In short, post-migration life places enormous demands on the individual. This chapter tells the stories of six persons who were forced to leave their home countries and seek asylum.

Forced migrants are distinguished from voluntary ones by the greater level of 'push' versus 'pull' factors that determine their decision to migrate. In other words, forced migrants flee to avoid aversive aspects of their home environment, whereas voluntary migrants are attracted by positive aspects of the host environment. The popular media in Western countries generally portray asylum seekers as voluntary migrants or 'bogus refugees' who move to Western countries because they are attracted by their strong economies or the possibility of living off their social welfare systems. This argument does not convince us. For the majority of asylum seekers, the decision to uproot themselves must be understood in terms of the difficult conditions of their home environment rather than expectations of better conditions in the host environment.

When individuals relocate to a new socio-cultural environment they have to make adjustments in how they meet their needs They also have to make changes in how they pursue their personal goals or in the actual goals themselves. In addition, migrants have to manage demands not encountered in their society of origin, such as language difficulties or racist abuse. *Migrant adaptation* is the process through which individuals seek to satisfy their needs, pursue their goals and manage demands encountered after relocating to a new society. The outcome of this process is determined by the individual's access to resources. Migration invariably has an impact on the individual's resource pool. In a fundamental sense, the study of migrant adaptation is an examination of factors which facilitate or constrain access to resources.

Situations that deprive needs, block goals or place excessive demands on the migrant's resources will result in psychological stress. From the handful of studies conducted in an Irish context, there is ample evidence that asylum seekers experience deprivation of their basic needs. For example, there have been reports of malnutrition among pregnant women and babies,[1] homelessness,[2] and accommodation with no heating.[3] Asylum seekers live in stressful environments, having to contend with overcrowding, high noise levels and lack of privacy. These conditions combined with legal status insecurity, forced exclusion from the work force and forced dependence on social welfare are a recipe for emotional suffering. It is no surprise that asylum seekers report extremely high levels of psychological distress.[4]

The accounts that follow are based on interviews the first author (D.R.) conducted as part of a larger research project.[5] After conducting a two-phase quantitative survey of forced migrants, I could put numbers on their levels of depression, fear and loneliness, but it was the human stories behind these numbers that were so shocking. Both within and outside the context of research, many participants had a strong desire to tell their story and to be listened to. While playing scrabble with a girl from Central Africa, she told me about the day a group of rebels came to her village and the devastation they left in their wake. A young man from another African country told me about how he had been forced into the army at a young age. I came to the realisation that there was more to learn from these stories than from the quantitative data I had collected. I decided to go back and interview some participants for a third time and write them up as case studies. I completed seven such studies, six of which are summarised here. A semi-structured interview schedule was used to guide the interview. It included questions on need satisfaction, goal pursuit and experiences of stress in both home and host countries. Since the participants were uncomfortable with the prospect of being recorded, I took hand-written notes. All the names used are fictitious.

Anna

Life in home country

Anna was born in the former Soviet Union. Her father was a member of the indigenous ethnic community and her mother was Jewish. She was an only child. Her parents had a good marriage and she had a happy childhood. In her words, 'I grew up surrounded by love. Nothing was refused to me.' Her father died when she was sixteen. Neither Anna nor her mother ever experienced financial strain. Anna's mother provided her with every opportunity to achieve her academic goals, and in this pursuit she excelled. After completing her education, Anna held a university teaching post for ten years. She then set up her own business. Anna had a busy but rewarding professional life, and a good social life.

One day two men from a nationalist political organisation came to Anna's office and suggested that she move the business to another location. Their real motive, Anna believes, was to appropriate the business because it was thriving. She refused to move and the men became verbally abusive. They were escorted off the premises by staff members. Following this incident, Anna received threatening phone calls, some company cars were vandalised and a staff member was threatened that she would be killed if she continued to work for a Jew. At a later date, two men forced their way into the house where she lived with her mother. They made physical threats regarding Anna, stating, 'You are old and will die yourself but we will kill your daughter.'

One evening when Anna was in her office she heard somebody breaking into the premises. She felt that the men who had threatened her before were looking for her, so she escaped through a back exit. When she arrived home she was attacked and badly beaten. On witnessing the scene, Anna's mother collapsed and was taken to hospital. She died the next day. Anna had also been hospitalised and was in a state of shock. After four days she returned home and locked herself indoors. She saw a programme which reported that a number of powerful people had fled the country. At this point she felt her life was in danger and decided to flee herself.

Flight

It took Anna three days to prepare for her flight. In retrospect, she was surprised that all she was thinking about at the time was escaping. She was not thinking about her mother's death or all that she would lose by leaving. The only document she had was her birth certificate, which she kept in a rucksack along with some clothes and a photo of herself as a child with her mother. She flew to Moscow and from there took a bus to the Polish border. At the border she saw a lot of police and became very frightened. While she was in a café, a waiter asked her if she was all right. She explained that she wanted to leave the country and asked him if he knew anybody who could help her. He said that he could put her in touch with somebody and asked her for $100. When Anna met the trafficker she was frightened. He told her that it would cost her $1,000 to be delivered to a safe place. She paid him and was put in the back of a jeep, where she was covered with a blanket. Throughout her journey Anna was confused and terrified.

After lying in the back of the jeep for two days, Anna was handed over to a second trafficker. He demanded a further $2,000 and Anna was put in the back of another jeep. The second journey lasted about twenty-four hours. When Anna got out of the jeep she could not walk. She felt dizzy and had lost her appetite. The trafficker gave her a bus ticket and put her on a bus without telling her where she was going. After some time she saw a signpost for Dublin. In her state of confusion, she had not realised that she had been on a ferry – a fact that would be questioned during her asylum interview.

Life in Ireland

When Anna got off the bus she was completely disoriented. She started looking for a police officer. An elderly man saw she was distressed and accompanied her to the Department of Justice, where she lodged her asylum application. After this she was sent to a reception centre in the Dublin area. After two weeks she was dispersed to a hostel outside Dublin.

She described her feelings about her new place of residence. 'I was lost. I was in a bedroom with two other people. I was a businesswoman and was used to a businesswoman's habits.' Anna found the constant presence of security guards stressful, stating that 'they are not here to protect us'. The food was bad, with little variety and not enough protein. There were few outlets for recreational activities, with no gym, computers, books, magazines or newspapers.

When I asked Anna about her most stressful experiences during her stay in the hostel, she described an incident that occurred one night when she was in bed ill. A fellow resident was having a telephone conversation outside her bedroom. The lady in question was shouting, so Anna's room mate popped her head outside the door and asked her to lower her voice. After some minutes they heard a knock on the door. When Anna opened it she was physically attacked by the woman who had been on the telephone, mistaking Anna for her room mate. The woman grabbed Anna's neck and began choking her but a number of residents intervened and, according to Anna, saved her life.

The incident had a detrimental effect on Anna's psychological well-being. She could no longer sleep and was startled by the slightest noise. She reported the incident to the manager, who refused to remove the assailant from the hostel. While she was interpreting for a friend during a medical visit, the doctor noticed she was not well. He began questioning her and she gave an account of the attack. On hearing her story, he wrote a letter recommending she be moved into private accommodation. After a lengthy process, Anna was granted permission to leave direct provision (i.e. state-provided full-board accommodation).

Anna was delighted at the prospects of moving into private accommodation. She moved to Dublin and rented a small flat. It was in bad repair but at least she was independent. When she went to her local social welfare office to sort out her welfare payments, she was told that the law had changed and she had no right to leave direct provision. To Anna's misfortune, section 13 of the Social Welfare (Miscellaneous Provisions) Act 2004 had come into effect just as she was making her move to Dublin. She was advised by a support organisation to move back to the town where she had been living. It seemed like she had no choice. She was penniless, having pooled all her money together with a loan from friends to pay the first month's rent and a deposit. However, she refused to leave and appealed against the decision of her social welfare office.

Anna's social welfare appeal was turned down. Again, she did not give up but appealed a second time. This time she had a letter from a medical doctor in Dublin which made a strong case for her being given the right to stay in private accommodation on health grounds. She spent four months in a state of destitution and insecurity but her tenacity paid off and she won her case.

At the same time Anna was fighting a second battle with her asylum case. Her first interview had to be postponed because of an illness. It was rescheduled during the period in which she had made her second appeal to social welfare. It was a traumatic experience for Anna. In her words:

> My first interview was dreadful. I wanted to forget everything. My memory – probably out of a natural protection – was blocked. I couldn't put my memories in order. I didn't want to. I cried when I started thinking about them.

She felt that her interviewer did not want to listen to her story and see her as a human being. The outcome of the interview was negative and Anna had to wait for nine months for her appeal.

I met Anna again and she was extremely hopeful that she would receive a positive outcome on her appeal. She had started attending a Bible group twice a week and borrowing books from a public library, two pursuits that helped her cope with stress. She described a conscious decision she made regarding how she dealt with stress in her life:

> I have reviewed my life and my attitudes towards other people. I try to block out memories of the past. I've thrown away the keys to my past life. I have some valuable things towards which I am striving. I haven't lost my self-respect.

Two weeks later Anna sent me a text message saying that she had lost her appeal.

Alex

Life in home country

Alex was born in an Eastern European country that was ravaged by war. Despite being a member of a persecuted ethnic minority, he had a peaceful and happy childhood. Before the war he was successfully pursuing his personal goals. He was married with two small children and had a secure job as a schoolteacher. He lived next door to his parents in his own house.

When the war erupted there was chaos. Alex did not feel his family was under direct threat because they were not members of the groups in conflict. As the war worsened they had to rely on international aid for basic provisions. One day Alex and his wife walked to the village for food. They could not carry everything in one trip, so Alex went to the village a second time. On his return he noticed smoke coming from his street. As he neared it he realised that both his own house and that of his parents were engulfed in flames. It was too late to do anything: his wife, parents and two children were dead. He personally found his wife's and children's bones among the smouldering ruins of his house. Most of his friends had been killed, too.

From then on Alex said he had no feelings. 'I was like a tiger in the jungle. My main goal was not to be seen by [the group who killed his family].' For almost two years he hid out in a mountainous region. He was constantly on the move, living off whatever scraps of food he could find. The winter months were particularly harsh. 'I had to dig a hole in the ground and live like a wolf.' His physical health deteriorated and head lice were a constant source of discomfort. In a state of emaciation, poor health and exhaustion, Alex was found by a group of international peacekeeping soldiers, who arranged for his passage to Ireland in the back of a lorry.

Life in Ireland

On arrival in Ireland Alex felt utterly lost. He thought he would have been better off at home because at least he knew his way around there. With the little English he had from school, he made his way to the Refugee Applications Centre. From there he was sent to a reception centre, where he received medical attention and was referred to a psychologist. The hostel staff were very supportive. Three months later he moved into private accommodation. Alex started attending his local church, where he made a number of friends. He took up a voluntary job, saying it was 'to keep myself busy and not think about the past'.

Five months after his arrival he had his first interview. 'It was extremely stressful. It felt like an interrogation but the commissioner was good and understanding.' The wait for a reply 'seemed like an eternity'. Three months later Alex got news of his positive asylum outcome:

> For a week I had wings – I was flying. It was a great relief, but then I started worrying. How am I going to get a job, a house, everything? I found out my university diploma is not recognised here. After the news, there were ups and downs. I was depressed and confused. I got into a new relationship that brought about a lot of stability but I think about the past a lot. I wish it was like a video-recorder where you could take the tape out and burn it.

Alex found part-time work for some months but was laid off. Since then he has held some temporary jobs, usually as a security guard. His main concern is rebuilding a family with his partner, with whom he is now cohabiting. He is still experiencing high levels of distress. His past haunts him through nightmares and he continues to have diffuculty sleeping. When I asked him what he thought about seeking help from a mental health professional he was sceptical, saying, 'I myself don't understand what I've been through.' Despite the painful memories, Alex's outlook for the future is hopeful.

The last time I met Alex he told me that he was planning to get married.

Kemi

Life in home country

Kemi was born in Africa. She was a bright child and performed brilliantly both at school and at university. After her studies she met with success in her professional career and was in a top managerial position in her company at a young age. She went on to marry Joseph and they had three children. They lived very comfortably in a suburban house on its own grounds.

Everything was going well for Kemi and her family before two incidents in which their home was attacked by armed robbers. On each occasion shots were fired and their children were threatened. Luckily, nobody had been hurt seriously during these attacks. However, Kemi and her husband did not want to risk facing a further attack with a more serious outcome or of having one of their children kidnapped. They left their home to stay with family members and started making plans to leave the country. They decided to move to Ireland because they felt it would be safe for their children and they would have a chance to rebuild their professional careers. They also decided that it would be best for Joseph to leave the country first with the eldest son so that they could set things up before moving the younger children over. Joseph and his son flew to Ireland and they lodged an application for asylum.

What was intended as a short family separation lasted for fourteen months. Joseph still had not received an asylum outcome when Kemi decided to leave with the other two children. Her departure was extremely stressful and the personal losses were huge. Kemi had to leave her mother and her friends. She had to give up a rewarding professional career that had been built up over years, and the family home she and her husband had built.

Life in Ireland

Kemi's initial adaptation to her new life in Ireland was facilitated by the fact that her husband had already established a strong network of friends before she arrived. They both joined a Church organisation and their pastor has become a personal friend and an important source of support. In the expectation that they would eventually be granted asylum, Kemi and her husband started studying for professional exams. Kemi's studies helped deal with the monotony of her daily life and gave her a sense of purpose. She became pregnant and sat her exams a few days before her baby was born. Despite being heavily pregnant, Kemi came top of her class.

Kemi's asylum application was turned down both at her first interview and on appeal. The negative outcome of her appeal came just a few days after the birth of her baby. She then entered the process for leave to remain on humanitarian grounds. Since her fourth child was born in Ireland, Kemi and her husband applied for residence on this basis. For a number of months Kemi felt relatively secure, believing that it was only a matter of time before her residence would come through and she could start rebuilding her life. These hopes were dashed after a legislation change at the beginning of 2003 when the right to residence on the basis of an Irish-born child was withdrawn.

After the birth of her baby Kemi had to abandon her studies. She is confined to the house most of the time and has put on weight. Even if she is eventually granted leave to remain, she feels that she will no longer be eligible for the type of job she is looking for because of her age. If Kemi is refused leave to remain on humanitarian grounds, she and her family will be deported. Regarding this prospect, she said, 'I don't even want to think about it.'

Salam

Life in home country

Salam was born in an African country devastated by civil war. Until the war his family was comfortably off. They had their own house and education was free. When the war broke out everything changed. They lost their family home and were separated from their father for three years. They were forced to leave their native city and live with relatives in the countryside. Life there was difficult: they often experienced a lack of food and their physical safety was in constant danger.

For a brief period of time when an international peacekeeping force was present Salam worked as an interpreter. On this income he was able to support his family. Unfortunately, the peacekeeping force withdrew from the region and Salam lost his job. His family were constantly on the move afterwards, since their physical safety was again in danger. For a period of time they were forced to live in a refugee camp in a neighbouring country because they had no food. After this they were given the protection of a tribe who were militarily strong but who treated them like slaves.

For some time Salam and his family had wished to leave the country but they did not have enough money. Their father was a respected member of their tribe and when he made a request for financial assistance from elders who had settled in the United States they readily agreed to help out. Their fellow tribesmen sent $4,000, which was enough to arrange travel to Europe for one person. Salam's family chose him because he was the eldest son and because of his knowledge of English. Salam had to spend three months in a neighbouring country before he could begin his journey. For its duration he was never in control and never knew what was happening. It was an extremely stressful time: 'I never thought I would make it.'

Life in Ireland

Salam arrived safely in Ireland and lodged his asylum application. From the outset he felt that he was not being given enough information. Before his dispersal he was given no details of the town he was being sent to. His major stress at this time was concern about the well-being and safety of his family back home. He was under pressure to send money back home to feed his family. With an income of €19.10 a week, he felt he had no choice but to work illegally. This brought with it the constant fear of being caught and losing everything he had been working towards.

Salam reported that his asylum interview was an extremely stressful experience. However, the outcome was positive and he applied for family reunification. When his work permit came through he found a full-time job. Salam was reunited with his wife, father and six brothers and sisters. His mother had died of natural causes just before the family left the country. A major source of stress for Salam was feeling responsible for the well-being of his whole family, none of whom spoke English. An incident in which two of his sisters were attacked and had their traditional headdress removed by six youths was extremely upsetting to Salam. From then on, he or his father escorted the girls wherever they went.

After the racist attack, Salam and his family moved to a safer area. His brothers and sisters have settled into their new schools and his father has established his own network of friends. Now that Salam has organised everybody else in his family, he is ready to pursue his personal goal of becoming an accountant. The last I time I spoke to him, he had applied for a full-time university course.

Magda

Life in home country

Magda was born in an African country in which ethnic tensions resulted in terrible atrocities. She has fond memories of her childhood.

> My mother loved me very much and I also got a lot of love from my father's side of the family. My grandfather had five wives, so there was a lot of female support for the children – mothers, aunts and mothers-in-law. I was blessed in that I came from a good family. There was no stress in my life. I was so completely naïve.

Magda got married and she and her husband were very happy together. They built their own house with a big garden. Magda was a full-time homemaker but she never experienced loneliness. She had plenty of hobbies and interests, her favourite one being gardening. They were well-off and could afford a good social life. With her large extended family there were always parties, weddings or other occasions for celebration. When she and her husband had two daughters, she could not have asked for more in life.

When the conflict broke out things would never be the same for Magda. Everything in her world changed and these experiences changed her. Regarding the war, she said:

I was never prepared for it. I was putting my clothes outside and the rain came and soaked me. All my family were killed [apart from her husband and daughters]. It's very hard when people die like dogs. Everybody I think about is dead. Some of the people who died are better off ... Before the war I was a completely different person. I was a trusting person. Now I have so many friends but I don't trust anybody. Nobody from this society can understand me. Nobody can understand me apart from people from [her native country].

Despite the atrocities that were committed, Magda and her husband went on living in their home. She always thought that her husband should leave the country but he did not want to. Magda's suffering did not end with the murder of her extended family. One evening when she was at home with her family gunmen burst through the door. Her daughters who were in the back of the house escaped through a window and ran away. Magda's husband was killed in front of her eyes and she was brutally raped.

Magda lost touch with her daughters for four months. During this period she felt suicidal. Eventually she found out that they were in a neighbouring country in the care of a relative. She decided that it was time for her to leave. Relatives gave her the $4,000 she needed to pay the traffickers. She was taken to a neighbouring country in a car and from there flew to Dublin. The journey was a terrifying experience for her.

Life in Ireland

The initial period in Ireland was extremely stressful. 'I didn't know anybody. I was very sick, tired and scared to death'. When she arrived at the Department of Justice Magda could not stop crying. She was sent to a reception centre for two weeks and from there to a hostel, where she got a lot of support. She was referred to a centre for rape counselling, which she attended twice a week for seven months.

After eleven months Magda was given permission to leave direct provision and decided to move to a town where a friend lived. She got her own flat and joined a Church group. For some time she continued travelling to her counsellor but eventually had to give up because she could not afford the bus fare. This was difficult for Magda because, in her words, 'I needed to be listened to and I didn't want to worry my friends.'

Magda described her first asylum interview as 'my most difficult experience in Ireland'. The interviewer began with the comment 'You don't look like your file.' Magda immediately felt that the interviewer did not trust her. Two weeks after her interview she was called a second time and was questioned for a further three hours. She found it almost impossible to talk, as she could not hold back her tears. She felt that her interviewers believed she was acting and that her crying was a charade. Some months later she got news that her asylum application had been refused.

Things did not go much better during her appeal. 'Just the look in her [the interviewer's] eyes made me not want to talk.' I met Magda the morning she got the negative result of her appeal and she was devastated. She cried incessantly and was inconsolable. The members of a local support organisation were shocked by the decision. They told her that she had a very strong case for a judicial review and helped her access legal support.

In the following weeks Magda's physical health deteriorated. She became depressed and lost all hope of ever rebuilding her life. Members of her Church organisation visited her regularly. Their support and prayers helped Magda back on her feet. However, she has chronic sleeping problems and goes for long walks in the evening to tire herself out before going to bed. She is afraid during these walks because she is often sexually harassed by men, some of whom ask her, 'Are you working?'

The last time I talked to Magda she had been in the asylum process for three years. She had been waiting two years for her case to go to court. In her words, 'the delay in the asylum process is killing people'. She had reached a stage where she no longer cared about her asylum case and had begun to lose hope that she could ever have a normal relationship with her daughters after what they had been through. She worries that if they are reunited, 'they will have got used to living their lives without me'. She lives with the constant regret that she did not convince her husband to leave before his brutal murder.

Tanya

Life in home country

Tanya was born to Russian parents in the Asian part of the former Soviet Union. Her physical appearance is visibly different from that of the majority population. In her words, 'My ethnic identity is written on my face.' Her father left the family home when Tanya was young and was not involved in her upbringing after that. She and her younger sister were brought up by their mother.

Problems started for Tanya when her country got its independence. It was not safe for Russians to go out after dark because of frequent attacks. These were not reported because the police did nothing about them. Tanya lost count of the number of times she herself was physically attacked, estimating that it occurred between twenty and thirty times in eleven years. The first attack was in the street near her home. It was extremely vicious, leaving her with a fractured skull. After a week in hospital she fled to her grandmother's house in another country to recover. On her return she was attacked by a neighbour. Since she knew the attacker this time, she reported the incident to the police. She found out that the attacker's cousin was a policeman and realised that she would get nowhere.

The later attacks became sexual. Tanya's first rape occurred at the age of nineteen at a job interview. 'Instead of the job interview, he raped me in his own office.' She believed Russian girls were easy targets because the perpetrators knew the authorities would not carry out a proper investigation. Four years later she and a friend were walking along the street when a van pulled up alongside them. Six men jumped out and forced the girls inside. Over a period of two days they were repeatedly raped by the six men and were badly beaten. When the men had fallen asleep, they managed to escape. They reported the incident but nobody was ever charged with the crime.

After a number of years Tanya had a baby but the father left her before he was born and never contributed in any way to the child's upbringing. Tanya's financial state worsened and she experienced periods in which there was a shortage of food in the house. Eventually she decided that she would have to leave the country. The lack of physical safety was a factor but her primary motivation was her inability to secure decent employment. As she put it, 'I left because I had no future. I was the only one in my family who could do it.'

Her family saved hard so that Tanya could leave and then arrange for her son, mother and sister to follow her. She paid $3,000 for a student visa and $650 for a flight to Dublin. She left expecting that it would take her at most a year before she would be reunited with her family.

Life in Ireland

For her first three weeks in Ireland Tanya attended an English course and stayed with an Irish family. From there she moved into an apartment with a girl from her country. She found a job in a warehouse. It was physically demanding and paid badly but she needed to start sending some money back home. She sustained a back injury at work but could not afford to take time off to recover.

When Tanya's visa expired she lost her job at the warehouse. She had no income for two months but then found illegal work as a cleaner. For five eleven-hour days a week Tanya brought home €200 (i.e. €3.64 per hour), which she thought was good considering she was illegal. On her two days off she had other cleaning jobs. She was satisfied with her work because she was treated well by her employers.

In order to cut down on the cost of accommodation, Tanya moved into a four-bedroom house with eleven other persons. It was not an ideal situation for a young woman. The men who lived there were often drunk and violent, and the occupants were changing constantly. Tanya did not feel safe and personal belongings were stolen a number of times. On one occasion all her shoes were stolen.

In the meantime Tanya had begun a relationship with a man from the former Soviet Union. She became pregnant and, as was the case with her first child, the father left her when he found out. Tanya worked hard throughout her pregnancy. Her contractions arrived when she was ironing for her employer. She went on ironing for two hours before she was rushed to the hospital, where her second son was born. 'I didn't have a chance to relax [before the birth] and do shopping like all women.'

Just before her son's birth, Tanya felt she had no choice but to enter the asylum process. She filled in her application alone. She reported, 'I was afraid when I applied for asylum – afraid of the interview. I didn't know what to expect.' Three days after her son's birth she moved into a hostel. It was much better than the accommodation she had left: 'The food was good. It was quiet and I liked it.' Three months later she moved into private accommodation.

After a negative decision on her first asylum interview, Tanya's expectations of a positive outcome on appeal were low. However, in the months prior to her appeal she was feeling hopeful. On the day, things did not turn out as she expected:

> I saw the judge didn't believe me. When I talked about my second rape he didn't pay attention to me. I expressed myself well but the solicitor didn't put my case forward well. I understood that nobody gave a shit. The judge got my story wrong [referring to her rape as 'attempted rape']. My case worker acknowledged there were mistakes in my appeal.

At the time of my final interview with Tanya she was awaiting news from her solicitor regarding the possibility of seeking a judicial review. However, he had not given her much hope. She was under considerable financial strain because she was sending most of her welfare allowance back to her mother so that she could look after her first son. Her separation from her family is extremely stressful for her. Once a week she can afford to talk to her mother on the phone for ten minutes. When stress started getting the better of her she went to a psychologist. It was good to talk to somebody but Tanya felt the person could not really help her.

Since her second son's birth Tanya has been away from him only on two occasions: her first asylum interview and her appeal. She bears the responsibilities of parenthood alone. Both being a single parent and having to send as much money as possible home have resulted in Tanya having no social life whatsoever. She experiences extreme loneliness and social isolation. She summed up her experience in Ireland as follows:

> I'm wasting my time for nothing. I'm not working – not building my social life. It's like living in a prison. It is a prison: I have free accommodation and three meals, but since it is a prison, I can do nothing. The government treats me like a prisoner. I steal their money and accommodation. I'm not wanted here. I have not seen my son in two and a half years. If I go on with the legal process it may take another two or three years. I haven't gained anything in Ireland. At least back home I had some respect ... My brain stopped working here. I put all my life on one card and I didn't win anything.

The last time I met Tanya her request for a judicial review had been turned down. Her only remaining possibility is leave to remain on humanitarian grounds, regarding which she holds little hope: 'Nobody gets it.'

Conclusion

People can be forced out of their home communities for many reasons. Each of the stories described here involved the deprivation of basic physiological and psychological needs prior to migration. For example, Alex, Salam and Tanya experienced food deprivation, and the safety needs of all six were not met in their home environment. The stories were also characterised by major personal loss, including the death of close family members in tragic circumstances, and the loss of family contact and support, a rewarding career, the family home and financial resources. In short, all the stories involved severe levels of psychological stress before arrival in Ireland.

The asylum process brought with it a whole new set of demands to contend with. Perhaps the key stress-inducing aspect of this process is the erosion of personal control. Anna's story highlights the lengths to which people are prepared to go in order to regain some control over their life conditions. She preferred to face destitution and live in a squalid flat than return to hostel life. Asylum also brings major financial strain. On an income of €19.10, Salam was left with no choice but to work illegally to support his family back home. In doing so he risked deportation, which would have resulted in the complete loss of the time and money invested in reaching Ireland, as well as jeopardising his family's safety.

Psychological well-being is intimately linked with the pursuit of life goals. For those who were still in the asylum process the pursuit of major goals was blocked. Magda and Tanya could not be actively involved in their children's upbringing. Kemi amd Anna – both successful career women – could not pursue their professional goals. On the other hand, those who had obtained a positive asylum outcome were getting on with their lives. Alex was starting to rebuild a family life and Salam was pursuing his academic goals.

This chapter examined experiences of psychological stress in the lives of forced migrants. A psychological study of this population could just as easily have focused on their resilience. However, we feel a more appropriate response from a host-society perspective is to examine ways in which we can reduce the demands that put such resilience to the test. The first step in doing so is to understand the nature and impact of stressful demands on the psychological well-being of forced migrants. In reaching such an understanding we need to listen to the forced migrants' own stories – something which is sorely lacking in both the academic literature and the popular media.

As host societies to forced migrants, we need to take a long and hard look at the psychological impact of our asylum policies. Whatever about the suffering that forced migrants experienced before arriving at our shores, the blame for any suffering rooted in asylum policies lies squarely on our shoulders.

Notes

1 B. Fanning, A. Veale and D. O'Connor, *Beyond the Pale: Asylum Seeking Children and Social Exclusion in Ireland* (Dublin: Irish Refugee Council, 2001).

2 African Refugee Network, *African Refugees Needs Analysis* (Dublin: African Refugee Network, 1999).

3 Vincentian Refugee Centre, *Housing and Refugees: The Real Picture* (Dublin: Vincentian Refugee Centre, 2004).

4 Two Irish studies that recruited samples or sub-samples of asylum seekers observed similar findings, with approximately 50% of the forced migrants in each case reporting severe distress: M. Begley, C. Garavan, M. Condon, I. Kelly, K. Holland and A. Staines, *Asylum in Ireland: A Public Health Perspective* (Dublin: Department of Public Health Medicine and Epidemiology, University College Dublin, 1999); O. Horgan, 'Seeking Refuge in Ireland: Acculturation Stress and Perceived Discrimination', in M. MacLachlan and M. O'Connell (eds), *Cultivating Pluralism: Psychological, Social and Cultural Perspectives on a Changing Ireland* (Dublin: Oak Tree Press, 2000).

5 D. Ryan, 'Psychological Stress and the Asylum Process in Ireland: A Longitudinal Study of Forced Migrants' (unpublished Ph.D. thesis, Department of Psychology, University College Dublin, 2004). This project was supervised by Professor Ciarán Benson and Dr Barbara Dooley. It was funded by the Irish Research Council for the Humanities and Social Sciences and the Department of Psychology, University College Dublin, Ireland. It consisted of face-to-face interviews with a sample of 162 forced migrants, seventy of whom were re-interviewed during a follow-up study.

9

Tuyen Pham: caught between two cultures

Vera Sheridan

The following interview with Tuyen Pham took place on 27 November 2001 at the Vietnamese–Irish Centre and is one of eighteen interviews investigating the long-term process of cross-cultural adaptation[1] by members of the Vietnamese community in Ireland.[2] This introduction provides the historical and socio-political context in which the exodus of the 'boat people' began from Vietnam in 1979, as this movement of refugees was the result of a series of internal events within Vietnam as well as external events stemming from relations with neighbouring states. It also outlines aspects of post-flight resettlement in Ireland from which cross-cultural adaptation issues emerge and which are discussed at length in the interview. As the interview progresses it becomes clear that both interviewer and interviewee have the common experience of having been young refugees and this common experience allows a detailed exploration of the complexities of Tuyen's story.

Tuyen arrived in Ireland in 1979 as a teenager and as one of 212 refugees from Vietnam who had been invited to Ireland through the government of the day's response to a call from the Secretary General of the United Nations in 1979. The Secretary General had requested governments to 'act in a decisive way'[3] in order to help ease the burden of the countries of first asylum such as Malaysia and Hong Kong. Consequently, of this original group of 212 refugees who came to Ireland, 109 came from Hong Kong and 103, including Tuyen, from the camps in Malaysia.[4] The mass exodus from Vietnam had already been preceded by a series of dramatic events within Vietnam following reunification in 1975 as the Communist forces of North Vietnam defeated the South Vietnamese regime. There followed a period of political change as the new state attempted to create loyal citizens in line with Communist doctrine. A time of political repression followed in the former South, focusing on people with any connection with the former regime who were sent to 're-education' camps, for instance, for the correction of their political views.

In 1978 an anti-bourgeois movement was initiated, including the seizure of property and business assets. There was a focus on the ethnic Chinese population in the former South, as they were a visibly wealthy minority. At this juncture external political factors also came into play as Vietnam invaded Kampuchea and ousted the Khmer Rouge regime of Pol Pot, whose forces had made numerous incursions into Vietnamese territory in the south. This decisive political action aggravated China, a supporter of the Khmer Rouge, and resulted in an invasion of Vietnam and a seventeen-day war. Though China withdrew into its own borders, the Vietnamese government exploited a wave of anti-Chinese sentiment. Violence against the minority Chinese population resulted in flight from both north and south of Vietnam, and over 200,000 crossed into China,[5] where the Chinese government took a long-term perspective on the resettlement of the refugees. Others also decided to flee at this time as there was no place for them in the new order: those released from the re-education camps, those tainted by any link with the previous regime or those with a Chinese spouse. From the south they fled in small, overcrowded boats, arriving mainly in Hong Kong or Malaysia. As numbers grew, an international conference was convened in Geneva on 20–21 July in 1979 and resulted in the Secretary General's request for countries to share the burden of this humanitarian crisis.

In Ireland the Department of Defence[6] made the arrangements concerning the new arrivals, who were initially housed in two reception centres run by the Red Cross, one in Blanchardstown at the James Connolly Memorial Hospital and the other in Swords. From there families and individuals were dispersed throughout the state and placed in local authority housing. Though the Vietnamese were the third group of refugees[7] to come to Ireland, following the Hungarians in 1956 and the Chileans in 1973, there was little experience of long-term resettlement or discussion of long-term cross-cultural adaptation in a society where cultural homogeneity was considered to be the norm. The interview with Tuyen reveals the personal consequences of this situation, not only for himself but for other young Vietnamese as they came to terms with a new life, a new language[8] and a new culture against the splintering of the specific Vietnamese cultural form that resides in social organisation by family[9] and family loyalty. The traditional Vietnamese family has its cultural origins in a blend of ancestor worship and Confucianism[10] and also draws on Buddhist, Catholic[11] and other spiritual sources.[12] Two particular features of the Vietnamese family are elder respect[13] and taking care of family elders, a responsibility that usually falls on the eldest son and his wife. Marriage is a moral duty, as it perpetuates the family, and Tuyen refers to these core values in Vietnamese culture during a discussion of marriage, where his sense of being caught between two cultures emerges.

The Vietnamese community in Ireland has now been in existence for a significant length of time during which individuals and families have been drawn to Dublin, where there is some sense of community with a shared past. This small community has changed the physical landscape of Irish society through the setting up of family-run enterprises as Chinese restaurants and take-aways in Dublin and in towns throughout the state, as the first submission made in 1995 by the Irish government to the OECD's annual report[14] on trends in international migration acknowledges. However, the report refers to Asians and others of the same nationalities whereas the take-up of citizenship by members of the Vietnamese community is high[15] so that the process of cross-cultural adaptation appears to be unidirectional in Irish society. Even so, contact with the new culture raises questions around the cultural roots of ethnicity and the formation of a continuum of identities where an individual can embrace both the past and the present: as Vietnamese, Chinese, an amalgam of both as well as being Irish by citizenship or birth.[16] Such new identities, created at both group and individual level, have implications for the younger and older generations, as Tuyen realises. At the same time the question of heritage language maintenance and assimilationary pressure[17] in Irish society will have a profound effect on the future third generation of this small community[18] in Ireland.

The interview

Vera. That should record us reasonably well, OK, um, and you were saying that you don't have anybody to teach them to read or write Vietnamese, [uhum], aren't there some classes up in Clondalkin?

Tuyen. Clondalkin? That I don't know anything about that in that area, just know in this area, probably they are teaching more Chinese,[19] [aha], in Clondalkin, than Vietnamese. I'm not too sure about that, what they teaching there at the moment. So, here we do need actually, we need financial support, in order to teach all our children to have, ah, better, you know, Vietnamese reading and writing skills and we also need qualified teachers as well, you know, qualified ones. That's why we haven't got a chance to ask for support, you know.

Vera. Yeah. Would there be anybody in the community ...

Tuyen. I think there should be somebody who is capable of teaching Vietnamese but they have their time of doing their own business or they have no time to come over here and teach us all. So in that way we have to look, somehow, to apply for a teacher.

Vera. OK, yes. So, I mean, that's quite difficult when it's so small.

Tuyen. Yes.

Vera. What I was going to do, then, was just talk a little bit about you, because I think you probably have quite an interesting history, er, because, again, it gives a nice background to the whole community. Anything you don't like you can turn it off, if you don't like, that's the way to turn it off.

Tuyen. Aha.

Vera. OK.

Tuyen. OK. Yes.

Vera. Right, so that's the one.

Tuyen. Nothing personal, is it?

Vera. No, no.

Tuyen. OK then.

Vera. Em, yeah. When did you come to Ireland? So how long have you been here?

Tuyen. I came here in October '79.

Vera. Really?

Tuyen. Yes.

Vera. So you're one of the first.

Tuyen. Yes, first few of the people, refugees arrived here in Ireland, yes.

Vera. And how old were you?

Tuyen. I were fourteen at the time.

Vera. So you can remember quite a lot about everything that happened before you came?

Tuyen. Er, no, not very much.

Vera. So, did you come – you came with some of your family?

Tuyen. I came with my two uncles and, um, his family, one of his families, one of my uncle's is married.

Vera. So you, presumably the family group paid somebody so that you could get a place on a boat?

Tuyen. No, actually my uncle was an organiser, so he get me a place, he just dealing with that, I don't know is he [?] or not because he an organiser, [that] I know.

Vera. So he got all of you a place on a boat?

Tuyen. Yes, yes.

Vera. So how long did it take?

Tuyen. Oh, it took quite a while, as I can remember it, it took me ah, oh, quite a dramatic, ah, you know, escaping, can't remember much but we ... On the way from Vietnam to Malaysia we met a storm, yes, a really big storm and Thai pirates as well ... And our boat was damaged by the Thai and our engines were broke down ... We were drifting on the sea for, for three days and three nights, yeah, three days and four nights. Probably I remember like that and we were saved by the, um, American oil rig in the middle of the sea, you know, in the China sea, you know where it is.

Vera. What did you do for water?

Tuyen. Water? We just brought enough water but food we ... a little bit, you know, just about, but we were saved by the boat, so we, we stayed in the oil rig for two days, I think, and then we got to the land, to Malaysia, by the navy, by the boat there.

Vera. So you stayed in a camp in Malaysia, there?

Tuyen. Yes. First we came to the reception camp in, um, in Kuala Lumpur. Stayed there for a month, where we stayed in a football camp. Just a field, a football field which was overcrowded and waiting for ... to be called or to be arranged to coming to the camp, refugee camp itself.

Vera. You must have felt quite terrified?

Tuyen. Oh, still, oh, everything so strange, everything was, you know, very frightened. When you first come there they put you into the football field, and overcrowded and they have the ... and at the time, when new arrival on the boat, being pulled out to sea again, you know, yes, by the local authorities there. It doesn't matter if you were accepted in the reception camp or not; if your name called up you will report into one boat with enough water and food, with one ... a compass and then they maybe will pull you out to the sea, towards the sea to, I don't know how long, and then jump off the rope and leave you floating there ... and say that you are not allowed to come back . But a lot have go back and then [they have come back], yes, yes [and then come back, I mean], yes, and then they return to the area, come back. They have nowhere to go, just come back, and finally, you know, they got accepted to stay at the refugee camp with the interfering of course probably by the UNHCR or by, you know, humanitarian organisations. Something like that.

Vera. But, I mean, it must have been just so, so scary.

Tuyen. Of course, I frightened my death because if my name or my family's name were called we were pulled out to sea again and my experience with the sea is peril. I got seasick and everything. I got pirates, you know, and we got storms. Our boats were broke down and damaged, water were coming in, we had to get it out by hand. All the engines were broke down, you know, a lot of things that your life would be terrible. Probably was feeding the fish.

Vera. So how long did you stay in the Malaysian camp?

Tuyen. Stayed there for, I arrived in May so ... arrived in May, I arrived here in October, it's five months, yes.

Vera. OK. So you were there May '79 and then October, you went to, you came to Ireland. Why did your family leave? If you don't mind my asking.

Tuyen. Ah, you know, they have to, to organise the whole family to go. First, you have to get the finances to pay for the place and the boat also, small when you are escaping, just enough people. You need money to buy food and water, oil, and for the escaping, for the journey …

Vera. Uhum [mobile rings], that's OK. You can answer it if you like. And, um, let's see. You arrived then in October [mobile rings] and how did you … Do you want to answer?

Tuyen. No, it's all right. I'll switch it off.

Vera. OK. Was it UNHCR or was it a religious organisation that contacted you or your family to, kind of, bring you to Ireland?

Tuyen. No, no, no, not at all. When I arrived here in Ireland I made the application for family reunification and they joined me ten years later.

Vera. OK, so it was ten years later. OK, and, um, you've still got family back in Vietnam? Do you still keep in touch?

Tuyen. Yes, I do have relatives. I have an aunt, an uncle still living in Vietnam. We stay in touch by letter or by phone.

Vera. So you have some link? [Yes.] And, but they're obviously going to stay there, they're not going to join you here?

Tuyen. Oh, very difficult, you know, because they're old, married, have children and they become, you know, grandparents themselves. If the Irish government will accept them, then it would be nice. Yes, I think it's very hard. I hope that the Irish government will open their hearts and accept my family over because they're feeling lonely. Because my grandparents are here and both sides, my maternal grandparents, my paternal grandparents, are here, my father, and uncle and aunts, are here as well.

Vera. Yes. So I mean, really, it's like …

Tuyen. It's all my family, so. The only two left in Vietnam are really, very small members, so I hope that if the Irish government, you know, would do me a favour, consider this area, you know, for me, for us here, it's very gratefully if they can join us here.

Vera. But that's a very tricky question because they said – it was a couple of years ago – it was supposed to be the final round, wasn't it?[20]

Tuyen. That's right, yes, and we got only the youngest family came over, which were —— person, yes.

Vera. Yes, is there a limit, something like the age of eighteen or [Yes.] or something about family groups …

Tuyen. Yes, they were qualified, all as independent children, you know.

Vera. So, I mean, you think you were lucky last time around?

Tuyen. Ah, yes. Well, most Vietnamese community here able to bring some members of their family over in the last final decision by the Irish government. You know what I mean. They issue around two hundred visa and that is their final grant, final decision.

[Tape turned off at this point by Vera.]

Vera. Let's carry on a little bit there. So, then you said a little bit, you applied for family reunification and your family came ten years later. Was that difficulties from here or difficulties organising everything in Vietnam?

Tuyen. What did you mean by that question? Is that by the visa or the waiting here?

Vera. Well, just getting the visas but then also maybe, you know, back in Vietnam you have things to do. I don't know. But, you know, ten years is a long time.

Tuyen. It is. Ten years quite a long time. I only applied when I was able to speak a little bit of English. Then I applied. Five years later and when the decision was agreed I was granted visa for my families. Five years, you know, making a decision by the Irish government and as soon as I got it granted, got the visa granted to my family to join me here in Ireland, I send it home to my parents. I've been told in Vietnam they went through the medical check-ups by the, um, you know, by the IOA,[21] which is the international organisation for migrants or something like that for migration.

Vera. They had to do, they did a medical check-up [Yes.] over there? Why?

Tuyen. And they arrange flight tickets and all that. I don't know who can pay, the Irish government pay for all the organisation, or that organisation pay for that, but I guess that the Irish government must have paid. Yes, that is their end of doing. In here, it took five years to get the decision done.

Vera. So you actually, you applied in a certain year and then five years later you actually got the decision? That is a very long time.

Tuyen. That some time before I, yes, quite a long time. First they answered me that, you know, because I was too young, and I was unable to support them if they coming over. That's why the length have been there. So a few years later, I don't know how, must be pushed, or must be a humanitarian, so maybe the application form was so long, they looked into the points and finally … I was delighted, anyway.

Vera. Well, yes, that was a good end to that, to that story. Of course, you weren't working in Vietnam were you?

Tuyen. No, no, no. Not at all. I was too young. I was at school before the Viet, before Saigon. After the fall of Saigon,[22] my family's ... my —— – was in a re-education camp for a while, to, to ... because he served in the South Vietnamese army, and my families were oppressed. I was off from school, because I had to stay home to support, to do some work, hard work and all that, helping the families. Haven't enough money to send all of us to school. So, I'm the oldest in the family, so I have to stay home.

Vera. So, I mean, your education really then was interrupted?

Tuyen. Interrupted for three years until I escaped in '79. In Ireland I started to go to Christian Brothers' school, in ——. Firstly, when I arrived in 1979 here, the government bring us, a group of about two hundred people, to a monastery in Swords, where we stayed there. I stayed there for three months and we got the, um, very kind Irish family that sponsored us to —— city, to —— county. And there my two uncles and families and myself went to ——, to stay there and I went to a Christian Brothers' school there.

Vera. Did you get any special help?

Tuyen. Yes, yes, in school I have special treatment from the principal, the teachers. I have a special, an hour, a private English class in school and the rest, I had to do exactly what I heard like the Irish kids did.

Vera. Did you have a good time or a bad time at school?

Tuyen. First I got a very bad time because I couldn't communicate with the children there. I got a very strange look from the local kids. They thought that I might be an alien coming down from somewhere, you know. They looked at me. I feel very, very embarrassed. I feel very scared but the teachers there have helped me through a lot of it by talking to the kids; do not look at me and treat me nicely and all that, and I get very good treatment from the kids afterwards. They offered me sweets and at lunchtime they offered to share with me their sandwiches and all, like this. I joined, I played football in school, yeah, and after school I played football, I even played some Gaelic football and I joined the school Gaelic team. And I travelled too, you know, playing against all the schools, having great fun.

Vera. So, I mean, that was quite good, then, because you got support from your teachers. So, so they tried to help the other kids to, to develop a reasonable attitude to you.

Tuyen. Yes, yes, yes. Thanks to the teachers there, you know, and they helped people a lot.

Vera. And this was a secondary school?

Tuyen. This was a – no, because I was, because I arrived, I was sent into the first, you know, not the secondary, primary school to get me a little bit of English first before I can go to the secondary school, you know.

Vera. So you spent a year in sixth class?[23]

Tuyen. Yes.

Vera. And then you went to secondary?

Tuyen. Yes.

Vera. So did you do all the secondary education?

Tuyen. Yes, I did, until ... when we moved to Dublin here. I can't remember ... it was '86 or something and I went to ... I continued my secondary school in —— school here in ——, where my English is so bad I couldn't cope with the subjects and the homework was a lot, so I quit when I doing my Leaving Cert. I haven't finished my Leaving Cert. but during the year of the Leaving Cert. I left and I joined FÀS[24] a year later.

Vera. So, what FÀS training did you do?

Tuyen. I went to Finglas. It called ANCO at the time, it wasn't called FÀS, and I did a computer course, electronics, for nine months.

Vera. Did you get a certificate?

Tuyen. Yes, City and Guilds certificate.

Vera. Oh, that's a good one.

Tuyen. And then I worked in Dun Laoghaire electronic company, for a German firm, it's called ——, for three years. After that I left and I joined UNHCR.

Vera. Oh, really! Is that because of your experiences?

Tuyen. Ah, well, I just applied. I don't know, I just heard that they needed interpreters in Hong Kong in the Vietnamese refugee camps, so I just – I don't know if I'm qualified or not – I just wrote to them and somehow I got an answer.

Vera. So, what year was that?

Tuyen. This was the end of 1990.

Vera. So were you quite excited by this?

Tuyen. I was nervous, actually.

Vera. 'What have I done?'

Tuyen. Yes! You know, going away again, you know, my first time again to go living abroad, no assistance, no knowledge of any Chinese. Luckily I have some Vietnamese there, so I settled down quite soon afterwards.

Vera. That was quite a difficult time to go out there because, if I remember rightly, in the '90s there were lots of issues coming up in the camps because people were being kept there or they weren't being moved. There were fights.

Tuyen. Yes, that's right, yes, um, that they have a bad life, for boat people who arrived ... If you come alone, if they arrived in Hong Kong before, um, oh, what's that time, for, let's see, what year was that, ... um, I don't know, some time in August 1988, they were automatically refugees.

Vera. Ah. OK.

Tuyen. After that time they have to go through a screening procedure. So if you passed that screening procedure you become political refugees. All the economic refugees are now asylum seekers. You will be refused for the first time and if you're refused for the first time you have a right to appeal.

Vera. OK. So, this is where the tension was created? [Yes.] Because it depended on this decision?

Tuyen. Yes, that's right.

Vera. And if your appeal failed?

Tuyen. You have a third appeal, the mandate by UNHCR. And UNHCR will look into your claim and see that you are a genuine refugee or not. If not then still you've failed and you will be sent home either voluntarily or by deportation.

Vera. Because I can remember quite late in the '90s when there was forced deportation.

Tuyen. That's right, yes, which mean that a lot of people are against that decision and there were a lot of fighting, disturbing everyone in the camps.

[Tape turned off.]

Vera. I didn't come here as a refugee. We went to Britain. We went from Hungary. You know, Hungary was a Communist country then but there was a revolution in 1956 and before the revolution my family had been in a bad situation because we were thought of being, you know, we weren't peasants ... and so my grandfather had a business, so we had a lot of problems, you know, and they kind of followed family.

Tuyen. Yes.

Vera. So my mother left and, she left by herself, then she paid a man to go back in to bring me out.

Tuyen. Oh, yes. So she left you behind?

Vera. Yeah, with my grandparents, because she went very late, the border had been closed, so at that time she had no idea, you know, was she going to get across, was she not? She was very lucky. She managed it. So ... [mutual laughter] ... so I stayed in two camps, a small one first, just inside the border, in Austria, then we were moved further in to a big camp called Traiskirchen which I didn't like.

Tuyen. Aah?

Vera. Big. And then we went to England, and then we stayed in a camp there, but not for too long.

Tuyen. So you automatically went as refugees anyway.

Vera. Yeah, well, at that time it was easier.

Tuyen. As Conventions?

Vera. Yes, exactly.

Tuyen. The Convention's only in '67, isn't it? [Um.] The Protocol's '54?[25]

Vera. Eh, they – they still did us under the '51.

Tuyen. Ah, yes.

Vera. I, I don't know how they did it but that's how it happened. Um, anyhow, back to you. So, how long did you work in Hong Kong?

Tuyen. I worked there for five years.

Vera. Five years.

Tuyen. Five years.

Vera. So, um, from '90, 19 ...?

Tuyen. From early '91, yes, early '91 till ... late '95.

Vera. And then, and you worked for UNHCR all the time?

Tuyen. All the time, yes.

Vera. Interpreting?

Tuyen. Interpreting. All in the refugee camps. I worked in both, various camps: detention camps, open camps and repatriation camps, you know, yes, and in drugs [?] camps, prisons, I guess, prisons as well ... amongst other things, yes.

Vera. So, I mean, you saw all of it?

Tuyen. Yes, yes. I saw most of it but I don't remember that much, I try not to remember. [Laughter.]

Vera. Yeah.

Tuyen. It's quite horrible.

Vera. I know. I mean, when we used to see all the news. Sometimes, it was quite horrible, to be honest.

Tuyen. Yes, you facing people with all their problems, with all their claims, you know, complaints to the management, camp management and all that, the way they treat people there. And day in day in you will see that people complained to us and we tried to solve their, UNHCR tried to interfere into that situation. But still it's not that much, you know, it's because the camp management have their way of ruling them. They get the big brothers, Vietnamese big brother within the camps to control the population inside the camp. So UNHCR cannot, you know, say anything if the camp management do something to the people. Then there will be human rights and all that. They will, you know, do for the people, but they use the, um, the inside, the people against the people itself' and it's very difficult for the UNHCR to intervene into that.

[Some interference.]

Vera. Um, yeah.

Tuyen. You know, very sad seeing that happen day after day, and, you know, badly treated. Food were bad as well, you know … it wasn't, you get the same routine of food, day after day, like Monday, for example. Monday you have chicken wings for your lunch, and you know, Tuesday, you have veg., a little veg. and all that, because … and so the routine goes, all towards the rights of food, you know. As the days and weeks and years[26] go by so people are kind of [?] the food sometimes. If anyone who have … aeh … the right to go overseas sometimes they have relatives. Then they're able to buy some food in the canteen.

Vera. So family support is always important?

Tuyen. Oh yes, to us, yes. [Mutual laughter.]

Vera. OK. Coming back to here, you came back here in 19—, you came back here did you … when you finished in Hong Kong?

Tuyen. Yes, I, um, because I, I kind of put my job [?]. I resigned and came back here to Ireland … and here I am. [Mutual laughter.]

Vera. Here you are. You didn't think, you didn't want to go back to Vietnam?

Tuyen. No. I went back again last, last year, just a few months ago, the beginning of this year, yes.

Vera. What was it like?

Tuyen. I've seen a lot of changes since I left.[27] Well … you know, it's a lot of changes … it's [?] and more open a little bit to foreigners, to tourists and it's no more strict like before. Like before, if you go back there, if you are a foreigner or you are a Vietnamese visitor going back there, you have to register with the local authority: where you're staying, how long you're going to stay for. But now you can move around without involving the local authorities. Unless when you move to some place and then you know what the story is … There must be a lot of corruption over there … it's the facts.

Vera. We have it here, too. [Mutual laughter.] That seems to be everywhere. OK, you saw quite a lot of change but you, you prefer to stay, to live here rather than there?

Tuyen. Since my family, most of them are here, I get used to the way of living here in Ireland.

Vera. And so, really, because your family's here, and you think you have a better standard of living here?

Tuyen. I think, yes, in the social way. The people here been looked after, than in Vietnam. But anywhere else, if you've got a job, to work, then … you might be, you know, safe, but here it's a freedom country:

you can do whatever you can, talk whatever you feel like, and go wherever you want to go and in Vietnam you don't have that chance, no chance. Of course life here is a lot better. To me, anyway, and I don't know about the others, but to me it is better. Probably, I grew up here, get used to it, I have friends here, Irish friends, and ... that's all. I go back to Vietnam, sometimes ... Of course, I can make friends in Vietnam but the weather is also a little bit too hot for me, probably. In here maybe too cold but I don't say it's cold, you know, I get used to it, and it's OK, but hot I cannot bear.

Vera. [Laugh.] OK, so you, that's gone, you've lost that. [Mutual laughter.]

Tuyen. Yeah, but not too hot, like hot, but warm is OK—you know, twenty degrees is OK, but other than that ... In Vietnam it's thirty-something degrees Celsius, so it really tore you apart in the middle of the day. [Laughter.]

Vera. And you have Irish friends, do you?

Tuyen. Yes, yes, I have Irish friends.

Vera. So what's the mix? You got more Vietnamese, more Irish or kind of half and half?

Tuyen. Of course I'm here in the Centre. so I know a lot of people, so yes ... but cannot say it's a friend. I only have a few Vietnamese friends about my own age and all that. And going out together, around, you know, thirty to fifty friends. But a lot, I know a lot of Vietnamese people, the elderlies, the youngs and all that. Compared to Irish friends I have more Vietnamese friends.

Vera. And your Irish friends, are they friends from school, or ... ?

Tuyen. Very few from school, but from neighbours, friends making social friends ... keeping in touch ... School friends. I have two school friends ... getting in touch, is often difficult, seeing each other, going out.

Vera. So you've kinda got a mixture of friends. What about ... say you were going to get married?

Tuyen. Aha. First I've got to meet the right one! [Mutual laughter.]

Vera. Does it matter if it's an Irish girl or a Vietnamese girl?

Tuyen. Doesn't matter! It doesn't matter to me but to my parents and elderlies' generation. The older generation, they might object to that. They are not racist but because of the culture, the way they want to teach me, especially to Asian people and the elderlies, the majority of the family, so I have to keep in the cultural way, you know.[28] They would prefer me to get a Vietnamese girl so that I can be looking after my parents when they get older, because that's the way, you know [laughter], but I'm looking for a lady [laughter]. But to the Irish people, a woman, they will not agree to that point, so it's my conflict, between ... I'm caught in the middle. It's senseless ... It's hard ... So if

I met the right one, it doesn't matter. I would marry whoever it was, you know.

Vera. But, I mean, there's always a little bit of pressure there, because your parents ... and you respect them, so ...

Tuyen. But of course, love is a different story. [Mutual laughter.]

Tuyen. I have to please them all. I will have to please myself also. I will not be selfish but it's the way it is. Life is misery, um!

Vera. Do you think many young, many people who've kind of, really, grown up here have this kind of, you know, you said it was a conflict, have this feeling that they're really torn?

Tuyen. Yes, I have seen, between the younger generations now ... don't speak fluent Vietnamese.[29] They speak very, very well English because they've grown up here and all that. And the way they live, they've adapted to the Irish culture and Irish life so they, most of them, have their Irish friends in school ... Asking the young one here, who grown up, to get married to a Vietnamese girl, that's quite difficult, because first, you have ...There's not much Vietnamese girls around anyway. And most of the Vietnamese girls will be kept at home by their parents and they're not allowed to go out so late at night, so they haven't really a chance to meet each other.[30] So I guess that most of them are meet the Irish friends and they, they, you know, they just meet. I know that some of my friends marry Irish, Irish women, yes, and have kids and all that. They will be OK. No problem at all.

Vera. And your friends who've married Irish girls, obviously the children, they're not going to speak Vietnamese?

Tuyen. No. The children speak very, very little because the mother is very close to them and the father is talking to the mother in the English language, so the children got lost.[31] That's why I would like to have some financial support to get some, a qualified Vietnamese teacher to teach the children if I could arrange that. I don't know what their status would be and I hope that the children would turn up for their classes. Otherwise, you know, something stop ... the children, because they go to school here five days a week. They have their homework to do. They have three languages at school to learn already – English, Irish and some foreign language – in order to qualify for university. And now, forcing them to learn another language which they have only Saturday and Sunday, they need a break. I don't know if they turn up or not. That cannot, their parents. to force them to do that. To force them, the parents have to bring them to the classes, otherwise they cannot on their own, going by their own. And the parents have their own business. Still, they're too busy and they haven't got time to bring them at weekends. So that is my problems.

Vera. It's a dilemma.

Tuyen. And a problem, in fact.

Vera. To make the time and everything else ... And, um, what about you? I mean, do you read Vietnamese books or listen to music? Is it easy to get?

Tuyen. Yes, I do read Vietnamese books, um, and listen to music. I can get them from America, or from France, yes.[32]

Vera. Is that because you have family there or because you know where to write?

Tuyen. Yes, I know where to write. I write to them and order, you know, a list of songs or CDs. So I can look and see what CDs to buy and pay them by cheques and send them the money. Within a little bit of time they will send back the CDs or videos. About reading books, I sometimes go into the Internet looking at the news from the Internet. That's why I need to do, you know, go in twice a week. If I have time I go then and have a look or having a little chat with all the Vietnamese around the world in the Internet. I'm also thinking that I try to get much of the ... issuing a weekly bulletin, you know, to distribute to the Vietnamese around here because, in general, the older generation of people, they don't read any English at all.[33] They don't know what's going on, so I'm thinking here it's quite, if I got a chance to answer for them as well. I can issue a weekly magazine or bulletin to send to the people. I, of course, I need a computer and a printer with paper, ink and stamps and finances to pay a part-time worker, you know, to edit, editing of the bulletin, to change it around. Yes, I feel, I think it's a good idea, because the older ones don't know what's going on, like the war here that happened, and I meet a lot of older people and they say, 'What's going on at the moment in Afghanistan?'

Vera. There must be some kind of government money, especially if it's for a local group. I don't know where you source it. I can always try to find out if you want me to. [Oh, yes.] I don't know who to contact but I'd find some way, um, because there are some people that help local groups and then you can get finance. You know, you'd have to keep financial records if you got a grant.

Tuyen. Probably I have to do one copy first and give them a general idea of what I'm going to do. And when I see the sources of where to apply to I can send a copy at that time of what I'm going to do.

Vera. Because, you know, I'm sure, for older people ... You know, in some families I visited the grandmother, you know, because now there are grandchildren, I mean, you know, we smile at each other and then, maybe. they say 'Hello,' and that's it, finished. There's no support. How do they know what's going on in the world?

Tuyen. Yes, that's right, know what's going on around them, because they also need to know what's going on in Vietnam as well. Maybe in the Internet when I see there's a lot of names from one area or other I can gather a little bit, not very detailed, but still there's some information for them to know what's going on ... I think that's a good idea ... but the financial ... [inaudible interruption] ... it's only a small grant ... because it's a small community here.

Vera. About eight hundred.

Tuyen. No, a thousand, a thousand. Well, I think a thousand. So half of them are the younger generation and half the older. Still the older ones feel very lonely, very sad, and they have no English. Imagine, they're just sitting there in their corner at home ... I can see that in my grandparents. I can see that, actually I can see that myself, and that is very sad. To go out is too cold for them, so I think, to talk to the neighbours, but they're unable, language barrier.[34] Going shopping, doesn't know what to buy, you know, doesn't know how to question: where can I find this and that? OK, they just happen to know. 'Oh, that's stationery. OK, go buy some paper.' Go to the stationery, look around, you know, go into a big supermarket ... they don't know where to put their stuff or buy some, you know, cups. They don't know where to go, and so they have to walk all around the supermarket in order to find the places. It's quite odd.

Vera. Because they can't read the signs.

Tuyen. Yes, so they're shy going out. They are lock themselves up in the corner at home. At least they have ease of mind by getting some information in Vietnamese.

Vera. It keeps the contact as well. So you keep the contact with the world. I think that's quite important, actually. OK, we can finish off slowly. In terms of culture, what's important to you? Do you celebrate Chinese new year, Vietnamese new year?[35]

Tuyen. Yes, we still keep in touch with Vietnamese new year for some time at the end of January or ... [February.] ... February, yes, something like that ... in between that time. And every year we celebrate Chinese new year, and we organise a party, a small party, either in the Centre here or in a hotel so that means the Vietnamese people come here and celebrate.

Vera. So it's pretty much a community celebration.

Tuyen. Yes. Compared to all the countries where the Vietnamese are, the celebrations are more important but in here it's a small group and we are eventually lost that kind of thing we do. But still, anyway, we still keep that, the greatest day of all our culture.

Vera. What about things like religion? I know some people are Catholic, some people are Buddhist, some people tell me they're nothing. [Mutual laughter.]

Tuyen. If they are not they are ancestor worshipper. And Catholics, very few Catholics are here. Buddhism, yes, that's right.

Vera. Because there's a Buddhist temple out in Clondalkin, isn't there?

Tuyen. Yes, that's what I heard also. There's a Buddhist temple, a little Buddhist temple, there and, you know, most people are ancestor worshippers, they worship their ancestors.

Vera. So you have a traditional altar in the home.

Tuyen. Yes, for Catholics they have an altar with a sign of the cross or Mary, mother of Jesus, pictures. In Buddhism you have different kinds of pictures and statues of the Buddha, an altar. Ancestors you have the urn and some incense with a picture of the dead, of your ancestor you worship ... and they worship them every single night, burn incense, and they pay their respects.

Vera. What about young people? Do they keep up things like that or is it no longer important?

Tuyen. For some families, I do know that they don't keep that at all. They go to school here and of course Irish is the Catholic country and most Irish schoolkids, when they're in third class, in fact, go through First Communion[36] and then ... What is it? [Confirmation.] Confirmation, yes, and the children also in that class, they also sometimes join in as well. It doesn't matter they're Catholic or not and their parents doesn't mind, either [incomprehensible interference] really in their own, we can do that, it doesn't really matter. Maybe they just follow all their classmates. I don't know if they understand what they're doing or not but I think they do learn religion in school. So they might know something about that and they don't keep the Sunday. [Mutual laughter.]

Vera. OK. So they might learn religion but it's probably not that important. What about things like food? I mean, obviously grandparents, parents, they're going to stick to traditional cooking, but are things changing again with youngsters?

Tuyen. Yes, of course, it's changed as well. We cook our own Vietnamese food at home to eat ... it's traditional. We're used to that kind, we have rice and meat or poultry cooking, or we ... I myself, I don't know how to cook, anyway, Irish food or Vietnamese food. [Mutual laughter.] I don't know, but that's how I am. [Mutual laughter.] Whatever I'm given at home I eat them. And my parents sometimes make Irish food, like beefsteak, boiled potatoes or mashed potatoes with soup and gravy. And at Christmas[37] we try to have turkey, dinner, like the Irish traditional one [mutual laughter], lamb and all that, yes, it changes once a week or twice a week at least we have Irish food.

Vera. So there's a little bit of a mixture going on?

Tuyen. A mixture, yes, as to the older ones. But the younger ones, they prefer what they have, like pizza, chips or, you know, mashed potatoes, boiled potatoes. If the parents are willing to cook it then they're happy to eat them but they do prefer that than Vietnamese food. If for those who are very easy to eat then it's OK, they don't mind what food they eat. But for some, they still have to, at least four a week, four Irish food a week, or they have every day because at schooltime they can go to the chipper to buy some cheap food and all the time bringing their sandwiches.

Vera. Yeah, they need to be like their friends. Um, if you have children what would you like them to know about the Vietnamese way of life? What do you think would be important?

Tuyen. I'd teach them as much as I know about Vietnamese culture, because I myself will eventually lost it. I don't know how to teach them. I think what's best for them is to leave them free to adapt to all the peoples around them.[38] Of course I will teach them whatever I know of my experience of my culture: to give them a little bit of advice, to honour the elderly people, respect their parents and remember the most important cultural days like the Moon festival,[39] the Vietnamese new year and some other Vietnamese cultural celebrations. If I can remember. [Mutual laughter.]

Vera. What do you think will happen in the future? Do you think more of the younger generation will marry Irish people, and do you think the community's going to disintegrate? Do you think there's enough to keep it together?

Tuyen. Oh, that I cannot predict, but I would imagine that the younger generation, eventually, they probably will lost their culture and they kind of, you know, mixed with the Irish people. In here in the Vietnamese Centre we try to, try to stick together until the younger are grown up. Then we can hand over to the younger ones so that they can mix, but they still have, or they can bring in, their Irish friends. That's exactly where the place for them to keep in touch with, and if someone is good enough or is very interested in Vietnamese culture, of course they can make something happen. They can invite people from Vietnam and with the help of them to bring cultural [events] in here, to show them what culture is like and to show a bit interesting ... if that's going to happen, and I hope that's going to happen.

Vera. We don't really know, it's a matter of wait-and-see. What about the language? [Mutual laughter.]

Tuyen. The English language or Vietnamese?

Vera. Vietnamese and Chinese. Do you think that's under pressure?

Tuyen. Yes. As I told you, now we need financial [assistance] to get a qualified teacher or get someone that free in their own time. And of course
we will pay that teacher with the support of the government here,
the Education Department, to teach Vietnamese to the younger ones
so they can read and write to their relatives or friends in Vietnam, if
they can make friends. Or they can go into the Internet and chat with
Vietnamese friends after work. It is very hard to set up, to set up the
school. The class is OK but the willingness of the students ... I don't
know how the percentage would be, what percentage ... So that issue
will go to next year and we'll talk about that because ... [inaudible] ...
so we leave everything until next year and try to organise that to see
[*Vera.* To see what comes of it.] or even if the children would come to
Vietnamese class during the summer time .

Vera. And, just going back to the language, just probably one of my
last questions now. Say you've got a family situation where children
have pretty much grown up here, do they speak Vietnamese to their
parents or English to parents? Vietnamese to each other, English to
each other? What have you seen?

Tuyen. What I have seen is: yes, they do speak Vietnamese to their
parents, with broken Vietnamese, to their parents. They sometimes
put in the English word. And to each other if they are brother and
sister at home there without their parents present, or without the
elderly people present, they're chatting in English. They're fighting in
English, they're talking in English.[40] You know, if something is a secret
between them they're coming to English so their parents won't understand it. And if the children think that their parents might understand
some English then they will talk about it in slang English! [Mutual
laughter.] They are quite good in that way, and, you know, they're
more Irish themselves, so that's how I see that. And they're getting
influenced: at school they're talking English going home, in their
spare time they're watching television, children go back to English.
Their parents are busy working at night time and they have no time
to talk to their children, so that way the children are talking to each
other in English. It's the parents' responsibility to tell their children
to speak Vietnamese to each other.

Vera. But difficult.

Tuyen. That's the family's, yeah, to keep an eye on them, because they
can be upstairs talking ... it can be all in English ... There's no way to
keep an eye on them unless you have twenty-four hours with them,
which can't be done.

Vera. What about employment? A lot of people work in the restaurants and take-aways.[41] What about the children now, the ones who've gone to school here? Are they going on to college or university, moving on to other jobs? What's kind of happening?

Tuyen. That, in a general view, I cannot answer personally, because each child, each children, their point of view, or they have the willingness to go to school or not.

Vera. What have you seen kind of happening from your own experience?

Tuyen. From my own experience I have seen my friend's children, my older people that I know and their children that have grown up here and go to school until they are doing their Leaving Cert. and after that they can pick their own career ... Some like school, some actually still continue with their schooling, but I have some ... Of course here in Ireland it's very difficult to tell Vietnamese children keeping their school or not, studying or not, because of the atmosphere. If they adapt into the Irish life then they will have fun at school. Then they will continue. If those who are more sided to their Asian culture and parents, a little, you know, a bit less, they can go out looking for a job but their job will be labourer, no qualified. That generation, that my generation.[42] Wait until another five to ten years' time, you will see then what will happen.

Vera. And you think more people will end up going to college and kind of moving out of restaurant work?

Tuyen. I think that's ... If they're thinking enough, yes, they will move out from the restaurant. The younger ones, I hope the younger ones will go to school, get some certificates and get an easy, just a day job, 'cos it's a more social life. Working in a restaurant, from experience I don't work there at all, I don't have to cook, but I see a lot of people cooking six days a week. They've got no social life at all, because in a restaurant you need to work night-time and weekends. So they're only off one day, whatever they pick, but cannot be off at weekends, so their social life with other people very, very difficult ... so I hope that the younger ones will see that as a difficulty and back up, try to do, learn in school, that's better. They should do that.

Vera. OK. Well, I think that's all the questions I have to ask you, unless there's anything else you want to say?

Tuyen. That's everything I can say. [Mutual laughter.]

Notes

I am most grateful to Tuyen Pham for giving me his time so that this interview could take place and so help form a deeper understanding of the long-term process of cross-cultural adaptation by members of the Vietnamese community in Ireland. Tuyen Pham has decided to use his own name for this book.

1 For a full discussion of cross-cultural issues, including theoretical perspectives, see Y. Y. Kim, *Becoming Intercultural* (Thousand Oaks, CA: Sage, 2001). Culture here is theoretically defined as the internal abstract representation of how individuals engage with each other in society though the term is used in a more general sense during the interview. For a long in-depth definition of culture see R. Keesing, 'Theories of Culture', *Annual Review of Anthropology*, 3 (1974), pp. 73–97, and G. Hofstede, *Culture's Consequences* (Thousand Oaks, CA: Sage, 2001).

2 V. Sheridan, 'With Loneliness and Satisfaction: Tracing the Path of Cross-cultural Adaptation by Members of the Vietnamese Community in Ireland', unpublished Ph.D. thesis (Dublin: School of Applied Language and Intercultural Studies, Dublin City University, 2005).

3 Office of the UNHCR meeting on refugees and displaced persons in South East Asia, convened by the Secretary General of the United Nations at Geneva, 20 and 21 July 1979, and subsequent developments (*Report of the Secretary General*, 1979), p. 2.

4 Refugee Agency information sheet, 1998.

5 T. Lam, 'The Exodus of Hoa Refugees from Vietnam and their Settlement in Guanxi: China's Refugee Settlement Strategies', *Journal of Refugee Studies*, 13: 4 (2000), pp. 374–90.

6 Note the military model which stems from post-World War II, when approximately 30 million displaced people were managed, initially along military lines. This approach was replaced by a humanitarian model with the creation of the United Nations High Commission for Refugees in 1951.

7 See B. Fanning, *Racism and Social Change in the Republic of Ireland* (Manchester: Manchester University Press, 2002).

8 See M. Dean, 'Some Sociolinguistic Implications of Vietnamese learning English in Ireland', in L. MacMathuna and D. Singleton (eds), *Language across Cultures: Proceedings of a Symposium held at St Patrick's College, Drumcondra, Dublin, 8–9 July 1983* (Dublin: Irish Association for Applied Linguistics, 1983), pp. 71–82, and also F. McGovern, 'The Education of a Linguistic and Cultural Minority: Vietnamese Children in Irish Schools, 1979–1989', *Irish Educational Studies*, 12 (1993), pp. 92–105, for the education of adults and children and revealing social comments.

9 See R. Smith, *Vietnam and the West* (London: 1968), for an insight into Vietnamese culture; G. Hofstede, *Culture's Consequences* (Thousand Oaks, CA: Sage, 1980/2001), for the organising principles of family collectivism; S. Gold, *Refugee Communities* (Newbury Park, CA: Sage, 1992), and D. Haines, D. Rutherford and P. Thomas, 'Family and Community among Vietnamese

Refugees', *International Migration Review*, 15 (1981), pp. 310–19, among others where the particular cultural form of the Vietnamese family also emerges in relation to culture contact.

10 See K. V. Nguyen, 'On the Historical Role of Confucianism', *Vietnamese Studies*, 94: 4 (1989), pp. 67–72.

11 Buddhism passed from China to the north of Vietnam as well as Confucianism. The Confucian system of rule persisted into modern times in the court of the last emperor, Bao Dai, who fled Hanoi in 1954. Missionary activity in the sixteenth and seventeenth centuries left the legacy of Catholicism in Vietnam. See T. L. H. Nguyen, 'No Discharge from that War: the Double Diaspora of Vietnam's Catholics', *Orbis* (fall), pp. 491–501, in relation to the partition of Vietnam in 1954.

12 For a discussion of harmony, order and bending stemming from Tam Giao, or the Triple Religion, a fusion of Confucianism, Taoism, Buddhism and ancient Vietnamese animism, see R. Smith, *Vietnam and the West* (London: Heinemann, 1968), and Smith *et al.*, *Area Handbook for South Vietnam* (Washington, DC: US Government Printing Office, 1967).

13 K. Sung, 'Elder Respect: Exploration of Ideals and Forms in East Asia', *Journal of Aging Studies*, 15 (2001), pp. 13–26.

14 OECD, *Annual Report: Trends in International Migration* (Paris: OECD), p. 97.

15 C. O'Regan, *Report of a Survey of the Vietnamese and Bosnian Refugee Communities in Ireland* (Dublin: Refugee Agency, 1998).

16 See J. O'Neill (the former head of the Refugee Agency), 'Integration of Refugees in Ireland. No Welcomes Here? Asylum Seekers and Refugees in Ireland and Britain', *Democratic Dialogue*, report No. 14 (2001) at www.democraticdialogue.org/report.

17 V. Sheridan, 'Quand "l'espoir vous fait vivre" : la communauté vietnamienne en Irlande', in E. Murphy-Lejeune (ed.), *Interculturel francophonies 5, Nouvelles mobilités, nouveaux voyageurs* (Lecce: Alliance Française, 2004), pp. 55–71.

18 The final official estimate of the size of the Vietnamese community was 823, including an Irish-born generation of 200 children and community links with the other diaspora countries such as the United States, Canada, Australia, the United Kingdom and France and others (Dublin: Refugee Agency, 2000).

19 The Vietnamese community is heterogeneous and contains both Vietnamese and ethnic Chinese members among others. This is a reference to Saturday morning classes which take place in Chinese and Vietnamese in north Dublin.

20 This refers to the final reunification programme for the Vietnamese and Bosnian communities made by the Irish government in 1998 when approximately 200 Vietnamese family members were to be admitted under the scheme. See the *Irish Times*, 3 December, p. 3. Both O'Regan and Baneham have noted communication difficulties between the Vietnamese community and the Irish government and Sheridan on a specific encounter with Irish government officials. See O'Regan, *Report of a Survey*, and B. Baneham,

'Waiting for Ho: A Study of family Separation in the Vietnamese Community', unpublished M.A. thesis (Dublin: University College), and V. Sheridan, 'The Effects of Social Distance on the Second Language Learning of Members of a Minority Group settling in Ireland', unpublished M.Phil. thesis (Dublin: Trinity College, 1998)

21 The International Organisation for Migration provides resettlement assistance.

22 A reference to the fall of Saigon in April 1975. President Duong Van Minh announced the unconditional surrender of the South Vietnamese government and its military forces to the Vietcong on the 30 April 1975.

23 The final year of primary school where most children would be aged thirteen, that is, younger than Tuyen at the time.

24 FÀS is the Irish national training and employment authority.

25 These are references to the Geneva Conventions of 1951 and 1954 and the New York Protocol of 1967. The 1951 Geneva Convention relating to the Status of Refugees contains the basic legal definition of refugee status. The 1967 Protocol relating to the Status of Refugees removed the post-World War II-linked time restriction and created a universal instrument of refugee law.

26 The last Hong Kong camp closed in 2000. C. O'Clery, *Irish Times*, 1 June 2000, p. 11.

27 The process of *moi doi* or 'economic restructuring' began in 1986 in Vietnam. See Y. Wu and T. Sun, 'Four Faces of Vietnamese Communism: Small Countries' Institutional Choice under Hegemony', *Communist and post-Communist Studies*, 31: 4 (1998), pp. 381–99.

28 Tuyen is the eldest and is particularly under pressure, as traditionally the eldest son has specific family responsibilities.

29 Note the relationship with language. With endogamy, that is, marriage within the group, both culture in its broadest sense and language are preserved within the family. See Sheridan, 'With Loneliness and Satisfaction', for a full discussion of language issues across the generations.

30 Traditionally there would be concern for a young woman's virtue. Young women would be expected to be chaste until marriage and it would not be considered decent behaviour for a young woman to smoke or drink. See H. Rydstrøm, 'Sexed Bodies, Gendered Bodies: Children and the Body in Vietnam', *Women's Studies International Forum*, 25: 3 (2002), pp. 359–72, for a discussion of the blending of Confucianism and Communism in modern Vietnamese society.

31 Note how the child is lost to language. See J. Fishman, *Handbook of Language and Ethnic Identity* (New York: Oxford University Press, 1999).

32 From the main diaspora countries with major Vietnamese populations and family connections within the diaspora.

33 The elderly face increasing isolation, which is alleviated by satellite television for some. See Sheridan, 'With Loneliness and Satisfaction', for the Irish context and also S. Su and C. Conaway, 'Information and a Forgotten Minority: Elderly Chinese Immigrants', *Library and Information Science Research*, 17: 1 (1995), pp. 69–86.

34 Language issues surfaced as early as 1981, as is indicated by the Minister of Defence's statement to the Dáil in February 1981 and Dean, 'Some Sociolinguistic Implications of Vietnamese learning English in Ireland'.

35 Vietnamese new year, or Têt, which means the first morning of the first day of the new year. The celebration lasts for seven days and homes are cleaned to remove bad fortune associated with the old year. Debts are paid, differences between family and friends are resolved and everyone receives new clothes. It is the most significant Vietnamese cultural celebration.

36 Also in McGovern, 'The Education of a Linguistic and Cultural Minority'.

37 Food and Christmas as markers of contact and change also in V. Sheridan, 'Social Distance and Language Training: a Case Study of the Irish–Vietnamese community', in R. Lentin (ed.), *The Expanding Nation: Towards a Multi-ethnic Ireland*, proceedings of a conference held in Trinity College (Dublin: Trinity College, 1998), pp. 55–65.

38 A reference to an intercultural identity. See Kim, *Becoming Intercultural*.

39 Têt-Trung-Thu, or the mid-autumn moon festival, which provides an opportunity for parents to show their love and appreciation for their children.

40 See U. Scheu, 'Cultural Constraints in Bilinguals' Code Switching', *International Journal of Intercultural Relations*, 24: 1 (2000), pp. 131–50.

41 Not all refugee groups open family businesses. For a cultural explanation of ethnic entrepreneurship in a Confucianist cultural context see J. Sanders and V. Nee, 'Immigrant Self-employment: the Family as Social Capital and the Value of Human Capital', *American Sociological Review*, 61: 2 (1996), pp. 231–49, and Sheridan, 'With Loneliness and Satisfaction', with regard to the Vietnamese in Ireland.

42 The result of assimilationary pressure in school.

10

The 'Bosnian project' in Ireland: a 'vision of divisions'

Maja Halilovic-Pastuovic

Following the decision by the government in July 1992 to allow them entry into the Irish state, a relatively small group of Bosnian programme refugees, fleeing the conflict in the former Yugoslavia, arrived in Ireland. Before their arrival, a long-term state-sponsored reception plan was put in place under the slogan 'refugees today – ethnic minorities tomorrow',[1] and from the moment they entered the state this reception and resettlement programme was followed. The main aim of this reception programme, or 'Bosnian project' as I will call it, was the long-term successful integration of Bosnian refugees into Irish society. According to a 2000 Irish government report entitled *Integration: A Two-way Process*, 'integration policy must be framed *to prepare individuals to function* in Irish society', since, 'afforded the appropriate support and opportunities, refugees will be enabled to demonstrate their talent, skills, enthusiasm and culture and to contribute to the social fabric of Ireland'.[2] The report argued that, for this to happen, 'there must be cohesion in delivery of services and the Government's commitment to integration must be clearly grounded in Government policy and driven by central Government'.[3]

This chapter examines the Bosnian experience in Ireland thirteen years after their arrival and argues that state-sponsored integration did not occur as planned. A 2005 review by the Bosnian Community Development Project identified the issues of integration and social inclusion as still the main problems facing Bosnians living in Ireland.[4] The chapter is based upon the interviews I conducted with Bosnian women during the summer of 2003[5] and on personal communication with the Community Development and Information Officers of the Bosnian Community Development Project in the autumn of 2005. In examining the 'Bosnian project' I argue that within the 'weak multiculturalism' that, according to Fanning,[6] dominates the politics of diversity within the Irish state, where 'the multicultural' is still stuck in the context of 'descriptive'[7] and where a *partnership-based* approach sought to manage the 'problem' of cultural diversity, the envisaged integration could not have happened.[8]

Instead of integrating, members of the Bosnian community have found their own way of negotiating their position in Ireland. Notably this has taken the form of annual summer migrations to Bosnia.[9]

Integration, multiculturalism and the *racial* state

Firstly I want to argue that the multicultural understanding of diversity in Ireland, as influenced by Taylor's 'politics of recognition',[10] still rests upon the essentialist[11] belief in cultural difference where there is a perceived dichotomy between the national ideal of Irishness, the official host culture, on the one hand, and all 'the others' on the other. The homogenisation of the Bosnian community within the 'Bosnian project' is a clear example of this essentialist approach to difference. I also argue that the *partnership* approach that the Irish state has adopted in dealing with Bosnian programme refugees is an example of what Goldberg terms 'historicism'[12] and, as such, is a part of the way the *racial* state operates. Indeed, the Bosnian Community Development Project was conceived by agents of the Irish government, funded by the state sources and managed by the director of the Refugee Agency, in order to prepare Bosnians *to function in Irish society* and successfully *integrate*.[13] To a considerable extent it was an extension of earlier historicist approaches to the assimilation of Travellers.

Multiculturalism emerged as a result of the realisation, originally in the United States, and then in Britain, that 'a "melting pot" does not melt' and that ethnic divisions get reproduced, albeit in different forms, from one generation to the next. The initial aim of the policies based upon the multicultural principle, located within this 'new' understanding of difference as reproducible, rather than assimilable, was to construct society as composed of a hegemonic homogeneous majority and a small number of 'unmeltable' minorities with 'their own essentially different communities and cultures which have to be understood, accepted and basically left alone'.[14] Although the understanding, and the policies based upon this understanding, have changed since the 1960s and 1970s with the effect that minority cultures are viewed in less essentialist terms today, the 'hegemonic majority versus marginalised minority' way of dealing with difference has not been abandoned. From a policy standpoint, multiculturalism, as a response to cultural diversity, still assumes that racism is caused by the 'strangeness' of incoming immigrant groups rather than by the 'host' society, and that by 'integrating, and eventually assimilating out-groups, the "problem" would disappear'.[15] Indeed, the belief was that by the recognition and integration of the Bosnian community into the 'new' multicultural Ireland the problem of their 'otherness' would eventually disappear. However, the Bosnian population in Ireland was far more complex and diverse than the Bosnian project could account for, as this chapter shows.

Goldberg argues that it is possible to define the nation-state as a more or less coherent entity in two related ways: as *state projects* 'underpinned and rationalised by a self-represented history as state memory' and as *state power(s)*'. Furthermore, it is precisely the power that the state *has*, or that the state *is*, which enables the state to define and carry out projects, and to authorise official narrations of historical memory. The state has a 'power to define the terms of its representations and to exercise itself and those over whom the authority is claimed in light of these terms'.[16]

Fanning argues that dominant constructions of Irishness were institutionalised in legislation and policy in numerous ways, where a dominant perceived ethno-religious homogeneity was won 'through a process of exclusionary nation-building'.[17] However, the older colonial, black-and-white dualism model cannot fully grasp the generational specificities of emerging inter-ethnic social relations in Ireland, or do justice to the location of Irishness within racialised discourses.[18] Kiberd argues that 'Irish culture is at once post-imperial (recognising the many Irish who helped build the British Empire) and post-colonial (due to the great role played by those who began its dismantling)'.[19] This contradictory power location of the Irish population within the modern nation-state system did not, however, prevent the reproduction of inequalities from occurring in Ireland and the construction of Irishness as Western and white. For a long time Ireland has had an 'official culture' written in the history, the literature and the Constitution, and this 'official culture' based on the construction of Ireland as a homogeneous society continues to permeate Irish society of today.[20] In addition, according to Loyal, the 'new Ireland' of the Celtic Tiger offers the harsh reality of capitalist production, exclusionary nationalism and growing xenophobia.[21]

Bosnian refugees in context

The war in the former Yugoslavia resulted in over 3 million displaced people.[22] The scale of displacement prompted the UNHCR, in July of 1992, to call for a response to the war which was 'comprehensive and humanitarian' whilst also recognising the 'temporary and emergency nature of the need for assistance'.[23] Several European countries offered protection to refugees fleeing the conflict; however, the approaches relating to the determination of their status within the host society varied greatly. Some, such as the Netherlands, Finland and France, decided to grant 'temporary residence permits' to the refugees of the former Yugoslavia, whereas other countries opted for 'temporary displaced person status' as in the case of Belgium, 'collective protection' in Norway, or 'tolerated status' in Germany. [24] In the United Kingdom a resettlement programme was set up in November 1992 tailored in response to the Bosnian population in particular, under which some 2,500 Bosnians were allowed to enter the country. However, under this programme the Bosnians were given temporary protection rather than full refugee status. [25]

With regard to the Nordic countries, Brochmann states that a change of direction in policy planning has taken place, sparked off by refugee movements stemming from the former Yugoslavia. [26] Although Brochmann notes that Sweden has been strikingly more 'liberal' [27] in relation to Bosnian refugees than both Denmark and Norway, she argues that a convergence of policies has happened in Scandinavia, where the focus is now placed upon voluntary repatriation and obligatory return, instead of the integration of refugees. Indeed, in Norway 'the Bosnian war refugees represented a "test" case for an activation of repatriation policy'. [28]

While countries differed in the status accorded to the refugees within their respective territories, most shared the temporary quality to their responses where the main agenda relating to the nature of the assistance given revolved around offering help as long as the conflict continued. Once the war was over, the refugees were supposed to 'go back home'. This may not be surprising considering the conceptual predominance of the modern system of nation-states whereby the nation is perceived as a 'natural' place of belonging and identity and culture are viewed as stable only 'at home'. [29] Consequently, refugees, viewed as 'people out of place', become 'an aberration of neat national categories, an anomaly in need of normalisation and control'.

The case of Ireland

Ireland responded to the UNHCR request for help by initially admitting around 200 programme refugees from the former Yugoslavia. The first group of Bosnian refugees arrived in September 1992. Since then, following different governmental decisions, of which the Family Reunification Scheme and Medical Evacuees were two, further groups of Bosnians arrived in Ireland. Currently there are over 1,700 Bosnians living in the Republic of Ireland, including 105 children born in Ireland. [30]

It is important to note that Ireland, unlike some of the countries discussed above, perceived incoming Bosnian refugees as a long-term commitment. Starting with the initial admission into the Cherry Orchard Reception Centre – a converted nurses' home – where Bosnian refugees could avail themselves of an educational programme including English language classes and counselling services in their native languages, and through the Resettlement Programme and the establishment of the Bosnian Community Development Project, the management committee in charge of Bosnian programme for refugees in Ireland has shaped services with future integration in mind.[31] The Cherry Orchard Reception Centre was set up, according to the Refugee Agency, in order to offer new arrivals the 'opportunity to settle down and become familiar with *their new country* in a safe environment, among a supportive community of *their own people* with a shared culture, before moving to independent living'.[32]

However, it is also important to note that, in essence, this initiative was characterised by perceiving the incoming Bosnian refugees as a *homogeneous* group despite its ethnic heterogeneity and urban–rural mix. The two main reports that have addressed the resettlement of Bosnian refugees in Ireland have been the *Report of the Survey of the Vietnamese and Bosnian Refugee Communities in Ireland* (1998) and *From Bosnia to Ireland's Private Rented Sector: A Study of Bosnian Housing Needs in Ireland* (1999).[33] Both failed to acknowledge the differences within the Bosnian population in Ireland in terms of identity and/or culture, as well as examining the possible impact these factors have upon the process of resettlement.[34] This homogenising community approach that Ireland adopted is similar in principle to that of Sweden, where the promotion of a development of Bosnian 'national consciousness', as advocated by the Swedish pluralist policy for immigrants and minorities, was encouraged by the state through funding Bosnian refugee associations.[35]

The Irish *partnership* approach is most clearly visible with regard to the creation of the Bosnian Community Development Project. This body,[36] established in 1995 by the Refugee Agency in association with the Irish Refugee Council and the Refugee Trust, aimed to provide community services and act as a resource centre for the Bosnian population in Ireland; its stated vision was to see 'the Bosnian Community in Ireland fully integrated, recognised and with equal opportunities and choices in Irish society'.[37] It was envisaged as bridge between the Bosnian community and Irish society and as opening a space for members of the Bosnian community where they could keep their culture, traditions and customs alive in the hope that with time 'integration' will happen. Yet, thirteen years on, integration has not 'happened'. Integration and social inclusion remain the main issues facing the Bosnian community in Ireland today. In addition to the lack of integration in Ireland, the majority – around 80% – of the Bosnians in Ireland are regularly spending their summers in Bosnia.[38] The Bosnian Community Development Project organises special charter flights to Bosnia and Herzegovina every year. The need for this to be organised yearly has been highlighted among the five main issues of the BCDP Working Plan for 2005–06.[39] Furthermore the Bosnian Community Development Project closes for the whole month of August each year because 'Bosnians are in Bosnia'. As put by two interviewees:

> Yes, yes, yes ... they ... [Bosnians] ... go every year...Because those Bosnians who are working[40] they proved themselves to be hardworking. They work day and night, more or less all the time and they don't take holidays during the year. Most of the Bosnians work in manual jobs as well, so you can make up hours ... by working weekends or double shifts. Lots of the women are unemployed, so they go as soon as the school finishes. Then the husbands join them there for as long as they can...For example, my stepfather does not take holidays during the whole year but takes them together in the summer...They ... [him and my mother] ... are there right now, they will stay for a month and a half. They have been doing it for years.

> ... lots of people are in Bosnia now, for two months ... maybe eight to ten weeks ... in September life starts again here.

It might be presumed that all immigrant communities are characterised by patterns of chain migration, meaning that new arrivals are following in the steps of earlier arrivals and gain support and advice from those people.[41] Kelly argues that such chain migration tends not to be evident amongst refugees, particularly those like programme refugees who arrive into the country *en masse*. Since there are often no pre-existing links between such refugees, communities are harder to develop.[42] Although Kelly's argument is drawn from the experience of Bosnian refugees in the United Kingdom, it pertains to the Irish case to a considerable extent. The Bosnians who arrived in Ireland did not know each other before arriving. Despite the fact that they were housed together in Cherry Orchard for a while there was no pre-established link between people. One way that refugees may respond to such policies is to form contingent communities, as Bosnian refugees have done in Britain.[43] I would suggest that something similar may be happening in Ireland, where, notwithstanding the fact that a formal association of Bosnian refugees exists (BCDP), informally there are no strong ties between Bosnians in Ireland. For instance, the issue of 'going home for the summer' seems of greater importance than building alliances here. Indeed, the Bosnian Community Development Project defines itself as a 'community of interest'.[44]

When discussing forced migration it might be useful to make a distinction between anticipatory refugee movements and acute refugee movements. Within anticipatory refugee movements refugees have time to prepare to leave their homeland and migrate before the situation prevents their departure. In contrast, acute refugee movements arise from sudden political changes or military activity, and under these conditions refugees often have no time to prepare for departure.[45] Furthermore, in relation to acute refugee movements, refugees often have no foresight with regard to the choice of the host country.[46] The Bosnians who arrived in Ireland as programme refugees came from a refugee centre in Austria, following a visit from an Irish government representative, after the 200 people quota was decided for Ireland.[47] Therefore when multicultural policies perceive refugees as 'ethnic minorities of tomorrow', the acknowledgement needs to be made of both the lack of choice refugees have in relation to the country of settlement and the interrelated issue of the acuteness of their flight. As put by one Bosnian woman:

> To the last minute I was saying 'I am not going anywhere' ... no, no, no ... but when it started, you had to go ... My husband went ... I went too ... I did not know what to think then ... When we arrived here ... I just thought that this is the end ... the end of everything ... the end of the world.

Yuval-Davis notes that a phenomenon common to most refugees is a state of 'permanent temporariness' in which 'life and identity before the war and the displacement gain a status of validity and permanence which any new life, constructed for however many years, can never replace. Being a permanent "outsider" in the new place of living sustains such a feeling'.[48] In her example of children born in Palestinian refugee camps in Lebanon, Yuval-Davis states that these children can often identify their place of origin as the village from which their parents were exiled. It is often this village, that may not be in existence for the last thirty or forty years, which is connected with their dream of 'return' and this village often becomes a passionate sentiment around which one's identity gets constructed.[49] In relation to Bosnian refugees in Ireland, the very act of 'going home for the summer' may be viewed as a sign of 'permanent temporariness' related to Bosnia before the war and life as it used to be there. However, it is important to note the ongoing marginalisation that Bosnians feel in Ireland. As expressed by two women interviewees:

> ... at the bottom of your soul you stay a refugee for ever ... I would always be a refugee here ... as long as I am here ... I personally think that that will stay like that for ever ... you are always going to be looked upon from above ... and you will stay below.

> ... Ireland gave us lots of good ... you can go to school if you want, and my children are going to school here ... However, you are always a foreigner here ... The other child is going to throw a stone on your child in the school, it will throw it on the Irish child as well ... but it is not the same, you are foreigner here ... It is not to say ... there are people who are better than Bosnians here, but there are the other ones too ... You just have to turn your head to the other side then.

The issue of marginalisation may not be surprising if one considers the extent to which the focus of Irish racism in the late 1990s was directed towards the refugee populations.[50] Loyal argues that there exists 'the semantic correlation of non-Irish immigrants with black asylum seekers or refugees' in Ireland which is 'an ideological effect of social relations of domination, specifically those of state and media discourses'.[51] Bosnians in Ireland speak of their alienation most poignantly. As put by two interviewees:

> When I think about living here ... there is one thing that bothers me ... I suppose ... yes ... that bothers me. Irish people always ask you, 'When will you go home?' I am not a refugee any more I have a passport, I have the citizenship ... Yet they always ask, 'When are you going to go home to your own country?'... It's like I am sitting in their own living room all the time.

> ... the integration will never happen ... never ... I had a friend, an Irish woman. I loved her a lot ... She died ... I love her to this day. After a few drinks she used to tell me ... 'You know what? This is not in relation to you but in relation to all other Bosnians here ... You see ... my son cannot find a job here (and her son was about to go travelling to Australia with his girlfriend). He has to go all the way to Australia because there is no jobs here. Bosnians have taken all the jobs here'... and she says ... 'Of course I don't mean this in relation to you. I know you, and love you. I mean it in relation to all other Bosnians.'... Why should I be an exception?

It is evident from the extracts above that Bosnian women I interviewed did not feel part of Irish society but instead perceived themselves as a racialised minority within it. Indeed, some Bosnians have encountered racism. The Bosnian Community Development project noted in 2005 that 'six Bosnian families who were accommodated by Fingal Co. Council have experienced racist verbal and physical attacks by their Irish neighbours ... Two families had to be relocated.'[52]

The complexity of the situation presented above speaks for itself. However, I want to argue that the homogenisation of the Bosnian population in Ireland in the embryonic stages of the Bosnian project did not help integration but rather reinforced Bosnians' social exclusion.

The problem of homogenisation

When talking about refugee populations coming from Bosnia and Herzegovina one needs to be aware of the extraordinary ethnic mixture of that particular republic when it was still part of the former Yugoslavia. Apart from Bosnian Orthodox and Bosnian Catholics, who might or might not think of themselves as respectively 'Serbs' or 'Croats', there were

Bosnian Muslims whose religious practice varied greatly, from practising individuals to individuals with a more secular orientation. There were also minorities of Jews, Germans, Hungarians and Roma populations in Bosnia and Herzegovina, all of whom were and are in themselves heterogeneous.[53]

Bosnia and Herzegovina had no one major ethnic group. One-third of the population was Orthodox, while one-sixth was of Catholic background, conceived in light of the Yugoslav ideology of containing nationalism, as having their 'homeland' in Serbia and Croatia respectively. The largest population group was made up of Bosnian Muslims, who accounted for just under half the population, and were viewed as 'coming from' nowhere but Bosnia.[54] It is also important to add that the Yugoslav census of 1961 furnished a new identification option, 'Muslim in the ethnic sense', while the 1971 census developed this official identity one step further by proposing the category of 'Muslim in the sense of nation'.[55] According to the *Working Plan Paper 2005–06* of the Bosnian Community Development Project, the Bosnian community in Ireland is now estimated to consist of Bosnian Muslims (75%), Bosnian Croats (12%) and Bosnian Serbs (8%), with the remaining 5% being made up of those in mixed marriages or others. Furthermore, those who considered themselves to be Bosnian Muslims differed in their own understandings of what that entails. As expressed by four interviewees:

> we are Muslims, but European progressive Muslims ... We eat all food, we don't separate ... the way we lived in Bosnia before the war, we live now. We changed nothing. We did not change into Muslims, we still don't go to the mosque, we still did not give up pork.

> when I say we ... [Bosnians] ... I think of us all, Muslims, Croats, Gypsies.

> we are not wearing veils, we are not that type of Muslims ... to be covered ... only people who work in the mosque are covered.

> when I say Bosnians I mean people from Bosnia ... regardless of their religion....

Anthias and Yuval-Davies argue that the most basic problem in constructions of multiculturalism is the assumption that all members of a specific cultural collective are equally committed to that culture.[56] Problems occur when the multicultural policies of the host society are based upon perceiving minority populations as homogeneous. It was this assumption of Bosnian cultural homogeneity – the other side of the coin being Irish homogeneity – that prompted the development of the Cherry Orchard Refugee Centre, where the Bosnians were initially placed in order to 'settle down ... among a supportive community of *their own* people'.[57] However, this was not what the Bosnians themselves thought. One interviewee described her experience of Cherry Orchard in the following terms:

> Initially it was horrible ... really horrible... in one place there were 182 people that you never met in your entire life. There were people there who differed in their traditions ... huge social differences ... Lots and lots of people came from rural areas ... It was really difficult to fit in. *It was so difficult to find somebody that you have something in common with* ... somebody you can just talk to, about unimportant things ... so you could relax, have a coffee. Everybody was tense, anxious, angry ... We all lost something.

Taylor argues that the politics of multiculturalism is about a demand for recognition by minority and subaltern groups. His thesis is based upon the assumption that our identity is partly shaped by the recognition of our own understanding of who we are, or the absence of that recognition. In addition, non-recognition or mis-recognition can inflict harm, and is a form of oppression. Since the mis-recognition can be so harmful, particularly if internalised by mis-recognised people – Taylor gives examples of black people and women here – 'real' recognition is not just courtesy, but 'a vital human need we owe to people'.[58] The challenge, according to Taylor, is how to 'deal with *their* sense of marginalisation without compromising *our* basic political principles'.[59] Or, in other words, the challenge becomes how to preserve *our* politics of universality when faced with *their* politics of particularity. And the answer becomes a search for a 'best' policy of multiculturalism to deal with *their* diversity without threatening *our* homogeneity, or, in Balibar's words, 'our illusion of national identity'.[60] This of course assumes both 'our' and 'their' homogeneity.

The Bosnian project as a strategy of managing diversity in Ireland exemplifies the sort of homogenised politics of recognition described by Taylor. In other words, for successful integration to happen Bosnians had to be recognised as an ethnic minority and helped as such to adjust to the Irish ways. This recognition, the symbol of which was the Bosnian project itself, led to the construction of a Bosnian community in Ireland. Indeed, within the dichotomy of essentialist understandings of both national identity and politics of particularity there is no space for the truly *multicultural*.[61] Additionally, if the logic of diversity is being institutionalised through the state's multicultural policies – where the agents of the 'official culture' have all the institutions of the state in their control and decisions of how and to whom the resources are allocated are made by them – talk about integration is really talk about assimilation or at least control.

As Loyal argues, 'exclusionary forms of nationalism cannot be simply replaced by anodyne notions of multiculturalism' if unequal forms of power stay in place.[62] In this context, the partnership between the Bosnian population and the Irish state is a partnership between the racialised and the *racial* state, and as such just another mechanism of state control. As Lentin and McVeigh argue, 'in Ireland the notion of *partnership* created the perfect excuse for continuing white privilege'. Starting with Travellers and extending this strategy when Black and other 'minorities' came along, the Irish state partnership approach is the 'classic case of what Goldberg calls "historicism" where Europeans are elevated over primitive or underdeveloped others as a victory of progress'.[63] In other words the *incoming other* is required to adopt to the Irish way of doing things through the necessary mimicry of the Eurocentre. Yet the racialised will never become the same – 'not quite/not white'.[64]

Conclusion

Thirteen years after their arrival the integration of Bosnians in Ireland had still not happened. Despite the plethora of possible factors that may have contributed to the lack of integration of the Bosnian community in Ireland it is important to situate the Bosnian project within the Irish state's multiculturalism policies – for it was the state that crafted it – and emphasise a couple of points. Bosnians were homogenised, constructed as a 'community' and, though invited to take part in the multicultural (intercultural) conversation with the Irish *racial* state, were not treated as equal citizens. Instead they were confined within the Bosnian Community Development Project and tied to the ethos of the *partnership* approach, where, under the guise of multiculturalism, historicist racism operates. Their response was to reject Ireland as 'home' and reaffirm Bosnia as 'home', choosing, however, to keep one foot in each place. The question which needs asking, and further study, is what choices the next generation of Bosnians in Ireland will make.

Notes

1 J. O'Neill, *Integration of Refugees in Ireland: Experience with Programme Refugees 1994–2000* (2000), www.democraticdialogue.org/report14/r14 oneill.htm.
2 Department of Justice Equality and Law Reform, *Integration: A Two-way Process* (Dublin: Official Publications, 2000), p. 42.
3 Ibid., p. 20.
4 Bosnian Community Development Project, *Working Plan Paper for the Period 2005–2006* (Dublin: BCDP, 2006), p. 1.
5 M. Halilovic-Pastuovic, '"Going home for the Summer": Bosnian Refugee

Women in "Intercultural" Ireland', M.Phil. in Ethnic and Racial Studies dissertation (Dublin: Trinity College, University of Dublin, 2003).

6 B. Fanning, *Racism and Social Change in the Republic of Ireland* (Manchester: Manchester University Press, 2002), p. 186.

7 As opposed to *normative multiculturalism* that insists on cultural diversity and proliferation of values at the expense of ideas of national cohesion, *descriptive multiculturalism* does not go beyond descriptions of the increasing heterogeneity in most post-1945 societies. D. T. Goldberg (ed.), *Multiculturalism: A Critical Reader* (Oxford: Blackwell, 1994), p. 1.

8 R. Lentin, '"Intercultural" Education for the University of Tomorrow?', in R. Lentin (ed.), *Working and Teaching in a Multicultural University* (Dublin: Trinity College, 2003), p. 9.

9 During my research with the Bosnian 'community' I discovered that their experience in Ireland centres largely around the 'going home for the summer' migrations. In other words, the majority of Bosnian people in Ireland tend to regularly go back to Bosnia during the summer months, while a large amount of their time and activity during the rest of the year revolves around preparation and anticipation of their 'summer migration'. See Halilovic-Pastuovic, '"Going Home for the Summer"'.

10 C. Taylor, 'The Politics of Recognition', in D. T. Goldberg (ed.), *Multiculturalism: A Critical Reader* (Oxford: Blackwell, 1994).

11 Essentialism refers to a theory of descriptions which states that definitions are descriptions of the essential properties of things, and that one can evaluate definitions in terms of falsity or truth of the descriptions given to them.

12 David Goldberg distinguishes between *naturalist* and *historicist* or *progressivist* racism as articulated within the context of the nation-state. Naturalist racism, based upon the belief of the inherent racial inferiority, was predominant from the seventeenth century well into the nineteenth, when it became accompanied by historicist racism which rests upon the belief of claims to different 'historical maturity'. Historicism elevates Europeans over racial 'others' but, unlike naturalism, views those racialised as actually capable of progress, but only through mimicking the Eurocentre. See Goldberg, *The Racial State*, p. 74.

13 When the Bosnian Community Development Project was established in 1995 by the Refugee Agency, in association with Irish Refugee Council and the Refugee Trust, the project planners hoped to hand the management of the project over to the Bosnian community as they 'became more familiar with Irish society'.

14 F. Anthias and N. Yuval-Davis, *Racialised Boundaries: Race, Nation, Gender, Colour and Class and the Anti-racist Struggle* (London: Routledge, 1992), p. 158.

15 R. Lentin, 'Anti-racist Responses to the Racialisation of Irishness: Disavowed Multiculturalism and its Discontents', in R. Lentin and R. McVeigh (eds), *Racism and Anti-racism in Ireland* (Belfast: Beyond the Pale, 2002), p. 29.

16 Goldberg, *The Racial State*, p. 8.

17 Fanning, *Racism and Social Change in the Republic of Ireland,* p. 185.

18 M. Mac an Ghaill, 'Beyond a Black–White Dualism: Racialisation and Racism in the Republic of Ireland and the Irish Diaspora Experience', *Irish Journal of Sociology*, 11: 2 (2002), p. 116.

19 D. Kiberd, 'Strangers in their own Country: Multi-culturalism in Ireland', in E. Longley and D. Kiberd (eds), *Multiculturalism: The View from the Two Irelands* (Cork: Cork University Press, 2001).

20 For further discussion regarding the issues relating to gender and the Irish Constitution see R. Lentin, 'Constitutionally Excluded: Citizenship and (some) Irish Women', in N. Yuval-Davis and P. Werbner (eds), *Women, Citizenship and Difference* (London: Zed Books, 1999).

21 S. Loyal, 'Welcome to the Celtic Tiger: Racism, Immigration and the State', in C. Coulter and S. Coleman (eds), *The End of Irish History? Critical Reflections on the Celtic Tiger* (Manchester: Manchester University Press, 2003), p. 74.

22 L. Kelly, D. Joly and C. Nettleton (eds), *Refugees in Europe: The Hostile New Agenda* (London: Minority Rights Group, 1997).

23 ECRE, 'Report of ECRE Biannual General Meeting', in ECRE, *Asylum in Europe: An Introduction* I (London: ECRE, 1993).

24 Kelly *et al.*, *Refugees in Europe*, p. 16.

25 K. Knox, *Credit to the Nation: A Study of Refugees in the United Kingdom* (London: Refugee Council, 1997).

26 G. Brochmann, 'Bosnian Refugees in the Scandinavian Countries: a Comparative Perspective on Immigration Control in the 1990s', *New Community*, 23: 4 (1997), pp. 495–510.

27 In June 1993 the government of Sweden decided that outstanding asylum applications from the citizens of Bosnia and Herzegovina would be handled generously, and almost all the applicants were given permanent residence permits. The number of permits given amounted to approximately 48,500. See Kelly *et al.*, *Refugees in Europe*, p. 16.

28 Brochmann, *Bosnian Refugees in the Scandinavian Countries*, p. 503.

29 Z. Bauman, 'Modernity and Ambivalence', in M. Featherstone (ed.), *Global Culture: Nationalism, Globalisation and Modernity* (London: Sage, 1990).

30 The census of 2002 identified 1,058 people from Bosnia and Herzegovina. Furthermore, areas with high Bosnian populations have been identified in Dublin 15 (Blanchardstown, Clonsilla, Mulhuddart, Castleknock), Tallaght, Swords, Lucan and the inner city.

31 Initially this committee consisted of representatives of the Department of Foreign Affairs, the Department of Health and Children, the Eastern Health Board and the Refugee Agency.

32 Refugee Agency, *Annual Report* (Dublin: Official Publications, 1998), p. 29.

33 C. O'Regan, *Report of a Survey of the Vietnamese and Bosnian Refugee Communities living in Ireland* (Dublin: Refugee Resettlement Research Project, Refugee Agency, 1998); S. Bradley and N. Humphries, *From Bosnia to Ireland's Private Rented Sector: A Study of Bosnian Housing Needs in Ireland* (Dublin: Clann Housing Association, 1999).

34 Both studies acknowledged the differences of gender, age and social status as possible deterrents, in certain circumstances, to successful integration. The O'Regan survey also registered differences in ethnic identification in relation to both communities; however, this was not developed further. See O'Regan, *Survey of Vietnamese and Bosnian Refugee Communities*, pp. 81–7.

35 M. Eastmond, 'Nationalistic Discourses and the Construction of Difference: Bosnian Muslim Refugees in Sweden', *Journal of Refugee Studies*, 11: 2 (1998), pp. 161–81.

36 The partnership model, as discussed by Lentin and McVeigh, *Racism and Anti-racism in Ireland*, focuses upon the development of ethnic and other community initiatives that act as a catalyst for voicing the issues concerning 'minority' populations. However, McVeigh argues that the issue of power still remains problematic.

37 Bosnian Community Development Project, *Working Plan Paper for the Period 2005–2006* (Dublin: BCDP, 2005), p. 7.

38 Personal communication with Community Development Officer, BCDP, 25 October 2005.

39 Bosnian Community Development Project, *Working Plan*, p. 12.

40 A number of the Bosnian population would be on disability benefit after the war, and would not be working in Ireland. See Halilovic-Pastuovic, '"Going Home for the Summer"', p. 51.

41 A. Shaw, *A Pakistani Community in Britain* (Oxford: Blackwell, 1988).

42 L. Kelly, 'Bosnian Refugees in Britain: Questioning Community', *Sociology*, 37: 1 (2003), pp. 35–49.

43 Ibid., p. 42.

44 Bosnian Community Development Project, *Working Plan Paper*, p. 1.

45 E. F. Kunz, 'The Refugee in Flight: Kinetic Models and Forms of Displacement', *International Migration Review*, 7: 2 (1973), pp. 125–46.

46 Kelly, 'Bosnian Refugees in Britain', p. 45.

47 Personal communication with management committee member of BCDP (9 July 2003).

48 N. Yuval-Davis, *Gender and Nation* (London: Sage, 1997), p. 110.

49 Ibid., p. 110.

50 Lentin and McVeigh, *Racism and Anti-racism in Ireland*.

51 Loyal, 'Welcome to the Celtic Tiger', p. 76.

52 Bosnian Community Development Project, *Working Plan Paper 2005–2006*, p. 4.

53 T. Bringa, *Being Muslim the Bosnian Way: Identity and Community in Central Bosnian Village* (Princeton, NJ: Princeton University Press, 1995).

54 C. Cookburn, *The Space between Us: Negotiating Gender and National Identities in Conflict* (London: Zed Books, 1999).

55 Bringa, *Being Muslim the Bosnian Way*. The first survey of perceptions of ethnic identity of the Bosnian population in Ireland found a similar heterogeneity within the sample. Although the largest proportion identified themselves as Muslim (39%), Bosnian (37%) and Bosnian Muslim (18%), the Croatian, Slav, Serbian and Yugoslav identifications were registered as

well. See O'Regan, *Survey of Vietnamese and Bosnian Communities*, p. 81.

56 Anthias and Yuval-Davis, *Racialised Boundaries*, p. 38.

57 Refugee Agency, *Annual Report* (Dublin: Official Publications, 1998), p. 29.

58 Taylor, 'The Politics of Recognition', p. 96.

59 Emphasis added. Ibid., p. 96.

60 E. Balibar, 'The Nation Form: History and Ideology', in E. Balibar and I. Wallerstein (eds), *Race, Nation, Class: Ambiguous Identities* (London: Verso, 1988), p. 86.

61 S. Hall, 'Conclusion: the Multi-cultural Question', in B. Hesse (ed.), *Un/settled Multiculturalisms: Diaspora, Entanglements, 'Transruptions'* (London: Zed Books, 2000).

62 Ibid., p. 90.

63 R. Lentin and R. McVeigh (eds) *After Optimism? Ireland, Racism and Globalisation* (Dublin: Metro Eireann, 2007).

64 Goldberg, *The Racial State*, p. 96.

11

African Pentecostals in twenty-first-century Ireland: identity and integration

Abel Ugba

Immigration has caused profound change to Ireland's religious landscape.[1] The evidence is in statistics as well as in the ways immigrant religious practices have provided new insights into concepts of identity, community and integration. While the numbers of people in Ireland that claim to be agnostics or atheists have grown in recent years, religious participation by immigrants, the majority of whom came into Ireland since the second half of the last decade, has provoked a resurgence in religious adherence. Statistically, the memberships of many mainstream churches, which had been either stagnant or declining, have increased as many immigrants joined these churches. According to the most recent census,[2] the Church of Ireland added 26,400 new members between 1991 and 2002, the Presbyterians gained 7,400 new members and Methodists added 5,000. During the same period the population of Muslims quadrupled from 3,900 to 19,100. The only major religious group that appeared not to have profited from the increased presence of immigrants is the Catholic.[3] However, the Roman Catholic remains the largest religious group, accounting for 88.4% of the population of the Republic of Ireland according to the 2002 census.[4]

While these statistics indicate a trend they do not address the complexity of the relationship between these churches and their new immigrant members. Empirical data from my investigation of African-led Pentecostal churches in Ireland suggests that membership of mainstream churches has, in some cases, been short-lived as immigrants who had joined these churches were compelled to relocate to churches led and mostly populated by immigrants due to the cold reception or racially based resentment they encountered in main-line churches. Others relocated because their expectation that a Christian community should also be a community of friends and of social solidarity were often not met in main-line Irish churches.

The second and more dramatic way immigrants have impacted on Ireland's religious landscape is through the formation of groups managed and mostly populated by them. Religious activism is one area where immigrant participation has been most voluntary and intense, less problematic and apparently unhindered by precarious residence status or length of time in Ireland. The constitutional guarantee of religious freedom and the relatively peaceful relationship among the various religious groups in Ireland in recent years have provided an atmosphere conducive to the birth of new religious groups, including ones set up by immigrants. Some immigrant churches have, in the early stages of their formation, received encouragement, material assistance and guidance from mainstream churches. In the case of immigrants from Africa, religious affiliation is one of the first relationships the majority cultivate or reactivate once they have arrived in Ireland. Other immigrant groups, apart from Africans, have also established churches. The Chinese, the Filipinos and migrants from the former communist bloc have set up places of worship in the Greater Dublin area. Membership of Orthodox churches, consisting mainly of immigrants from Romania and Russia, has continued to grow rapidly. Whereas there were about 400 members in 1991, there were over 10,000 in 2002.[5]

This chapter is based on data from my empirical investigation[6] and it describes the history and demographic characteristics of African-led Pentecostal groups in Ireland. It also examines the impact of beliefs on self identity and on the relations members of these groups maintain with other groups, including the majority society. While acknowledging the centrality of Pentecostal doctrines to the place and gaze of this sub-group of African immigrants, it challenges their unitary and coherent definition of self that emphasises Pentecostalism as the primary, and perhaps their only, identity marker. It argues for recognition of other identity markers like nationality, ethnicity, race and immigrant or exile status. The next section begins with a brief historical and substantive analysis of Pentecostalism as a way of contextualising the presence and practices of Ireland's African Pentecostals.

What is Pentecostalism?

Pentecostal believers and analysts have struggled with limited successes to articulate a universal and encompassing definition of Pentecostalism. It is perhaps easier to say who the Pentecostals are than to articulate a universal and coherent definition of Pentecostalism. Pentecostals are those who profess to be Pentecostals. Put differently, people are Pentecostals if they say they are. There are no universal or even clear-cut criteria for determining who is a Pentecostal. Outsiders, including researchers and academics, have generally relied on the testimony or self-confession of believers or that of their leaders or fellow believers. Pentecostals, even in small group settings, do not generally carry official identity cards. Membership of a group is established and affirmed by the regularity and level of involvement in group activities, outward demonstration of fidelity to group beliefs and principles and loyalty to the leadership.

Pentecostalism, on the other hand, is a generic term for a wide variety of practices based on or inspired by the holy ghost experience of the first-century Christians, as recorded in the Acts of the Apostles (Acts 2:1–36). The account states:

> Now while the day of the [festival of] Pentecost was in progress they were all together at the same place, [2] and suddenly there occurred from heaven a noise just like that of a rushing stiff breeze, and it filled the whole house in which they were sitting.[3] And tongues as if of fire became visible to them and were distributed about, and one sat upon each one of them,[4] and they all became filled with holy spirit and started to speak with different tongues, just as the spirit was granting them to make utterance.[7]

Pentecostals believe the event that took place in the first century had been foretold by the prophet Joel in the Old Testament:

> And after that it must occur that I shall pour out my spirit on every sort of flesh, and your sons and your daughters will certainly prophesy. As for your old men, dreams they will dream. As for your young men, visions they will see.[29] And even on the menservants and on the maidservants in those days I shall pour out my spirit.[8]

Although most Pentecostals cite the above passages as the inspiration or the reference for their unique practices, there is great divergence of interpretations and application. The different interpretations and the conscious efforts of many groups to contextualise or make Pentecostal doctrines respond to and reflect their unique cultures and socio-political situations have created a motley collection of groups and churches across space and time under the Pentecostal banner. As Corten and Marshall-Fratani notes, 'each society, each group invests Pentecostalism with its own meanings'.[9] The divergences and differences within Pentecostalism are doctrinal, methodical, structural as well as racial. Pentecostal believers, as Anderson puts it, 'range from the fundamentalist and white middle-class "mega–churches" to indigenous movements in the Third World that have adapted to their cultural and religious contexts to such an extent that many Western Pentecostals would probably doubt their qualifications as "Christian" movements'.[10]

Also contentious are the origin and history of the modern-day world-wide Pentecostal movement. There are two main contending schools of thought. One school believes Pentecostalism was started in Los Angeles in 1906 by William Joseph Seymour, the self-taught son of a former slave. The other school attributes the origin of the movement to the efforts of Charles Parham, a white American racist and antisemitic, who rigidly enforced segregation in his church.[11] Most sources situate the birth of the movement in America and in the period between the last two decades of the nineteenth century and first decade of the twentieth.

Despite these controversies and divergence of views, Pentecostals are unified by what Margaret Poloma describes as 'a particular Christian world-view that reverts to a non-European epistemology from the European one that has dominated Christianity for centuries'.[12] There are other traits and practices that are common to most or even all Pentecostal groups. They believe in the Bible as God-inspired and adhere to a literal interpretation of it. The Bible has relevance to everyday conduct and experience and it serves as a guidebook for life's processes. Poloma puts it like this: 'The Word of the Scriptures and the Spirit of the living God are in dialogical relationship, playing incessantly within and among individuals as well as within the larger world'.[13] The natural interacts seamlessly with the supernatural in the world of Pentecostals, and dreams, visions and trance constitute additional or alternative means of communication and interaction. These out-of-body experiences are very often embedded in the public and personal worship of many Pentecostals. Theirs is a world 'of miracles and mystery, where healings, prophecy and divine serendipity are woven into the fabric of everyday life'.[14] God intervenes in all situations to reward or punish or merely to have his purpose accomplished.

The arrival and spread of Pentecostalism in Africa are less clouded in controversy than its history and doctrines. Pentecostalism was introduced to West Africa in the early twentieth century mostly through the efforts of African-American Pentecostal missionaries who arrived in the region to spread the gospel in their ancestral land. The Faith Tabernacle and the Apostolic Church were some of the earliest Pentecostal churches established in western Nigeria, while in eastern Nigeria the Assemblies of God was one of the pioneering groups.[15] Other Pentecostal churches came mostly from the United States into Nigeria in the 1940s and 1950s. Many of these churches incubated in university campuses in the 1970s and students and lecturers played leading roles in propagating their doctrines both within and outside the university campuses.

During this period of its early development in Nigeria and the West African coast, Pentecostalism attracted intellectuals and students.[16] African students that had returned from the United States and the United Kingdom played a leading role in spreading the Pentecostal ideals. Pentecostal and charismatic revivals became more widespread in Nigeria in the 1980s as the number of universities and other tertiary institutions increased. Some leaders of the early Pentecostal and evangelical groups on the campuses later became church leaders with large followings. Examples include W. F. Kumuyi, a former mathematics lecturer in the University of Lagos, who founded the Deeper Christian Life Ministry, one of the earliest and largest Pentecostal groups in Nigeria, and Enoch Adeboye, also a former lecturer in the same university and founder of Redeem Christian Church of God, the largest African-led Pentecostal group in Ireland and probably in Europe and America.

The arrival in Europe of Pentecostal groups led by Africans signalled their intention to gain a foothold in the global spiritual market place.[17] Churches led by African immigrants first made their appearance in Britain in the 1920s. In the 1960s indigenous Pentecostal-like churches such as the Church of the Lord – Aladura, the Cherubim and Seraphim, and the Celestial Church of God were established in Britain mostly through the efforts of African students. The social and demographic characteristics of these churches have changed as the numbers and categories of African immigrants in Europe have increased. The Redeemed Christian Church of God and Deeper Christian Life Church were set up in Britain in the 1970s and 1980s as overseas branches of established groups in Nigeria or other African countries.

African immigrants in continental Europe soon started to copy the examples set by their counterparts in Britain. Since the 1970s the numbers of African-led religious groups have increased in places like Germany as more Africans came to Europe to study, work or seek political asylum. Hamburg, which has experienced a longer presence of Africans than most cities in Germany, has one of the highest numbers of churches in that country. Other German cities like Berlin, Cologne and Frankfurt are also home to many of these churches. Gerrie ter Haar[18] has documented the presence and activities of African Christian congregations, especially those formed by immigrants from Ghana, in the Netherlands. Most of the groups were formed in the 1990s and they are located in or near urban centres where a large percentage of African immigrants live and work. As far back as 1997 African immigrants had established as many as forty Christian groups in Amsterdam alone.[19]

The growth of African-led Pentecostal groups in Ireland

The presence and spread of Pentecostalism among Africans in Ireland has taken place against the backdrop of the increased presence, since the mid-1990s, of African immigrants in the country. Until the late 1990s the numbers and categories of African immigrants in Ireland were few and they consisted mainly of students and spouses of Irish or EU citizens. The majority of those that have arrived since the increase in in-migrations are asylum seekers, students and workers.[20] Until the 2002 census, most estimates of the total number of Africans in Ireland were haphazard and based mainly on asylum applications, work permits and student statistics. According to the 2002 census results, 20,981 people claiming nationality of an African country were living in Ireland in 2002 and more than one-third of them (or 8,969) were Nigerians, while 4,185 came from South Africa.[21] While these figures represent the strongest official indication of the number of Africans in Ireland, they most likely do not reflect the true statistical strength of the community. For example, they do not include Africans who are also Irish citizens or those who are citizens of European countries even though they are active members of African groups and organisations. The 2004 population estimates show that 7% (or 3,535) of the 50,500 immigrants who came into Ireland between April 2002 and April 2003 were nationals of African countries.[22]

Although the activities of African-led Pentecostal groups did not catch the attention of the media until about 2000, the first of these groups was set up in Dublin in 1996 by Congolese-born Remba Oshengo, who had migrated to Ireland that same year. Since then many African-led Pentecostal groups have been established, first in the Greater Dublin area and later in other parts of Ireland. Their diffusion to regions outside the Greater Dublin area has been facilitated by a government policy, initiated in 2001, of 'dispersing' asylum seekers all over Ireland. The majority of asylum seekers were located in the Greater Dublin area before this policy came into effect.[23] The number of African-led Pentecostal groups established outside the Greater Dublin area has increased as 'dispersed' asylum seekers and other Africans form new groups or set up outreach posts of Dublin-based groups. The spread of these groups has also been a deliberate strategy by church leaders to take their message to more people and fulfil what they say is their God-given commission to preach the gospel in the whole of Ireland before the imminent end of the world.

The Redeemed Christian Church of God is generally acknowledged as the largest and the most widespread African-led Pentecostal church in Ireland. Registered in 1998, the church now has about forty branches in Ireland. The other large and prominent African-led Pentecostal churches include the Mountain of Fire and Miracles Ministry (MFMM), the Christ Apostolic Church (CAC), the Gospel Faith Mission International (GFM), Christ Co-workers in Mission (CCM), Hope and Glory Ministries (HGM) and Christ Ambassadors Ministries. In the absence of official census, the exact numbers of these churches and total population of worshippers have been a matter of guesstimates and media speculation. As far back as 2001 *Metro Eireann,* Ireland's multicultural newspaper, reported that over forty of these churches had been established in the Greater Dublin area.[24] A report by the Irish Council of Churches in February 2003 estimated the number of African immigrants in what it called 'Black Majority churches' to be over 10,000,[25] while the Moderator of the Presbyterian Church of Ireland, Dr Ivan McKay, estimated the number to be 30,000 in 2004.[26] Information published by the Company Registration Office (CRO) on its Web site buttresses the fact that many groups have been established since 2000.[27] Most churches are registered as companies limited by guarantee and a few have attained charity status.

Although the beliefs, activities and administrative structure of these churches are similar, African-led Pentecostal groups in Ireland can be categorised into three broad groups based on their historical background and the transnational links they maintain. The other basis for creating a distinction is the self-perception of these churches and their interpretation of their unique roles in the Irish society and in the lives of their members. On the basis of history, one category is churches established by African immigrants with no support from or links, at least in the initial stages, with groups in Africa or elsewhere. Examples of such churches include Christ Co-workers in Mission and the Gospel Faith Mission. Immigrants that have spear-headed such initiatives are usually experienced Pentecostals who had been active members of Pentecostal groups in their home countries and have had some experience of leadership in a religious setting or in a secular occupation. The majority came to Ireland to seek political asylum, and the period before they gained refugee status, when government policy prevented them from gainful employment and formal education, provided ample opportunity and the incentives for spiritual devotion and religious activism.

The second category consists of churches established by disgruntled members of existing African-led Pentecostal churches. For example, the pastor and leader of Christ Glory Ministries had been the pastor of Christ Apostolic Church (CAC) and his present church is located not far from his former one. Disgruntled officials who leave to form splinter groups often take some members of the congregation with them. Usually they do not see themselves as rebels or disgruntled but persons called by God to fulfil a different and often greater mission from that being fulfilled by the group they have deserted. On the surface, those who stayed appear not to harbour resentment against those who left and those who left still see those they forsook as members of one large family of God's children. This, however, is not to minimise the impact of these disagreements and schisms, some of which have been very acrimonious. As one member of CAC put it, 'It was a difficult time for the church when the pastor suddenly decided to leave but God saw us through.'

The third category consists of churches like the Christ Apostolic Church, Redeem Christian Church of God and the Mountain of Fire and Miracles, which have their parent bodies in Africa. They were started either by trained pastors sent by the parent bodies or by ordinary members of the church who, when they arrived in Ireland, found no other Christian group that suited their style, beliefs and expectations. The spiritual and material requirements needed to set up these churches flowed directly from the parent bodies or their European headquarters, usually in the United Kingdom. Such support included the exchange of personnel and training of pastors and other church officials. The churches in this category continue to maintain close links with the parent bodies and other branches. For example, the pastor of Mountain of Fire and Miracles attends the yearly international convention of the church in Nigeria.

Demographic characteristics

Demographically, African-led Pentecostal churches are a microcosm of the larger African communities[28] and the demographic profile of one church tends not to differ considerably from that of the other. Generally there are more women than men and every church has a large number of children. The large number of children is not surprising, given that over 75% of those who participated in my survey said they have children.[29] More than 72% are married although the spouses of some were still in their home countries or outside Ireland. In the majority (85%) of cases, husband and wife belong to the same Christian group but more than six out of ten of the 15% who said their spouses were not members of their groups were women. Perhaps this indicates that women are less successful in convincing their husbands to join their groups or that men are generally less inclined to this kind of religiosity. Olusola Fasan, pastor of Gospel Faith Mission, believes women have shown a greater tendency to spirituality dating back to the days when Christ walked the earth: 'If you look at the scriptures you'll find that many places that our lord Jesus Christ went, women went there.'

Half the respondents in my survey identified themselves as immigrants. They consist of work permit holders and those who have gained residence status by other means, including parentage of a child/children born in Ireland. About 15% were Irish citizens or citizens of an EU country. Although educational and professional attainments are quite high (see Figure 11.1) among African Pentecostals in Ireland the unemployment

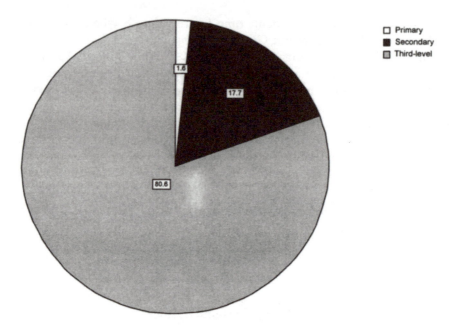

Figure 11.1 Ireland's African-led Pentecostal groups: educational qualifications of members

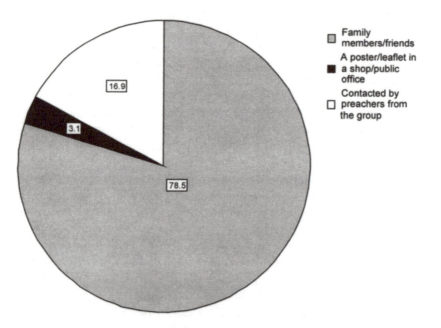

Figure 11.2 Sources of initial information about African-led Pentecostal groups

rate, at 31%, is also quite high. More than eight in ten have third-level educational qualifications and their occupational profile ranges from medical and veterinary doctors, nurses, accountants, computer specialists and teachers to diplomats, engineers, medical technicians and writers.

Publicity and the recruitment of new members are conducted mainly by word of mouth, and church members invite their friends and relatives. Close to 79% of the seventy respondents who said they became members of their groups after they arrived in Ireland either received their initial information through family members/friends or were influenced by them (see Figure 11.2). The vast majority of members have joined these churches because they believe that Pentecostal beliefs and activities foster a much cherished experiential knowledge of and relationship with the Supreme Being. Many of them are not encountering Pentecostalism for the first time. My survey shows that 44% had been members of their particular Pentecostal group before they arrived in Ireland. Many more had been Pentecostals although they associated with different groups before they came to Ireland. To qualify as Pentecostals they have had to renounce all prior religious experience and knowledge and undergo the 'rebirth' experience. Rebirth, or born again, they say, signalled the commencement of a personal and deeper relationship with the Supreme Being. They also believe that Pentecostal doctrines and practices uniquely help to safeguard, feed and nurture this relationship with God. It is therefore not surprising that they search for Pentecostal churches once they have arrived in Ireland or that they do not feel satisfied and comfortable in mainstream churches.

In Ireland many of them have chosen to associate with African-led Pentecostal groups rather than ones led by Irish persons because the former resonate with their experience of Pentecostal practices. Mr Fasan had associated with an Irish-led Pentecostal group before he formed the Gospel Faith Mission with five other Nigerians. He deserted the Irish-led group because 'their way of worship was quite different from the way we pray in Africa'. Moreover, African-led groups in Ireland have contextualised their activities, making them relevant to their unique social and political circumstances. Themes in songs, prayers and sermons emphasise their desire to survive and thrive in an increasingly difficult social and political climate where fear of racially motivated attacks and precarious residence status have weighed constantly on the minds of many.

Some members see the church as a place of refuge from the problems, hostilities and rejection they face in the larger society. For others, the church does not serve as a mere distraction from the harsh realities of living as strangers in a strange land but as a channel for receiving real solutions to various kinds of real problems. Mercy, a mother of three, was awaiting decision on her application for a residence permit when I interviewed her and her husband. Her two younger children had been born in Ireland and her application for residence permit was made on that basis. But after the government abolished the policy of granting residence status to parents of children born in Ireland she and about 12,000 others were caught in an immigration quagmire.[30] In her moments of anxiety and uncertainty the church provided guidance:

> Since I came into this country, it has been one problem or the other. Today, the government will say 'We're not giving you paper,' tomorrow they will say 'We're giving you.' In times like these when I get to the church there are some messages that I hear that will help me to keep calm, that will give me some encouragement. Through these messages I can see that God is still there for me. In this country, there is nobody there for you except God.

For the vast majority of members, particularly those holding prominent positions in the church, their membership compensates for the lack of recognition or the diminished social status that they experience in the larger society. Many members, including pastors and top officials, had enjoyed societal respect and recognition as successful professionals or business persons before they came to Ireland to seek asylum. Official and public attitudes to asylum seekers and most categories of African immigrants are a far cry from the respect and recognition they had enjoyed.[31] The acceptance and recognition members find in these churches help to restore the sense of self-worth they had experienced in their home countries. Jacob, an official of Christ Apostolic Church, had been an estate surveyor and a successful banker before he came to Ireland. He believes, 'people go to places where they are appreciated, they want to be understood and they want to feel that they are important and relevant'.

In the case of female members, Mr Fasan says the church provides solace, comfort and succour in the face of mounting domestic problems. Some female participants in my research say membership of the church or the intervention of church officials has saved their marriage, helped them through periods when their children or husband was sick and inculcated strong moral values in their children in the absence of their husband or a father figure. For instance, Adenike looked after her five children on her own for about three years before her husband joined her. He says the task was made easier because of the strong moral guidance the Bible provides:

> The Irish society, with all its permissiveness and immoralities, is not an easy place to raise children. At sixteen, children are supposed to be free to do what they like. But the Christian values that I've taught my children since infancy have made them amenable to my advice and instructions. If not

for these Christian principles, things would have been a lot harder. I know of many Africans that have lost their children. Their children are with the Social Welfare authorities, they are living in hostels because they revolted against their parents. It takes the grace of God to bring up children in the Western world.

Ilori believes single mothers and women living apart from their husbands find strong social network and emotional support in the church. While she waited for her husband to join her in Ireland, Maggie immersed herself in church activities and enlisted the prayers of the pastors and those of fellow worshippers for a speedy and safe reunion with her husband. She found companionship and acceptance in the church at a time when she was lonely at home and rejected by the larger society. During a special service at the church the speaker prophesised that the prayers of a woman in the church who had been 'waiting on the Lord' for her husband to join her had been answered and that the husband would soon join her. Maggie concluded that the prophecy referred to her although many other women in the group were in a similar situation. 'I immediately claimed the prophecy for myself,' she says. About a week after the prophecy was uttered her husband arrived from Nigeria through the Netherlands on a fake passport and after two failed attempts.

Maggie's story is the story of many women members of African-led Pentecostal groups and the direct consequence of a citizenship policy (abolished since January 2005) that conferred automatic citizenship on every child, including children of immigrants, born in Ireland.[32] At one time the parents of such children could apply for a residence permit. Once they had established legal residence, they could apply for their husband or the father of their child to join them. In practice the process was long, cumbersome and frustrating, especially as more immigrants took to this route to gain citizenship and legal residence. The frustration and uncertainties increased when the government announced in early 2003[33] that it was abandoning the policy of granting residence permits solely on the basis of parentage of a child born in Ireland. However, it did not say what it wanted to do about the outstanding applications and the long wait that followed tested the patience and tenacity of many immigrants, including members of these churches.

In prayers and songs church members expressed their desire to be free of these immigration problems. These desires also became recurrent themes in Sunday and mid-week worship sessions and in night vigils. The women and men caught in this immigration quagmire found not only friendship and spiritual guidance in the church but also professional advice. Church members who could not afford high legal fees relied on free advice from legal professionals within the church. In early 2005 the government implemented a new policy that paved the way for those caught in this immigration debacle to apply for residence permit under certain conditions.[34] For many African Pentecostals the new policy was God's direct intervention and the answer to their prayers. As a lady member of the Gospel Faith Mission put it, 'The hearts of the kings, even that of a hard-hearted Justice Minister, is in the hands of God. God is able to save his children from the enemy. We were always sure that He would do something about the problem. We give all the glory to God.'

Identity and integration

The concept of a 'new beginning' or 'rebirth' is a prerequisite for membership of a Pentecostal group and it is central to the self-perception of African Pentecostals in Dublin. Although the overwhelming majority have a Christian background, having being introduced to Bible doctrines and customs very early in life, the term 'new beginning' or 'born again' is used to describe not their initial contact with or acceptance of Christian beliefs but rather acceptance of and devotion to the unique Pentecostal interpretation of the Bible which emphasises 'experience and practice'.[35] 'New beginning' is appropriated in a manner that not only disavows prior religious and other experiences but also denies, or at least significantly attenuates, other relationships or identities.

For them the 'new beginning' does not only signify the beginning of a deeper and personal relationship with God but also a new and heightened consciousness of their privileges and duties as 'children of God'. Who they are and want to be, by their own definition, is only remotely connected with who they were and with the other facets of their lives. For instance, received identity markers like skin colour, nationality and race pale into insignificance and they are replaced with a relationship with God and Jesus Christ which allows them to escape what Paul Gilroy has described as 'the body-coded order of identification and differentiation'.[36] Commenting on Olaudah Equiano's encounter with Christianity and slavery, Paul Gilroy noted that Olaudah shed 'the superficial differences of gender and social status, race and caste, marked on the body by the trifling order of man' when he was immersed in 'the welcoming, baptismal waters of his new Christian faith'.[37] As Charles, an African Pentecostal and itinerant preacher, put it, 'I'm a child of God. That is what I am. It is the only thing that is relevant to me.'

For this category of African immigrants Pentecostalism has become an alternative basis (different from and superior to other identity markers like nationality, skin colour and immigrant status) for negotiating or constructing oneness and difference. The 'other' in the articulation of

African Pentecostals in Ireland is the unregenerate world or people, including non-Pentecostal African immigrants, outside the Pentecostal cosmos. They say their interaction with the 'other' in the Irish society, including the African 'other', is determined primarily or perhaps solely by their Pentecostal identity. They see themselves firstly and primarily as Pentecostal Christians.

However, I contest the 'essentialist' qualities implied in this construction of self and argue that identity is conceptually and experientially more fluid, fractured and multi-dimensional than their self-definition admits. The validity of this interpretation is more obvious in situations of voluntary or involuntary exile like the one African immigrants inhabit. Though African Pentecostals portray Pentecostalism as their essential and only window on the world and the only mirror for self-analysis and projection, I argue that this window coexists with other windows or prisms. Although 'rebirth' implies the renunciation of identity markers related to 'blood and soil', and African Pentecostals speak of their new self-ascribed identity as coherent and unitary, Woodward reminds us that 'there is never one fixed, coherent identity but several in play'.[38] She further argues that identity 'emerges in a number of different forms through a series of identifications which combine and emerge in an infinite number of forms'.[39]

The construction and projection of a single overwhelmingly dominant and coherent identity negates the contradictions and complexities of identities inherent in any subject, including African Pentecostals in Ireland. Although they invest the 'new personality' with essentialist attributes, I argue that other identities are implied or manifest in their conversation, dress codes, worship, songs and in many other aspects of their everyday conduct. The other realities of their existence in Ireland, especially their status as immigrants and a minority ethnic group that have been the subject of racially motivated attacks and discrimination, present an irrefutable case for a more nuanced articulation of the identity of African Pentecostals in twenty-first-century Ireland.

Relationship with the larger society

Though African Pentecostals depend in important and practical ways on the larger Irish society, they repudiate major social trends and habits of this society. They are opposed to alcohol consumption (in whatever quantity), visits to pubs (except to preach the gospel), sex before or outside marriage, homosexuality, attendance at non-Christian music concerts and the use of foul or dirty language. Given that most of these ideas and practices are widespread, or at least tolerated, in the larger culture and society, one might suggest that African Pentecostals in Ireland have created a social and moral universe that is parallel to that of the majority society as well as the ones inhabited by other sub-groups, including non-Pentecostal African immigrants. However, theirs is a universal that is connected with and even dependent upon the majority society in many significant ways. Their involvement in the mainstream economy and dependence on the social infrastructures of the dominant society provide a few examples of the interfaces or connections between their universe and the larger Irish society.

Some participants in my research have pointed to these interfaces or links to buttress the argument that the parallel universe they inhabit will not hinder their relationship with and integration into the larger Irish society. For example, as put by Remi, a medical laboratory technician and an official of Christ Apostolic Church:

> There is no way our involvement with the church will cut us off from the immediate day-to-day environment or prevent us from getting involved in the wider society. Even if we're in the church twenty-four hours a day, seven days a week, we still have to live in a neighbourhood, shop and work with people from other ethnic groups. We'll find ways to get involved in the system and work within it, otherwise we'll not survive.

Jacob believes church membership and activities are helping to prepare African immigrants for the long and arduous task of integration. In these churches members are able to gain the confidence and skills they need to cope with the demands the larger society. The leader of Christ Co-workers in Mission, Mr Oshengo, supports this view and he says the church is providing the conducive environment for African immigrants to devise and implement strategies of socio-economic mobility and active political participation. He foresees a future when the churches will offer political direction to the entire African communities and be breeding grounds for political and civic activists.

Conclusion

The realisation of that future depends not only on the self-perception and desire of African Pentecostals but also on how they are perceived by the 'other' in the Irish society as well as developments in the larger African communities. As Woodward notes, 'How I see myself and how others see me do not always fit.'[40] At the beginning of the twenty-first century, however, it is difficult to foresee the eventual transformation of the ghettoised universal of Ireland's African Pentecostals and their full integration into the majority society and culture.

Notes

1 See A. Ugba, 'African Churches in Ireland', *Asyland* (Dublin: Irish Refugee Council, autumn 2003). Whereas the academic community has paid little or no attention to the religious activities of immigrants in Ireland, media attention has grown in recent times. For example, an article by Paul Cullen, 'Vibrant Africans overcome the threat of racism', *Irish Times*, 30 July 2002.

2 Central Statistics Office, Census Results (2002), www.cso.ie/census.

3 For a detailed discussion of the declining membership and influence of the Catholic Church in Ireland see T. Inglis, *Moral Monopoly: The Rise and Fall of the Catholic Church in Modern Ireland* (Dublin: University College Dublin Press, 1998).

4 Ibid.

5 Ibid.

6 My empirical investigation has focused on African-led Pentecostal groups in the Greater Dublin area and it consists of the following methods: ethnographic observation, qualitative interviews with church members, a survey of 127 members across four groups and analysis of secondary documents. The information contained in this chapter is based on the interviews and the survey.

7 This is taken from New World Translation (NWT) of the Holy Bible.

8 Ibid.

9 A. Corten and R. Marshall-Fratani (eds), *Between Babel and Pentecost: Transnational Pentecostalism in Africa and Latin America* (London: Hurst, 2001), p. 7.

10 A. Anderson, 'Introduction: World Pentecostalism at a Crossroads', in A. Anderson and W. J. Hollenweger (eds), *Pentecostals after a Century: Global Perspectives on a Movement in Transition* (Sheffield: Sheffield Academic Press, 1999).

11 For accounts of the origins and spread of modern worldwide Pentecostal movements the following texts are useful: Anderson and Hollenweger, *Pentecostals after a Century*, H. Cox, *Fire from Heaven: The Rise of Pentecostal Spirituality and the Reshaping of Religion in the Twenty-first Century* (London: Cassell, 1996); W. Hollenweger, *The Pentecostals* (London: SCM Press, 1972); I. MacRobert, *The Black Roots and White Racism of early Pentecostalism in the USA* (Basingstoke: Macmillan, 1998), and A. J. Raboteau, *Canaan Land: A Religious History of African Americans* (Oxford: Oxford University Press, 2001).

12 M. M. Poloma, '"The Spirit bade me go": Pentecostalism and Global Religion', paper prepared for presentation at the Association for the Sociology of Religion annual meetings, Washington DC, 11–13 August 2000, pp. 5–7.

13 Ibid., p. 6.

14 Ibid.

15 A. O. Matthews, 'The Contextual Significance of the Charismatic Movements in Independent Nigeria', *Africa*, 58: 2 (1980), pp. 23–27.

16 Ibid.

17 A. Adogame, 'Betwixt Identity and Security: African New Religious Movements and the Politics of Religious Networking in Europe', *Novo Religio*, 7: 2 (2003), pp. 24–41.

18 T. G. Haar, 'The African Diaspora in Europe: some Important Themes and Issues', in G. ter Haar (ed.), *Strangers and Sojourners: Religious Communities in the Diaspora* (Leuven: Peeters, 1998).

19 Ibid.

20 For detailed information on Ireland's African communities see a report by A. Ugba, *A Quantitative Profile Analysis of African Immigrants in Twenty-first-century Dublin* (2004), www.tcd.ie/sociology/mphil/prelim-findings-2.pdf.

21 Central Statistics Office, Census Results (2002), www.cso.ie/census.

22 Central Statistics Office, *Population and Migration Estimates, April 2003* (Dublin: CSO, 2003).

23 See *Refugees and Asylum Seekers: A Challenge to Solidarity*, published by Tróicare and the Irish Commission for Justice and Peace in 2002.

24 *Metro Eireann*, 'New African churches arrive here with vibrating ovations', June–July 2000, p. 18.

25 ICC, *Black Immigrant Churches in the Republic of Ireland*, www.irish-churches.org/ (2003).

26 'Immigrants praised for "huge impact" on Church', *Irish Times*, 24 February 2004.

27 See www.cro.ie, office website of Company Registration Office.

28 Ugba, *A Quantitative Profile Analysis of African Immigrants*.

29 This survey involved 127 members of four churches in the Greater Dublin area. It was conducted from January to December 2004.

30 Developments in immigration law at the time received wide coverage in the mass media. See 'Residents of limbo', *Irish Times*, 7 June 2003.

31 Among other reports, the one published by the Irish office of Amnesty International in 2001 documents the racism experiences of immigrant and minority ethnic groups in Ireland. But see R. Lentin and R. McVeigh (eds), *Racism and Anti-racism in Ireland* (Belfast: Beyond the Pale, 2002), for a comprehensive and detailed analysis of this issue.

32 See Irish Nationality and Citizenship Act 2004, Dublin: Department of Justice Equality and Law Reforms.

33 See N. Haughey, 'State contesting right of non-EU parents of Irish children to stay', *Irish Times*, 9 January 2002; 'Residents of limbo', *Irish Times*, 7 June 2003.

34 See Irish Nationality and Citizenship Act 2004, Dublin: Department of Justice, Equality and Law Reforms.

35 Anderson and Hollenweger, *Pentecostals after a Century*.

36 P. Gilroy, *Between Camps* (London: Penguin Books, 2000), pp. 119–20.

37 Ibid.

38 K. Woodward (ed.), *Questioning Identity: Gender, Class, Ethnicity* (London: Routledge, 2004), p. 6.

39 Ibid., p. 6.

40 Ibid., p. 7.

12

Getting into politics

Neltah Chadamoyo, Bryan Fanning and Fidèle Mutwarasibo

This chapter describes efforts of the Africa Solidarity Centre (ASC) to promote responsiveness by Irish political parties to immigrants in the run-up to the 2004 local government elections. It also recounts how these contributed to the development of the ASC as an immigrant lead organisation. A research idea emerged from a discussion between Fidele Murtwarasibo and Bryan Fanning. The main aim of the proposed study, later named *Positive Politics: Participation of Immigrants and Ethnic Minorities in the Electoral Process*, was to encourage Irish political parties to think of immigrants as potential voters and supporters. It was influenced by campaigns in the United Kingdom aimed at addressing underrepresentation of black and minority ethnic communities in British political parties.[1] At the time most immigrants were not citizens yet non-citizens resident six months or more in the state were entitled to vote in Irish local government elections.[2] It was proposed to highlight the presence of a growing immigrant electorate as an alternative to anti-immigrant political populism. *Positive Politics* was envisaged as a 'shot across the bows' of political parties tempted to exploit racism in the 2004 local government elections. As things turned out, the politics of the 2004 election were overwhelmed, late in the day, by the calling of the Referendum on Citizenship.

In the run-up to the 2002 general election political parties signed an anti-racism protocol.[3] In the main the protocol was observed.[4] However, it was flouted in North Cork, where, arguably, the 'race card' was played by Fianna Fail candidate Noel O'Flynn.[5] According to a rival candidate, Senator John Minihan, O'Flynn topped the poll because he struck an anti-asylum seeker position close to the date of the election. Flynn had described asylum seekers in Cork as ' freeloaders', 'people screwing the system' who were 'thumbing their noses at Irish hospitality'.[6] Senator Minihan described the impact of Flynn's populist rhetoric on people from immigrant and minority ethnic communities living in Cork:

A university student visited me in a distressed state. Her father was from

Hong Kong, her mother was born and educated in Cork, and resided there. She was as much a Corkonian as I am. However, because of her different ethnic looks, she was now a victim of racial taunts. A mother of two foreign adopted children contacted me. Her children had settled into school and had been in Ireland since they were a few months old. They were now being taunted in the school yard. Cork people who had married non-nationals who had become integrated into the community, and who had worked and lived in Cork for a number of years, contributing to our society, were now being racially abused. Elderly ladies living alone were in fear of being assaulted or raped by non-nationals who according to myth were rampant on the streets of Cork. This was a result of stirring it up, of playing with people's emotions. Fuelled by some local journalists, the myths and tensions grew.

O'Flynn received no sanction from Fianna Fail. Elsewhere overtly anti-immigrant politics met with less success. The Irish People's Party, which promoted racism against African immigrants in Dublin, was short-lived; to all intents and purposes it was confined to the Internet. One independent candidate, Aine Ni Chonnail of the Immigration Control Platform, obtained just 926 first preference votes in Dublin South Central out of a total poll of 44,768 (under 2.1%). She was eliminated on the fifth count. Those who voted for Ni Chonnail indicate preferences for candidates from various mainstream political parties. Under the proportional representation system just under 21% of her transfers (the second preferences of those who voted for her) went to Fianna Fail, just under 12.5% to Fine Gael, almost 19% to Labour, almost 24% to Sinn Fein, just over 9% to the Green Party and just over 7% to the Progressive Democrats.[7] Although anti-immigrant racism was less demonstrable in Irish politics than it was at the time in many other European countries, there were grounds for concern that Irish parties would exploit racism for electoral gain.[8]

From Fidele Murtwarasibo's perspective the proposed research was part of a larger project of promoting immigrant civic participation. He had initially trained as a forester in Rwanda. then became a secondary school teacher and had subsequently worked on a 'Training for Transformation' community development programme. Before coming to Ireland he was employed by an NGO in a refugee camp in the Congo. The camp had a population of 400,000. In Ireland, employed as a community development officer, he worked predominantly with 'indigenous' marginal goups, including people with disabilities. In 2000 he co-authored a study of Africans in Ireland that examined barriers to participation in Irish society experienced by respondents. These were found to include racism and cultural and communication differences; notably difficulties with the perceived formality of the dominant community.[9] His experiences in working with disadvantaged groups in Africa and in Ireland convinced him of the importance of civic and political participation:

> Following my research with the African Cultural Project, I realised that to move beyond token participation requires community development within ethnic minority communities. Although Travellers are indigenous to Ireland their needs had been for a long time neglected. It is only recently when they started to organise that changes started to happen. Today we have a Traveller health strategy and a Travellers accommodation strategy. This did not happen by accident. Ethnic minorities can only overcome the difficulties they face by engaging with policy makers. Failure to do this will result in their marginalisation. I personally feel that I have to look beyond myself and try to play a part in shaping a society in which my children, the second generation, and future generations of immigrants will be proud of their heritage and not be treated like second-class citizens.

The idea of setting up Africa Solidarity Centre came about in the late 1990s. In 2001 work started in earnest to produce a memorandum of association and put in place a constitution. The Centre was launched officially in September 2001. The few grants that the Centre had been able to attract from Irish sources came from bodies that had a remit for overseas development such as the Department of Foreign Affairs. So little support had been forthcoming from mainstream Irish sources that there was a debate about dropping the word 'solidarity' from the name of the organisation. The perception was that potential Irish funders did not seem to respond well to it.[10] During 2002, as voluntary director of the newly founded Africa Solidarity Centre, Fidele Murtwarasibo proposed the development of a leadership training programme for members of African communities living in Ireland. The initiative could not be progressed because of lack of funding. In December 2002 the board of the ASC agreed an organisational goal of promoting civic and political activism amongst Africans in Ireland. The board agreed that the proposed *Positive Politics* project was compatible with this. In March 2003 a research proposal was drawn up by Bryan Fanning and Fidele Murtwarasibo. In May 2003 a funding bid was submitted to the government's Know Racism campaign in response to an invitation for bids from community organisations to fund initiatives aimed at tackling racism. The ASC proposal combined a research element with the development of an information pack for immigrants on voting rights in Ireland. In July 2003 the bid was turned down. A second bid to a EU funding initiative for pilot projects for integration of third-country nationals was also unsuccessful.

The ASC board decided to proceed with the research without funding for a research assistant. Throughout this period the ASC was extremely impoverished but set aside €1,000 for the project. Most aspects of the research were undertaken by unpaid members of the ASC, including design of the subsequent publication and its publication on the ASC Web site. One thousand copies of the *Positive Politics* report were printed. The printer agreed to defer payment.[11] The chairman of the ASC, Rev. Sahr Yambasu, and Fidele Murtwarasibo wrote letters of appeal to Church of Ireland and Methodist parishes in Dublin in an effort to raise the additional €4,000 needed to cover the cost of publication and that of a proposed conference on immigrant political participation.[12] Some donations were received. The ASC's sole staff member, an intern funded by the European Research Fund, left at the beginning of the research period. Her replacement Neltah Chadamoyo worked as an unpaid volunteer. As she recalled:

> My involvement in the research was by pure chance. I was unemployed looking for something to do besides sitting at home and became a volunteer for Africa Centre. The organisations' structure, set-up and vision were appealing, since it included Africans and non-Africans. The research had already been discussed and the first survey letters sent out to political parties before I became involved. It was felt that despite funding problems the research should carry on and each obstacle dealt with as it arose.

The *Positive Politics* survey consisted of four questions addressed to each of the six main political parties, Fianna Fail, Fine Gael, Labour, Progressive Democrats, Green Party and Sinn Fein). The questions sought to identify the extent to which they had adopted good practices and specific policies aimed at promoting the inclusion of and responsiveness to immigrants and ethnic minorities.[13] Detailed responses were sought to each specific question:

1 What policies or good practices has the party adopted to encourage members of immigrant communities and ethnic minority groups to become party members?
2 What policies or good practices have been adopted by the party to oppose racism in Irish society?
3 Has the party selected candidates from immigrant and ethnic minority communities to stand in the June 2004 local elections?
4 What initiatives are proposed by the party to canvas for support amongst immigrant and ethnic minority communities in the June 2004 elections?

Neltah Chadamayo took charge of liaising with the central offices of the six political parties. None of the six replied to the initial correspondence from the Africa Solidarity Centre. Follow-up letters were sent in September 2003. These stated that the unwillingness of parties to respond to the survey would be publicised by the ASC. Neltah Chadamayo made repeated telephone contacts with the political parties in her efforts to secure responses. She considered she that was not taken seriously by a number of officials from various parties she contacted either as an African woman or as a representative of an African organisation. In some cases she was quizzed at length by administrators and gatekeepers about where she was from (Zimbabwe) and about why she had come to Ireland (to escape from Mugabe) but found it difficult to get access to senior officials who could speak about party policies:

> It was revelation to realise that most of the people involved had never dealt with an African woman researcher before. It meant change of tactics in dealing with the parties. For example, when making calls I had to be firmer with requests, more eloquent and exact but at the same time not 'turning into a man'. A tough feat but easier to manage, especially over the phone because the other person could not see how much of an effort the other is making.

She found Sinn Fein to be the notable exception. Sinn Fein were the only party whose gatekeepers provided her access to senior party officials without having to make repeated efforts. In a few cases it was concluded – after multiple efforts – that party officials were unwilling to discuss the research questions with members of the Africa Solidarity Centre. Subsequently these responded promptly to queries from the sole academic (and only white person) on the research team. Overall, members of the research team were surprised by the lack of professionalism of the majority of parties in fielding queries and in articulating their policies. When it came to written replies to the research questions the two exceptions were Fianna Fail and Sinn Fein. The responses of both of these were considerably more polished than those of the other parties contacted even if, in the case of the former, there was little or no engagement with the specific research questions.

What was surprising (in an era of political spin) was the extent to which the responses of the others were unguarded and dismissive. A written reply from the Labour Party merely directed the researchers to its Web site. Senior officials from a number of parties remarked in telephone conversations that they had never given the issue of immigrant participation in politics any thought. Some patently struggled to understand the questions being put to their organisations. It became clear that many of the political parties contacted did not take the ASC survey seriously. In a number of cases there was little sense that party officials understood that an unwillingness or inability to address social diversity was either an issue for internal concern or a potential source of external criticism.

Table 12.1 Positive Politics survey, September 2003

Question	Fianna Fail	Progressive Democrats	Fine Gael	Labour Party	Sinn Fein	Greens
Policies/good practices encouraging members of immigrant communities and ethnic-minority groups to become party members	None	None	None	None	None	None
Policies/good practices adopted to oppose racism in Irish society	Some	Some	Some	Some	Some	Some
Candidates selected from immigrant and ethnic minority communities to stand in the June 2004 local elections?	None	None	None	None	None	None
Initiatives to canvas for support amongst immigrant and ethnic minority communities in the June 2004 elections	None	None	None	None	Some	Some

In their responses none of the six main political parties, including Fianna Fail and the Progressive Democrats, their partners in government, identified specific policies or good practices adopted to encourage members of immigrant communities and ethnic minority groups to become party members (Table 12.1). The written response of Fianna Fail, the main government party, was the most extensive received but it made no reference at all to immigrants and ethnic minorities. Instead it outlined a general ethos of inclusion grounded in the democratic republican ideals of the party. The Progressive Democrats wrote that its party constitution contained a provision that prevented people who were not Irish or EU member state citizens from becoming party members.

The *Positive Politics* report was launched on 2 December 2003. Fianna Fail facilitated a photo call at the Taoiseach's office in Dail Eireann. The print and radio media picked up immediately on the exclusionary provisions in the constitution of the Progressive Democrats.[14] However, most of the findings of the study received little serious attention. Media criticism was specifically directed at Michael McDowell, party president

Table 12.2 Second *Positive Politics* survey, February 2004

Party	New policies and practices identified by parties aimed at improving responsiveness to ethnic minorities and immigrants
Fianna Fail	Some party material to be translated into community languages Advertising in immigrant and ethnic minority media
Progressive Democrats	Party constitution amended to permit non-EU nationals to join. Five such persons have joined the party
Labour	Some party material to be translated into community languages
Fine Gael	Some party material to be translated into community language Advertising in immigrant and ethnic minority media
Green Party	Anti-racism training for candidates Some party material to be translated into community languages
Sinn Fein	Anti-racism training for candidates Promotion of an anti-racism charter for local authorities in some areas

of the Progressive Democrats, who, as Minister of Justice Equality and Law Reform, was responsible for Irish immigration policy.[15] The Africa Solidarity Centre argued that parties that prevented non-citizens from joining could potentially be open to legal challenge on human rights grounds.[16] It emphasised that the British Labour Party had overturned a ban on members from Northern Ireland at its 2003 conference following legal advice that it had a weak case on such grounds[17]. The Progressive Democrats very promptly agreed to amend their constitution.[18]

A follow-up survey in February 2004 repeated the same questions. The aim was to gauge shifts in the responsiveness of political parties to immigrants as potential voters, members or candidates. The responses to the second survey indicated general willingness by the six political parties to consider limited initiatives. For example, Fianna Fail replied that it aimed to create a society based on the principles of equality and dignity and that it welcomed support from all people regardless of race or religion. The party reported that it had begun to advertise in *Metro Eireann*, a newspaper widely read by immigrant communities, inviting people to become members. It also reported the inclusion of an anti-racism section into the local elections manual that was supplied to all its candidates. This included a definition of institutional racism as 'Processes that consciously or unconsciously result in the systematic exclusion of ethnic minorities ... visible in the inequitable outcomes for minority ethnic groups from the policies and practices of organisations and institutions throughout society'.[19]

The Progressive Democrats, having removed their prohibition on non-EU citizens becoming party members, reported that they had now had recruited 'five such persons, including two Chinese nationals, into the Party's constituency organisation in Dublin South East'. The Labour Party emphasised that its public representatives were outspoken about racism in society. It reported that it was standing one candidate from an ethnic minority community. Fine Gael stated that it is open to having 'members of the immigrant community and ethnic minority communities' stand as candidates in the local elections. Fine Gael stated that it has advertised in publications focused on immigrant groups with the aim of encouraging them to become party members and to vote for the party. However, Fine Gael had not identified any such members and was standing no such candidates in the 2004 local government elections. The Green Party stated that it was encouraging members from ethnic minority communities to become party members. It invited independent candidates from ethnic minority groups to attend in a workshop that covered racism and the elections entitled 'Addressing Racism: for the Candidate on the Campaign Trail'. The Green Party stated that it planned to put together a flyer explaining rights to participate in the election in several languages.

Sinn Fein stated that local party organisations had stepped up their voter registration campaigns – 'all canvassers carry voter registration forms' – all the party's local election candidates would undergo anti-racism training. Sinn Fein reported that it had sought to introduce an anti-racism charter (developed by the party in Belfast) in some Republic of Ireland local authority areas. This suggested that Sinn Fein in the Republic of Ireland was conversant with UK policy norms and expectations about addressing racism in politics.

The publication of the second report and the planned seminar on immigrant participation in Irish politics – indeed, the *Positive Politics* project as a whole – were overshadowed by the announcement in March 2004 of a referendum on the removal of the constitutional right to citizenship from the Irish-born children of immigrants. This was to be held on the same date as the local government and European elections. Inevitably, immigration became the central issue of the 2004 elections. The referendum proposal was endorsed by the two parties in government, Fianna Fail and the Progressive Democrats, and by Fine Gael, the largest opposition party. In this context, the focus of the second ASC publication was expanded in order to address concerns by Africans about the citizenship referendum. These concerns were reflected in its title, *Negative Politics, Positive Vision: Immigration and the 2004 Elections*. The report argued that the proposal to hold the citizenship referendum could be legitimately perceived to be 'racist in effect' and that 'The ideological message being put to African people living in Ireland, including those with Irish children, is that they must remain outside the nation because they do not have "Irish" blood and are not part of the Irish "race"'.[20]

Negative Politics, Positive Vision noted that political participation by immigrants had been impeded by the way voter registration was administered.. Concern raised by NGOs several months in advance of the election that non-citizen immigrants entitled to vote in the local government elections would encounter difficulties in registering to vote proved justified. As late as 22 April asylum seekers entitled to vote were prevented from registering to vote in the June 2004 elections. This happened because of the incompatibility between procedures operated by the Department of Justice Equality and Law Reform and the requirements of the Department of Environment and Local Government.[21] The identity cards issued by the Department of Justice Equality and Law Reform to asylum seekers stated that these were not to be accepted for the purposes of legal identification. The result was that many people entitled to vote were prevented from including their names on the register of electors. It took several requests to the Department of Justice Equality and Law Reform and the Department of Environment and Local Government before clarification regarding how such people could register was forthcoming. A statement by the Irish Refugee Council, issued prior to the amendment, summed up the problem in the following terms:

> The strength of any democracy is in the extent to which all who are entitled to vote are encouraged and enabled to do so. In this regard the Irish government has, to date, singularly failed Ireland's immigrant communities. A failure to rectify this situation will be a missed opportunity for significantly enhancing the integration of Ireland's new communities into Irish society'.[22]

On 22 April 2004 the Minister for the Environment Heritage and Local Government amended the electoral regulations to allow recognition of temporary resident certificate and National Immigration Bureau cards.[23]

The seminar to mark the launch of *Negative Politics, Positive Vision* was held on 3 June 2004.[24] It was addressed by two immigrant candidates standing as independents and by a representative of the UK-based Operation Black Vote. One of the candidates recounted how her election agent had defected from Fine Gael to manage her campaign because as the Irish grandmother of 'a mixed-race child' she could not support the party's support of the referendum. Of the six political parties invited to send representatives to the seminar only Sinn Fein sent delegates. The seminar received no media coverage, in part because it clashed with an event held on the same evening by the Campaign against the Deportation of Irish Children. The sole journalist who attended from a national newspaper informed members of the ASC that his articles on the seminar and on the findings of *Negative Politics: Positive Vision* had been rejected by his editor two days running. The newspaper in question subsequently supported the government's position on the referendum.

Much of the activism by immigrant advocacy groups in the run-up to the June 2004 referendum focused upon concern about the deportation of Irish born children of immigrants and their families. This centred on the establishment of a Coalition against the Deportation of Irish Children (CADIC).[25] This activism focused on 'non-Irish Irish-born' child citizens at risk of deportation following the Lobe Supreme Court judgement in 2003. Prior to the Lobe ruling (see Chapter 3) persons with Irish-born children entitled to Irish citizenship were granted leave to remain by the Minister of Justice. Many of these children were African.

Seven independent candidates from immigrant communities stood in the 2004 local government elections. Two were elected, Dr Taiwo Matthew to Ennis Urban District Council and Rotimi Adebari in Portlaoise, Co. Laois. In May 2004 the Africa Solidarity Centre won an award for best group project at the annual *Metro Eireann* Media and Multicultural Awards (MAMA). The award of €5.000 was earmarked for strategic planning by the ASC. The research contributed significantly to the development of the Africa Solidarity Centre. In June 2004 Solidarity Centre received a £70,000 grant from the UK-based Joseph Rowntree Charitable Trust to develop the organisation and to progress civic and political inclusion work. The proposed development work included the employment of a co-ordinator to direct the strategic development of the ASC and the development of a civic and political participation programme for Africans living in Ireland. Neltah Chadmayo's assessment was that the research project contributed significantly to the development of the ASC:

> Regardless of how the report was received the impact it had on the organisation was huge. It helped the board, members and other interested parties see that the organisation had committed people who would work hard regardless of circumstances to produce good results. The two reports helped to get funding for the centre and as a result it could employ one full-time person. The research was done using the cheapest and simplest means and the results were very good and positive. A lot of people now have come to

realise the Africa Centre is a force to be reckoned with and the members have gotten new confidence. The organisation is on the rise.

Against this some members of the centre considered that the research project was achieved at considerable potential cost to the Africa Solidarity Centre. Following the receipt of funding from the Joseph Rowntree Charitable Trust the ASC worked to develop a strategic plan. The demands imposed upon members by this work on top of those caused by the research provoked debate amongst members about the future of the organisation. The mood in the immediate aftermath of the referendum was one of pessimism. As put by Neltah Chadamayo:

> The reports also brought their own problems. It was felt that the centre has failed to attract funding from the government after the two reports because of the impact they made. Some within the organisation have been complaining that demands being made, for example the requirement for a strategic plan, are just means and ways of refusing the organisation funding in case it produces further reports that do not reflect well on the government and the bigger parties. This brought about speculation in some quarters of whether or not the Centre would continue doing research.

However, further research was identified as central to the strategic plan. So too was an ongoing focus on the participation of immigrants in Irish politics. The successful ASC bid to Joseph Rowntree proposed a civic education project and shadowing scheme to allow representatives of the immigrant population to better understand the workings of the Irish political system. These proposals were implemented and the ASC has undertaken follow-up research on civic participation by immigrants in Irish society. The activism of the ASC has formed part of a wider participation by immigrants in Irish civil society. This broader context is addressed in the next chapter.

Notes

1 This included liaison with Operation Black Vote in the United Kingdom, www.obv.org. The Africa Solidarity Centre research was influenced by the recommendations of a 2002 report on racism and ethnic underrepresentation in British politics. These included a high-profile state-funded cross-party leadership programme aimed at ensuring the ongoing emergence of electoral candidates from different ethnic groups, 'rigorous goals' for minority representation on lists of candidates, the establishment of a unit to provide support and mentoring for ethnic minority candidates and reform of practices within political parties aimed at tackling ethnic underrepresentation. See A. Rushanara and C. O'Cinneide, *Our House? Race and Representation in British Politics* (London: Institute of Public Policy Research, 2002).

2 The Electoral Act 1992 provides that a national of any country ordinarily resident in the local electoral area who is over eighteen years old and who is on the electoral register is entitled to vote in local government elections. See N. Whelan, *Politics, Elections and the Law* (Dublin: Blackhall, 2000), p. 8.

3 In the run-up to the 2002 elections each of the six main political parties endorsed an anti-racism protocol. This outlined commitments to send 'consistent and clear' messages that signatories rejected racism, to condemn campaign material susceptible to inciting hatred on the grounds of 'race', colour, nationality, ethnic origin or religious belief. National Consultative Committee on Racism and Interculturalism, *Anti-racism Protocol for Political Parties*, www.nccri.ie.

4 B. Fanning, 'The Political Currency of Irish Racism, 1997–2002', *Studies*, 91, pp. 319–28.

5 S. Loyal, 'Welcome to the Celtic Tiger: Racism, Immigration and the State', in C. Coulter and S. Coleman (eds), *The End of History? Critical Reflections on the Celtic Tiger* (Manchester; Manchester University Press, 2003), p. 85.

6 *Irish Times*, 29 January 2002.

7 Fanning, 'The Political Currency of Irish Racism', p. 325.

8 For example, in Italy the 'neo-fascist' Alleanz Nazionale achieved 12% of the vote in the 2001 election; a fall from 16% in 1996, the Danish People's Platform, a new anti-immigrant party, took 12% of the national vote in 2001, the Austrian Freedom Party won 27% of the vote in 1999 under the leadership of Jorg Haider, the List Pym Fortuyn in the Netherlands obtained 40% of the vote in 2002 and the Front Nationale was supported by 18% (6 million voters) in France in May 2002. See M. O'Connell, *Right-wing Ireland? The rise of Populism in Ireland and Europe* (Dublin: Liffey Press, 2003).

9 S. Smith and F. Mutwarasibo, *Africans in Ireland: Developing Communities* (Dublin: African Cultural Project, 2000).

10 Africa Solidarity Centre annual general meeting, 2004.

11 Ken Rue of Fodhla Print in Dublin.

12 Africa Solidarity Centre received donations from parishes of the Church of Ireland and the Methodist Church. Thanks for the connections of Fidele and Dr Sahr Yambasu within the two Churches. These donations were boosted by a generous anonymous donation to the Centre.

13 Parties were written to on 18 August and 25 September 2003. Letters detailing the research questions were repeatedly followed up by e-mail and telephone.

14 The Progressive Democrat issue appeared as a front-page story in the *Irish Examiner* on 2 December 2003. It was also the subject of an editorial criticising Michael McDowell. The launch was also reported in the *Irish Times*, the *Independent* and the *Star*. A number of radio stations also covered the story.

15 Editorial, *The Examiner*, 2 December 2003.

16 B. Fanning, F. Murtwarasibo and N. Chaymayo, *Positive Politics: Participation of Immigrants and Ethnic Minorities in the Electoral Process* (Dublin: Africa Solidarity Centre), p. 13.

17 Fanning *et al.*, *Positive Politics*, p. 13.
18 The rule was changed by the party's National Executive at its meeting on 4 December 2003.
19 Fianna Fail, *Handbook for Local Election Candidates* (Dublin: Fianna Fail, 2004).
20 B. Fanning, F. Murtwarasibo and N. Chaymayo, *Negative Politics, Positive Vision: Immigration and the 2004 Elections* (Dublin: Africa Solidarity Centre, 2004).
21 *Irish Independent*, 14 April 2004.
22 Joint statement by Integrating Ireland and the Irish Refugee Council, 13 April 2004.
23 Statutory Instrument 175.2004 (Dublin: Stationery Office, 2004).
24 It was hosted collectively by Africa Solidarity Centre, Amnesty International and Immigrant Council of Ireland.
25 Members included Amnesty International (Irish section), the Children's Rights Alliance, Conference of the Religious in Ireland (CORI), Free Legal Advice Centres (FLAC), Irish Council for Civil Liberties (IRC), Jesuit Refugee Service, National Women's Council of Ireland and trade unions.

13

Immigrant civic mobilisation

Alice Feldman

This chapter considers the emergence of immigrant-led civic mobilisation in Ireland and its subsequent role in the social and institutional
transformations related to ethnic diversity, integration and social change.
It draws on new research that examines the circumstances surrounding
the emergence of immigrant-led community and voluntary organisations (hereafter, ILOs), the dynamics of their engagement with key stakeholders and community and voluntary sector actors, and the impacts of
these activities on the wider civil society arena.[1]

Citizenship, civil society and social capital have received increasing
attention in both academic and political arenas in the face of rising
inequalities, the retreat of the welfare state, and the realities of global
transformations. Soysal observes that citizenship is the major organising
principle of membership in contemporary polities.[2] It serves as the basis
for constructing and debating national identity and sets out civic obligations for participation in the public sphere.[3] As a relational mediator
– between the state and citizens, between citizens and non-citizens
– citizenship is more than simply a legal category indicative of access
to rights, but constitutes a critical element of democratic praxis.[4] Social
capital refers to the array of resources inherent in communities, networks
and relationships that generate the 'shared norms, values and understandings that facilitate co-operation within or among groups'.[5] Activities such as volunteering, political participation, community engagement
and efficacy and informal social support are considered central to the
cultivation of trust in social as well as institutional relationships and
activities.

Global migration flows have catalysed ever more substantial social
and institutional transformations, particularly as they relate to the ethnic
diversification of destination countries. These dynamics pose fundamental
challenges to conventional principles and policies underpinning citizenship and social capital and the role of civil society in these contexts.
Approaches to citizenship have been traditionally based on notions of

the territorially delimited nation-state that serves a mythically unified national populace. This framework and its associated discourses and institutions have long been identified by scholars as a central component of the state's propensity to racialise minority ethnic communities and the 'immigrationisation' of citizenship.[6] Nowadays, political and economic refugees and other migrants, who have been considered temporary residents of their 'host' societies, form large, often permanent, communities within host societies.[7] They must therefore set about the business of 'home-building' and 'place-making'[8] against the backdrop of a hostile political environment and restrictive policy[9] and within the wider 'culture of suspicion'.[10]

The civic mobilisation of immigrant or 'new minority ethnic communities' that these circumstances galvanise contributes to the adoption of new forms of incorporation which then shape the subsequent structures of opportunities for such activity.[11] It is no longer a common blood or lineage, or even loyalty to a particular state or common national interest, that constitutes the basis for claiming rightful membership to the host polity. Rather, as Rundell argues, it is the cultivation of 'a shared public, social space, a set of abstract principles and responsibilities ... and the rationalised organisation and routine of everyday praxis ...'[12] This highlights the shift in the conceptualisation of citizenship, from an emphasis on categorical definition and legal status to one that highlights the social solidarity, cohesion, civic commitment and social capital that underpin the relations framed by citizenship and other categories of national membership. That civil society can provide a space for those who belong to the most marginalised and disenfranchised to act in this fashion – regardless of their formal legal status – ensures that the changes set in motion by migration will become enduring features of social, policy and academic arenas.

These issues and dynamics have particular resonance in the Republic of Ireland. Concerns about the decline in civic participation and social capital in the wake of the Celtic Tiger have focused attention on the role of civil society and social capital in national well-being, equality and sustainable competitiveness.[13] Increasingly, the notion of 'active citizenship' has found its way into popular political discourse. It currently serves as a vehicle for (1) articulating a public philosophy and (2) developing new structures of governance and social partnership to redress the growing disconnection between the polity and the system of democracy.[14] And, as discussed in chapters throughout the present volume, these discussions are taking place in a highly politicised environment shaped by often hostile debates concerning immigration on the one hand and substantial civil and political innovations on the other.

ILO start-up and development

Of the twenty-three ILOs participating in this study, sixteen are based in the Irish Republic and seven in Northern Ireland. This includes twelve 'single community' or 'country-specific' organisations (including such regions as Eastern Europe/the former Soviet Republic, Africa/the Middle East, South East Asia, Pacific/Far East), five 'mixed community', refugee/asylum seeker organisations, and six 'pan' or umbrella organisations that serve or represent multiple communities. [15] Among those interviewed, ILO founders are typically well educated and often have relevant experience and training from their home countries, whether with respect to sector-based work (community development, campaigning, politics) or organisational work (business, management, accounting). This reflects a general level of expertise that stands in stark contrast to common perceptions and assumptions that these organisations and their members suffer from lack of capacity and professionalism. In establishing their organisations ILO founders were responding to a wide range of issues, including addressing needs associated with community formation (i.e. family, social and religious life, and changing community demographics) and social change at national level (e.g. racism, culturally appropriate service provision, global awareness, and so on). Their organisational mission statements emphasise such objectives as promoting awareness raising and anti-racism, cross-cultural exchange and integration, improving policies and services, and the means of self-representation and political participation.

ILOs experience many of the organisational problems common to all community and voluntary groups, like struggling to cultivate effective leadership, representative structures and community participation. They must also contend with the same institutional obstacles stemming from the social exclusion and discrimination to which existing policies have yet to respond effectively and the lack of access to decision makers. ILOs, however, are subject to additional obstacles and barriers. Here, MSO representatives interviewed in this study emphasised the negative impact of racism and the vulnerability of minority ethnic communities that often cause them to 'keep their heads down' and avoid being controversial or being seen as 'troublemakers'. Other factors include the diasporic and dispersed nature of their communities. These circumstances require ILOs to juggle such demands as maintaining their own community identities, dealing with homeland politics and suspicion among the various 'new' communities, all while they are struggling to be included in and recognised as part of the wider society.

The NGO staff interviewed acknowledged that ILOs are under extraordinary pressure to address the many urgent needs of their communities and to effectively represent large and diverse memberships. ILOs can experience further challenges because they do not have sufficient time to develop effective strategic plans and do not command high levels of trust on the part of funders and agencies. It was noted that the poor track record of one or two ILOs often reflects negatively on all others and contributes to a bias in favour of more established MSOs. These factors make ILOs even more vulnerable to funding-led influences. Because funding remits are largely policy-driven, the criteria for submissions are ever changing and ILOs struggle to 'fit' funders' mandates which typically provide only once-off project funding for single issues (e.g. poverty, anti-racism, development education). Although typically small-scale organisations, most ILOs are involved in a wide array of activities – campaigning, classes, cultural and social activities, drop-in centres, information and support services, research – and are thus constantly overstretched. For example, all twenty-three ILOs participating in the study undertake activities in at least two or more programmatic areas of work: twenty-two are involved in awareness-raising/intercultural education, seventeen in community development, sixteen in service provision, fourteen in lobbying/advocacy and six provided information services.

Relations between ILOs, MSOs and funders

Following the shift towards substantial in-migration during the 1990s, civil society in the Republic of Ireland experienced a veritable explosion of MSO activities in relation to 'new minority ethnic communities', alongside the flourishing of the race relations industry and growing policy infrastructure. These organisations have also been significant sites for the participation of asylum seekers, refugees and members of new minority ethnic communities through (1) volunteering – both to assist in the integration process and in order to battle the boredom and hopelessness from being denied the right to work and (2) employment – because many have done such work in their home countries, but also because many are channelled into sector-related work as the professional qualifications they obtained in other industries elsewhere are not recognised for work in Ireland. In light of the extent of this activity, research was undertaken to assess refugees' and asylum seekers' views on their participation in these activities.[16] Many involved in this work felt that they were exploited by MSOs which draw on their uncompensated knowledge and expertise but provide no direct benefit, capacity building or opportunity for genuine participation in the process. They also argued that their involvement in MSOs' programming circumvents the development and funding of their own organisations, particularly in light of the bias in favour of the more well known or well established organisations.

In recent years, many members of immigrant/'new' minority ethnic communities have begun to leave MSOs to form their own organisations, in effect depriving them of their expertise, insights and contacts as well as creating new competition for the same resources. This, in turn, has created further opportunities for conflict and tension. For example, ILO members report concerns stemming from the ways in which their interaction with MSOs and other mainstream stakeholders often leads to their ideas being 'poached'. This issue was raised in both the current and previous research and the accusation is not limited to MSOs. One ILO representative reported noticing a trend in which ideas set out in funding proposals which were unsuccessful seemed to be being taken forward by other organisations and agencies which were subsequently funded to do so.

The roles and interests of MSOs and the ways they engage with ILOs and immigrant communities are therefore subject to much more scrutiny and critique. There is no doubt that work and collaboration with MSOs provide important benefits for ILOs. This includes resources, expertise and training, increased credibility, clout and visibility, as well as opportunities to extend their involvement to national level through networks, platforms and other policy forums. The MSOs involved in this study were diverse in the types of work that they undertake, ranging from community development, development education, local governance, solidarity and advocacy, information and service provision, and so on. Regardless of the types of activity in question, MSO staff shared the belief that equal partnership with ILOs is essential given that ILOs have the most knowledge of their cultures and needs and the impact such work will have on their communities. There was acknowledgement that, while quality relations with ILOs are important to most or many MSOs, they have not always lived up to their aspirations or responsibilities. They struggle with the conflict 'between achieving something quickly and following through on a principle that is strong but time consuming and resource heavy'. This also applies to the need for outreach by key sector organisations which work primarily with the more well established constituencies and national organisations such as women, youth, rural and disability. Because they operate mostly through the maintenance of large databases, ILOs tend to fall outside the 'radar' if they are not registered, recognised or visible in the mainstream.

It is often assumed that organisations that employ community development strategies are more participatory and have better relations with ILOs as a result. Yet such organisations do not always include ILO or community representation at management or board level, despite their ethos and practices. Similarly, MSOs involved in service provision, policy or advocacy work (and which typically do not use participatory strategies) often do, even though they have less engagement with them in their actual work. In many cases, however, consultation with and direct participation of ILOs and community members are not always necessary, worth while or appropriate in MSOs' work. They may not have sufficient resources to properly support this type of working relationship (e.g. paying for travel, child care, and so on). The high level of burnout and over-commitment among key ILO representatives stemming from such in-depth involvement must also be taken into consideration. And, while community expertise may be necessary to inform the project or service, it may not be necessary or appropriate to support the creation of an ILO for the purpose or as part of the project in question.

Yet, having said this, it should also be noted that, in this study, these types of organisations tended to have little or to have mediated contact with ILOs or their communities. And, in the contexts of the interview discussions, those MSOs that did not employ capacity-building or community development principles seemed less reflexive and less articulate concerning the nuances of the challenges and contributions made with regard to cultural diversity in the sector. Thus, on one hand, community development approaches are not necessarily always empowering, and, on the other, just because ILOs or community representatives may not be involved with MSO work from start to finish does not mean the practice or provision is ill informed or paternalistic. These issues must, however, be considered against the backdrop of the problematic relations between ILOs and MSOs, and their implications for ILOs' success in the sector.

In contrast to the extensive involvement of MSOs with immigrant issues, communities and organisations, for most funders the grant work they undertake and the policy infrastructure within which they operate are quite new. In some cases, for statutory-based funders especially, the branch, agency or even the post they occupy has been only recently established. Combined with the issue-specific nature of their remits, and the generally distant relationship between government and the sector overall, it is not surprising that such staff may lack the in-depth knowledge of both the sector and immigrant/'new' minority ethnic communities. This lack of familiarity both leads to and is exacerbated by the tendency of funders to maintain a greater level of distance in their engagement with ILOs. This distance impedes the development of closer relations and the effectiveness of the funding process as a whole. It also has important implications for ILO organisation and development, in terms of how ILOs are viewed and – most important – assessed.

Such circumstances seem to have led to the funding process being seen as adversarial, and, as a result, the participation of ILOs (and other MSOs) in the application process is kept to a minimum. For example, members of these organisations would not generally be included on advisory or evaluation committees. Interviewees from funding agencies felt that this is necessary to ensure transparency – and that it would be awkward to excuse a member of the committee if a conflict of interest arose while grant proposals were being reviewed. One interviewee noted that it would be too difficult for those left on the panel to turn it down, even when the representative was absent from the discussion. While most funders provide at least some sort of pre-application information or consultation, in some cases funders would decline to provide any assistance in the application process for fear that such involvement would not hold up to 'public scrutiny'.

One of the consistent problems facing ILOs in the Republic of Ireland has been their inability to attract funding. The funders interviewed for this research tend to prefer to grant resources to projects involving partnerships and joint efforts, both to help streamline their own work as well as to encourage the sharing of expertise and long-term sustainability. Moreover, given the limitations of their available budgets, they seek to support organisations that they know can co-ordinate efforts in a much larger area and reach more communities to ensure added value. As a result, interviewees identified such organisations as immigrant women's groups and partnerships between immigrant- and majority-led women's groups, for example, as being particularly rewarding to fund or effective in the grant-making process. This is because they have well established participatory structures and, as such, work in coalition with other women's organisations, do outreach as part of their work, and typically address a wide range of issues.

Such discourse around issues of 'efficiency' and 'accountability' are common with respect to the sector as a whole. However, at this time, many funders who manage schemes that are central to ILOs lack even the most basic knowledge about immigrant/'new' minority ethnic communities. They cannot distinguish between the different organisations representing them – other than those who are particularly well known. The lack of engagement beyond mailing lists and information seminars perpetuates the development of a group of 'usual suspects' which constrains the growth of ILO participation and innovation, and undermines the effectiveness of investment.

Finally, relationships and collective efforts among ILOs, particularly regarding the establishment of a national umbrella body, have been the subject of ongoing debate. Only a few participants claimed to have strong, ongoing relations with other ILOs. While all have a high regard for each other's work and support each other whenever possible, the struggle to survive competition over available resources inhibit the development of stronger working relations. Representatives are aware that while the growing number and diversity of their organisations are an indication of the richness and value of their work, they also pose a potential problem in terms of long-term success and political effectiveness. This is made more complex by the fact that new minority ethnic communities are themselves in the process of formation and have yet to cultivate clear identities and constituencies. One representative observed that, for example, there may be a group of organisations which might be considered '"all Eastern European" but even those cultures have little in common even at the level of religious practice, different languages ... The only common element is that we are all foreigners, but this element is not strong enough to unite us.'

There is general agreement that a national-level body is necessary. However, participants were concerned about the ability to maintain equity, accountability, independence and distinct identities whilst being able to achieve a common vision or mission and avoiding the imposition of agendas by individuals. Ultimately the main obstacle to the advancement of such structures has stemmed from the stresses of organisational survival. To date, there has simply not been enough time or resources to pursue the establishment of an additional organisation. The lack of a national-level representative forum, however, renders ILOs and communities unable to take full advantage of the existing social partnership structure, leaving them subject to the mediation by other established NGOs and agencies of their interests.

The impact and wider role of immigrant-led civic mobilisation

'Institutionalised underdevelopment' and the reach of ILOs
Overall, MSOs and funders observed that ILOs are just starting up and need to build up structures and resources before they can achieve independence. Their current struggles reflect what most felt are developmental stages common to all community and voluntary organisations – which usually means starting at the bottom. Many interviewees felt that ILOs must form their own identities as groups to create the sense of confidence and solidarity that underpins collective action. Such coalescence, it was felt, is necessary for ILOs to move beyond a community focus to broader equality and discrimination issues. This is important, as policy responses to these issues are evolving from being 'add-ons' to more integrated approaches. These stakeholders observed that ILOs need to develop mixed groups and intercultural models or alliances, otherwise

they will fail to harness the common ground that exists within other policy areas and groups. Such strategies, in turn, help build strong bridges that contribute to the mainstreaming of new/immigrant community issues as well as engagement with wider sector politics and debates.

This raises the question of what the 'wider' issues are to which ILOs should focus their efforts. MSOs and funders noted that issues pertaining to 'difference' and 'identity' will always be a concern for people who are making a life in a new place and are faced with the challenge of being accepted. But, while racism is therefore a key and underpinning issue, anti-racism, as an umbrella struggle or campaign, may not be enough. Many across stakeholder groups consider anti-racism to be unproductively 'negative' and unrepresentative of the cross-cutting nature of new minority ethnic communities' struggles. They also express concern about their issues and contributions being ghettoised within the race relations remit. As one ILO representative noted,

> It's very important for people from ethnic minorities to live a normal life … because always we are involved in talking about racism and criticising the state and criticising others – but maybe we don't take part outside these activities. For example, how many of us are involved in environmental issues … with antisocial behaviour in our areas? There are many meetings being called for such things and I always go and people are surprised to see me there but I want to make a point: they shouldn't assume that we shouldn't take part in these things. I think with more time we will be accepted and people will realise that we are here, just living normal lives. All issues which concern the wider community concern us.

Single issues – asylum seekers' right to work or the rights of Irish-born children and their families, for example – can provide a solid basis for consensus among ILOs and other groups. Broader platforms, such as social inclusion, for example, can create a common thread across ILO aims and activities, as they involve issues concerning both the politics of identity/difference as well as overall quality of life.

Most MSOs and funders are at pains to emphasise the importance of ILOs' work, their expertise and the value of their contribution. Such statements, however, are often followed by the observation that ILOs are, in some way 'deficient' and unable to jump successfully through the institutional 'hoops' necessary to achieve funding, sustainability or other measures of 'development'. There is a striking difference between the perceptions, expectations and evaluations of ILOs among the different players. ILOs identify organisational survival in itself as a main goal and emphasise they are happy simply to be still in existence. Because they are doing so in what they characterise as a hostile environment, they strive to maintain their independence at all costs, typically with little more than their dedication, expertise and good fortune. This has led, in part, to the proliferation of organisations that are preoccupied with community-specific issues, and which are unable to engage fully with the wider sector. Yet this scenario was identified by MSOs as constituting an 'early phase' of development from which ILOs will eventually move on. MSOs see partnerships and mentorships as both natural and necessary means of achieving more 'mature' civil society engagement. They did not, however, tend to view such relations as a gateway to exploitation, circumvention and the theft of ideas, as many ILOs do. Funders tended to emphasise the need for accountability and representativeness – and the achievement of the ever elusive criteria of 'the professional organisation' in their calculation of ILO achievement.

ILOs are, thus, caught in a Catch 22 situation. They need to have a proven track record to obtain funding, but there are few financial supports or structures of engagement for establishing it. While this is not a situation unique to immigrant communities, it takes on a particular resonance when one considers the relative immaturity of policy infrastructures in relation to immigration, race equality and the third sector, which converge to create a condition of 'institutionalised underdevelopment' for ILOs. The fact that the 'hoops' themselves may be misaligned in relation to ILOs' position and trajectory is often overlooked. As such, at this time, ILOs remained locked in a focus on micro-organisational and community-level issues. From the perspective of ILO founders and staff, their avenues to alliance building and involvement in broader coalitions are limited, if not closed down. To make matters worse, the lack of a national-level representative minority ethnic/immigrant organisation in key policy-making fora, which is necessary to help change these circumstances (and other policy gaps) cannot be achieved in the absence of strong individual organisations.

Intercultural capital

The difficulties outlined above suggest an absence of reflexivity on the parts of mainstream sector stakeholders with respect to the complex ways in which ethnic diversification is reshaping Irish civil society and their own roles in this process. However, interviews with MSO members (and funders from Northern Ireland) also revealed the extent to which immigrant civic mobilisation has in fact set in motion a process of intercultural transformation that belies its current material and political limitations. When asked about what they have gained from working with immigrant-led organisations and communities, mainstream stakeholders identified changes at personal, organisational and national levels.[17] The ways in which people were affected personally by their work with ILOs also stimulated reflexivity in terms of their organisations' principles and practices. Working with ILOs required them to stand back and reflect – to be open to accepting criticism and the challenge of changing and adapting their practices. In doing so MSOs reaped significant rewards that enhanced their own capacity, effectiveness and strength of representation. Moreover, as one interviewee noted, 'if we can support them to represent themselves and to take on the role of advocates for their own communities, that makes the rest of the system work better'. This type of narrative demonstrates the ways in which 'capacity building' can go in both, or many, directions.

Participants also described the ways in which immigrant civic mobilisation has also had important consequences for the conceptualisations of Irish national identity and the nature of a multi-ethnic Irish society. Participants noted that interaction with ILOs through sector activities is 'helping us get over ourselves' and rise above 'parochial' issues, combating negative images and racism and increasing cross-cultural understanding. It has engendered 'new learning about ourselves', for example by reopening debates about Irish emigration and its impact on Irish society. According to interviewees, ILO-related work draws attention to the 'wider world' – the rethinking the global order as well as Ireland's role within it. It is a reminder that the global has arrived here: 'they've changed the perception … from… "we only deal with people from, for example, from African countries through the charity box"'. Immigrant civic mobilisation has served to emphasise the 'multiplicity of society', and cultivate understandings of the ways 'people have different requirements in terms of sustaining their local communities and themselves'.

In terms of politics and policy making, sector stakeholders felt that ILOs are generating new role models and providing better ways of addressing issues that are important to everyone. Engagement with ILOs leads to different perspectives at all levels of social need, getting people to address the issues with more complexity, and broadens areas of interest within community development. They also help make other organisations challenge their own assumptions and working practices, both in terms of the specific issue of meeting minority ethnic community needs, but also in relation to broader issues of inclusion and exclusion.

Discussions with sector stakeholders highlighted the extent to which the ability to address and negotiate cultural differences is fast becoming part of the 'work' of MSOs and agencies. It is increasingly a central component of their legitimacy and effectiveness, with the resulting changes becoming part of the normal process through which sector practices evolve and are cultivated. As ILO staff and their community members learn the ropes and become more effective actors through their engagement in the sector, other stakeholders not only expand their work repertoires but become more knowledgeable and confident in their cross-community and intercultural understanding and skills. This growth then positively influences their relationships with ILOs.

This 'intercultural capital' implies going beyond developing 'under-standing' and 'inclusion' of cultural differences (as is most common in sector work) and cultivating 'trust' on the basis of doing so. It is a process whereby those differences stimulate reflexivity concerning taken-for-granted principles and practices by those involved, and which lead to change at personal as well as organisational levels. It is also a process upon which both 'majority' *and* immigrant actors are dependent for their success and viability. In this fashion, the measure of intercultural capital, along with its economic and political consequences, becomes a funda-mental element, indicator and positive outcome of integration and essen-tial to the growth of a healthy multi-ethnic and democratic society

Conclusion

This examination of the development and impact of immigrant-led civil society organisations sheds light on (1) the formation and incorporation of 'new' minority ethnic communities (2) the nature of the third sector as a whole, and (3) the evolution of a multi-ethnic society in Ireland at a number of different levels. First, immigrant civic mobilisation demon-strates the potential of the sector to provide spaces and opportunities for the most marginalised to assert themselves and contribute to the public sphere. It also highlights the impact of the cultural and political histories of the sector on civil society in general and on the formation of ethnic minority communities in particular as it is advanced through civic activi-ties. Here, the role of the state also becomes clear in both promoting and impeding integration, as well as shaping the formation of minority ethnic communities through its regulation of sector actors and activities.

Second, the research highlights the ways immigrant civic mobilisa-tion can effect concrete changes in sector practices. ILO experiences draw attention to the variability of definitions, strategies and impacts associated with such central and taken-for-granted practices and princi-ples as 'community development', 'partnership', and so on. They raise the issue of the ongoing necessity for self-reflection, even among seasoned practitioners/actors and the encouragement of 'learning organisations'. Finally, the interviewees' views and experiences illustrate the links between community stability, civil society activity and effective policy making and implementation. These links are typically overlooked in the general discussions of social capital and active citizenship currently taking place. Innovations in the practice of interculturalism – and the effective transition to a multi-ethnic society more generally – are reliant upon both immigrant community mobilisation and empowerment and the development of effective structures of engagement and resourcing necessary to sustain them.

Overall, these findings also speak to a number of popular debates concerning citizenship and social capital – and debates concerning immigration which are often couched in such language. ILO activities show clearly the inseparability of the rights of citizenship and their associated responsibilities. They also illustrate the ways in which civic mobilisation that is undertaken by new communities in order to realise their due entitlements goes hand-in-hand with living up to the duties of citizenship – such as making contributions to the civic community. These two strands are often constructed as being mutually exclusive in criticisms that accuse immigrants of demanding rights and entitlements without being willing to fulfil their obligations to Irish society.

The work discussed here helps to deconstruct populist discourses about the cultivation and preservation of common Irish and European values and beliefs, commitments and identities.[18] These norms and constructs are often based on unstated assumptions of a fundamental 'difference' that exists between Irish/European people and recent immigrants, and that immigrants are unwilling or unable to 'integrate'. The research therefore also highlights the necessity of moving beyond essentialist constructions of the immigrant-as-always-only-negative-projection-of-self-and-nation. This is important, as such binary structures and adversarial constructions of difference are implicated in popular expressions of cultural racism and social theory alike.

The analysis of ILO development adds further analytical resources upon which to base assessment and critique of the notions and implications for policy and practice of social capital that are increasingly being incorporated within Irish political discourse. Zetter *et al.* have argued, for example, that popularised scholarship concerning social capital fails to consider the impact of wider structural obstacles to participation and presents a romanticised picture of social capital. As such, this work tends to obscure the realities in which the development of social capital is typically more the product of crisis and social breakdown, and desperation on the parts of immigrant communities.[19] The focus on the contemporary processes of ethnic diversification and introduction of concepts that draw on interculturalist dynamics demonstrate the need to expand the conceptualisation and analysis of social capital. This shift serves to centre the need to respond more effectively to the complexity of ethnic and cultural diversification within agendas addressing globalisation. It also brings to the fore the ways in which the development of the social and economic 'capital' of immigrant/'new' minority ethnic communities is inextricably linked with that of all communities on the island, and to the cultivation of the national resources necessary for Ireland to be a successful global actor.

It is therefore essential to shift the focus of debate away from the exclusive, issue-specific (albeit important) debates concerning racism and border control, where immigrants/'new' minority ethnic communities are regarded only as guests of the state, threats to national security or victims of racism. As such, discussion and debate regarding ethnic diversity, immigration and the development of 'new' minority ethnic communities must be 'joined up' with the development and implementation of policy initiatives relating to equality and anti-discrimination, social inclusion and cohesion more broadly. Considering their efforts as new sector actors provides an important opportunity not only to examine the challenges related to ethnic diversity. Working through issues concerning immigration, ethnic diversification and integration shifts the basis for official and popular discourses concerning national belonging and stimulates much needed reflection on 'who "we" are' as a polity, a country, a world player, and the social and institutional expectations and demands that come with them. Such mobilisation also speaks to the general 'health' of Irish civil society and democracy, invigorating discussions and debates concerning 'active citizenship' and participative democracy by posing pressing questions over what 'citizenship' means in the present global era.

Notes

This chapter is based on research funded by the Royal Irish Academy Third Sector Research Programme and the Joseph Rowntree Charitable Trust. The final report, A. Feldman, D. Ndakengerwa, A. Nolan and C. Frese, *Diversity and Civil Society in Ireland: A North–South Comparison of the Role of Immigrant/'New' Minority Ethnic Community and Voluntary Organisations* (Dublin: MCRI, Geary Institute, University College, 2005), was published by the Migration and Citizenship Research Initiative (www.ucd.ie/geary/research/mcri.html) and is available on line.

1 The fieldwork for this project was conducted between May 2003 and February 2004. It included interviews with twenty-three ILOs, eighteen MSOs and twelve funders. While interviews were conducted in Northern Ireland and the Republic of Ireland, this chapter is limited to discussion of the Republic only.

2 Y. Soysal, *Limits of Citizenship: Migrants and Postnational Membership in Europe* (Chicago: University of Chicago Press, 1994), p. 164.

3 Ibid., pp. 13–28. E. Jelin, 'Citizenship and Alterity', *Latin American Perspectives*, 129: 30 (2003), p. 316.

4 G. Lewis, '"Do not go gently ..." Terrains of Citizenship and Landscapes of the Personal', in G. Lewis (ed.), *Citizenship: Personal Lives and Social Policy* (Buckingham: Open University Press, 2004), p. 3; Jelin, 'Citizenship and Alterity', p. 310; J. Rundell, 'Strangers, Citizens And Outsiders: Otherness, Multiculturalism and the Cosmopolitan Imaginary in Mobile Societies', *Thesis Eleven*, 78 (2004), p. 89.

5 National Economic and Social Forum, *The Policy Implications of Social Capital* (Dublin: NESF, 2003), p. 3.

6 Lewis, *Citizenship*, p. 29; S. Castles and A. Davidson, *Citizenship and Migration: Globalisation and the Politics of Belonging* (New York: Routledge, 2000), pp. 130, 82; Rundell, 'Strangers, Citizens and Outsiders', p. 92.

7 Soysal, *Limits of Citizenship*, p. 2, 166.

8 Castles and Davidson, *Citizenship and Migration*, p. 130.

9 R. Zetter, D. Griffiths, N. Sigona, D. Flynn, T. Pasha and R. Beynon, 'Immigration, Social Cohesion and Social Capital: What are the Links?' Concepts Paper (York: Joseph Rowntree Charitable Trust, 2005), pp. 1, 9; R. Penninx and M. Martiniello, 'Integration Processes and Policies: State of the Art and Lessons', in R. Penninx, K. Kraal, M. Martiniello and S. Vertovec (eds), *Citizenship in European Cities: Immigrants, Local Politics and Integration Policies* (Aldershot: Ashgate, 2004), p. 141.

10 Lewis, *Citizenship*, p. 28.

11 Soysal, *Limits of Citizenship*, p. 29–44; Penninx and Martiniello, *Integration Processes*, pp. 142–4; Castles and Davidson, *Citizenship and Migration*, p. 129.

12 Rundell, 'Strangers, citizens and outsiders', p. 166.

13 See B. Ahern, speech presented at the launch of the NESF report *The Policy Implications of Social Capital*, Government Buildings, Dublin, 29 October 2003; N. Treacy, address, annual meeting of the Clann Credo Social Investors, Alexander Hotel, Dublin, 6 April 2005; A. O'Connor, 'Taoiseach anxious about "death of the community"', *Sunday Business Post*, www.sbpost.ie/post/pages/p/story.aspx-qqqid=9640–qqqx=1.asp.

14 C. Harris (ed.), *The Report of the Democracy Commission: Engaging Citizens* (Dublin: TASC, 2005), p. 6; NESF, *Policy Implications of Social Capital*, p. 5.

15 Six organisations were established through the joint efforts of people from both immigrant and Irish communities, but are immigrant-led. In order to maintain confidentiality for those who participated in the study, this breakdown is necessarily vague.

16 See A. Feldman, C. Frese and T. Yousif, *Research, Development and Critical Intercuturalism* (Dublin: Social Science Research Centre, University College, 2002), and A. Feldman, *Developing a Code of Practice for Research and Development Work with Minority Ethnic Communities* (Dublin: Social Science Research Centre, University College, 2003).

17 See Feldman *et al.*, *Diversity and Civil Society*, pp. 73–6.

18 Yet such primordialist claims of national identity and difference with respect to foreign-born immigrants and citizens often stands in stark contrast to people's inability to provide clear articulations of what constitutes an Irish national identity or to ascribe to a 'European' identity (see A. Feldman, 'Racism and Belonging in Diaspora Space: Changing Irish Identities and 'Race'-making in the 'Age of Migration', in N. Yuval-Davis, K. Kannabiran and U. Vieten (eds), *Situating Contemporary Politics of Belonging* (London: Sage, 2006)).

19 Zetter *et al.*, 'Immigration and Social Capital', p. 9.

14

Integration models and choices

Piaras Mac Éinrí

European peripheral countries such as Ireland, Portugal, Spain, Italy and Greece have all changed in the relatively recent past from being states with strong traditions of emigration to being receiving societies, experiencing substantial, diverse and ongoing inward migration. Because the phenomenon is recent, they tend to lack the landscape of ideology, policy, legislation, services, support structures and existing migrant and ethnic communities comparable to those which have been in place for decades now in core European receiving societies such as France, Belgium, the Netherlands, Germany and Britain. The characteristic feature of the latter group of countries, however different their policies, is that they have experienced relatively large-scale immigration, at least since the close of the Second World War, and that multi-generational ethnic minorities are therefore a reality for a comparatively long time.

In the case of Ireland in particular, recent levels of immigration are striking. To cite just one statistic, 133,258 social insurance numbers were issued to immigrant workers from the new accession states between 1 May 2004 and 30 September 2005.[1] It is not possible to say how many have remained in the country and the limited evidence available suggests a high turnover rate.[2] In the United Kingdom, a country whose population is fifteen times that of Ireland, the figure for the same period was 293,000.[3] To put it another way, the United States receives up to one million immigrants per annum under its various visa programmes[4] but the Irish figure just quoted would be the equivalent on an annualised basis of 6.75 million for the United States. Moreover, that statistic of 130,000 does not include persons who migrated to Ireland from outside the European Union with work permits (27,136 for January–December 2005),[5] or work visas/authorisations;[6] international students; workers and individuals from the other fourteen 'old' EU member states; and the non-economically active spouses and families of any of these categories of migrants. A final interesting comparison is with New Zealand, a country whose population is almost identical to that of Ireland but where the annual rate of immigration in 2004/2005, including family reunification, was 48,815.[7]

It is clear that Ireland is experiencing particularly dramatic rates of immigration at present but as yet, while immigrant *flows* are substantial, we do not know how this will translate into immigrant *stocks*, i.e. the portion of the permanent resident population composed of people born outside Ireland. At the very least, however, we may state with confidence that Ireland is no longer a country where immigration can be regarded as a short-term or transient issue. The country has now definitively joined the European mainstream as a society where a population of mixed ethnic backgrounds is the norm.

The debate in new immigration societies such as Ireland has naturally focused up to now on who gets in and on the conditions of entry. But there is now an increasing focus on *integration* – what happens to people once they are here? Will they be expected, as used to be said about Ireland's various immigrants in earlier centuries, to become 'more Irish than the Irish themselves'? Or will new immigrant countries such as Ireland move towards a more multicultural model? If they do, what are the core values which all members of society might be expected to accept and how can conflicts be negotiated and consensus be arrived at?

The challenges posed by these issues are compounded by the fact that Ireland shares the traditions of the European nation-state, often defining itself in exclusionary ways and grounded in cultural, linguistic and historical experiences reflecting what has been called a WHISC (white, heterosexual, Irish, settled, Catholic) discourse.[8] Tracy quotes the well known Irish journalist John Waters:

> I think there was always this official insistence on the idea that, you know, you kind of had to tick off on your list of qualities, you know; Catholicism – yes, nationalism – yes, GAA – yes, Irish language – yes, you know, that the more of these boxes you ticked the more Irish you were.[9]

The WHISC is a social construct rather than a fact and does not adequately represent the realities of a country that, contrary to myth, has always had some immigration. As explained by Tracy:

> It is possible that some WHISCs actually do exist in Ireland. However, this is not the point, the reality is that in debates the term Irish or Irishness refers to the WHISC. This prototypical WHISC, much like the WASP in the USA, has become the 'invisible centre' in discourses of Irishness. I have chosen to locate these characteristics and created an acronym for the most commonly recognised attributes of Irishness because these characteristics are taken for granted.[10]

For Tracy such a hegemonic discourse certainly makes it difficult to develop a new and more inclusive definition of Irishness.

The European context – two different models of integration?

In looking at approaches to integration in Europe in the present day it is possible crudely to distinguish between two models. One is assimilationist, the other aims for a certain degree of multiculturalism. Although no one country could be said to be entirely multiculturalist or entirely assimilationist, most can be located somewhere along a spectrum; a few may even reflect policy approaches based on both of these two perspectives. For convenience, and bearing recent events in mind in particular, we may call the assimilationist perspective the French model, even though France has attempted in recent years to adopt an approach to integration which purports to incorporate a multicultural element. In the European context we can refer to the multicultural perspective as the British model, even though Britain has not formally legislated for multiculturalism (unlike Canada and Australia) and one could equally have chosen a country such as the Netherlands as another European example of a multicultural approach. I shall be arguing that the differences between the two models, in the European context anyway, are more apparent than real.

One might argue that a third model has also existed – the *Gastarbeiter* model, which denied the reality of immigration and saw the migrant as temporary and merely of economic value. Such an approach has most typically been associated with Germany, although all European states have used variations of this model, such as the temporary programmes for seasonal agricultural workers found in a range of countries. Moreover, European countries have tended to see the presence of migrants as a threat and have been slow to extend the same framework of rights and entitlements as are available to citizens. Thus Greece makes it extremely difficult for a migrant to become politically integrated through citizenship. It is not proposed to deal with such issues here, however, because such approaches, by definition, reflect an anti-integration standpoint.

The choice of France as a point of departure is appropriate, as the assimilationist *v.* multicultural argument can also be seen in terms of eighteenth-century Enlightenment universalism, on one hand, and its nineteenth-century opposite, Romantic particularism, on the other. The emphasis of the Enlightenment philosophers was on the emancipation, legally guaranteed by a contract between state and citizen, of the atomised *individual* subject, within a universalist framework of citizenship. The nineteenth century saw a reaction in the form of an essentialising discourse of *community*, most frequently expressed in the various movements for political self-determination but also found in the cultural domain with the emphasis on the *Volk* as constituting a community of people whose shared history, culture and language bound them together. Malik sees the contemporary debate in similar terms, with a universalist discourse of equality and rights being opposed to an emphasis on the celebration of difference. He argues that 'multiculturalism as lived experience enriches our lives. But multiculturalism as a political ideology has helped create a tribal Britain with no political or moral centre'.[11]

For him this marks the failure of the equality agenda and its replacement by the notion of the acceptance of difference and the reification of boundaries behind a politics of identity which militates against real equality.

Multiculturalism, Jacoby concludes, 'has become ... the ideology of an era without ideology'. What began in the 1960s as a way of organising against oppression had ended up by the 1990s as way of rationalising the impotence of the left. Romanticism was born in the late eighteenth century out of the fear of the radical change unleashed by the Enlightenment and the French revolution and out of the desire for the safe anchor of ancient traditions. In the late twentieth century it was the fading of the possibilities of social transformation that led many radicals, albeit unwittingly, back to a Romantic view of the world.[12]

However, others have argued that the failure to recognise identity is itself a constitutive factor in the type of alienation experienced, say, by British Muslims and which led in turn to the rejection by a minority within that minority of the values of mainstream British society. Such a view is dominant in British official thinking.[13] More recently British official attitudes have tended to emphasise the need for a revalorisation of core values of 'Britishness'. Examples of such an approach include American-style citizenship ceremonies,[14] compulsory tests designed to explore immigrant knowledge of British values[15] and a new emphasis on Britishness stressing 'liberty, responsibility and fairness' as central values.[16]

Ireland is seeking to formulate a way forward against the backdrop of a rapidly developing pan-European debate on these issues, which includes but is not confined to Britain, France, the Netherlands and Sweden. This debate seeks to engage with the challenge of managing societies composed of ever more diverse communities – diverse in terms of culture, ethnic origin, religion, language, custom and practice. Whereas France has maintained an officially assimilationist approach – notably in its insistence on the secularism of the public domain – there has been sustained criticism of the multicultural model in countries such as Britain and the Netherlands, with a belief that such societies have become multicultural but not intercultural and that multiculturalism may itself be part of the problem.

Debate in Ireland is, as yet, at an early stage, although some have argued[17] that the country is adopting, *de facto*, an unthinking and untheorised version of the UK model, derived in turn from the Canadian model and the 'politics of recognition' advocated by Charles Taylor.[18] I propose to look briefly at some of the issues thrown up by these debates, notably in France and the United Kingdom, and to consider their possible relevance to Ireland. Developments at EU level, where the issue of integration is rapidly moving up the political agenda and a platform of 'common basic principles' (CBPs) has been adopted, will also be considered.

My central point is that a politics of radical multiculturalism is possible and even essential *provided* that it is constructed as a multi-locational interrogation of the central hegemonic discourses governing Irish society and of its constituent parts, including minority communities themselves. Multiculturalism need not inevitably lead to reification, as Shohat and Stam remind us:

> The celebration of multiculturalism and the critique of Eurocentrism are for us inseparable concepts. Multiculturalism without the critique of Eurocentrism runs the risk of being merely accretive – a shopping mall summa of the world's cultures – while the critique of Eurocentrism without multiculturalism runs the risk of simply inverting rather than profoundly unsettling and rearticulating existing hierarchies. The goal of what we call 'polycentric' multiculturalism is to eliminate, as far as possible and in our own specific sphere of action, the long-term cultural legacies of Eurocentrism and white supremacy.[19]

Such an approach is necessarily disruptive, as it subverts the comfort of received wisdoms and traditions for a significant part of the majority population as well as for the 'gatekeepers' of minority communities. It is also potentially liberatory in so far as it may allow the creation of new spaces where the voices of all the people can be heard, including the voices of the suppressed *within* mainstream society. But the disruption and re-inscribing of new possibilities of identity can have meaning only if it is accompanied by an equally radical emphasis on rights and equality and on articulating and implementing the core values of a civilised, diverse society, sensitive to the various realities of gender, ethnicity, age, ability, class and culture.

The French model

In 1791 the Comte de Clermont-Tonnerre outlined the principles that subsequently pertained to French republican responses to integration:

> Il faut tout refuser aux juifs comme nation et tout leur accorder comme individus; il faut qu'ils ne fassent dans l'État ni un corps politique, ni un ordre : il faut qu'ils soient individuellement citoyens.[20]

> The Jews must be refused everything as a nation but granted everything as individuals; they must not form a political grouping or specific category in the State; they must become citizens individually.

The meaning of this statement – a radical one for the time, in view of the equal treatment accorded to Jews by the new French republic in contrast to widespread antisemitism, discrimination and ghettoisation elsewhere – is clear. Citizenship, the foundation of all freedoms, is essentially a contract between the individual and the state. The individual's ethnicity (which is probably as close as one can get to the term *nation* in the sense in which it was used by Clermont-Tonnerre) or culture, or religion, is a matter for the private domain. Thus the 2004 law forbidding the wearing of ostentatious signs of religious identity, such as the *hijab*, in state schools follows perfectly the republican logic of a neutral public domain in which religion is an exclusively private affair.[21] Moreover the law was supported by the majority of French parliamentarians, on the left as well as on the right.

French republican citizenship is seen, then, as universalist and egalitarian; so much so that in France statistical data-gathering exercises such as the census do not even include a category for ethnic identity or colour. One is simply French or foreign. In the strict sense, therefore, there cannot be such a concept as a minority ethnic community in France. One may speak of *social* exclusion or poverty, but the fact that it might have something to do with the ethnic backgrounds of the poor and the marginalised is not to be mentioned. The ideological denial described here can lead to a rather unreal climate of public and political debate. The philosophy underlying French universalist republicanism is admirable, embodying as it does the principles of *liberté, égalité* and *fraternité*. But there can be no denying that in practice many French-born citizens of minority ethnic background, especially those whose families come from North or sub-Saharan Africa, do experience systematic marginalisation and exclusion in French society.

Yet the denial of the reality of ethnic discrimination is pervasive in French society. People are regularly described as 'immigrants' even though they may be second- or third-generation French citizens of ethnic minority origin. The use of such terminology is one way of marking their continuing exclusion from the mainstream. The bitter experience of the *harkis*[22] is also worth noting. Although they had risked everything and ultimately had to leave an Algeria which did not want them, their reception in France was cold at best and frequently hostile. Nearly two generations later their children's children increasingly make common cause with other *beurs*,[23] young French people of North African origin who see themselves as socially and racially excluded from French society.

In the French case there are thus a number of problems to be addressed. First, racism and discrimination in France are quite widespread, as indeed they are in most societies. Exclusion, racism and discrimination are all facts of life, yet the universalist doctrine can entail a denial of these facts. Second, the *non-dit* or non-naming of ethnicity as a constitutive element of social exclusion exacerbates the situation and makes it more difficult to address it effectively. For instance, minority ethnic representation in the French police, political classes and media is very modest, but some kind of US-style affirmative action programme to address these lacunae would not fit with the philosophy that individuals, and not communities, are equal in law and in society. It is perhaps ironic that the only politician who has proposed an affirmative action programme is Nicolas Sarkozy, the hard-line Interior Minister whose inflammatory language and actions poured fuel on the fire in the 2006 riots in France. Thirdly, the 'politics of identity' may well, as suggested earlier, dominate much of the debate about these matters in the English-speaking world, privileging the significance of personal and communal identities to an excessive extent over, say, socio-economic status. But, by contrast, it is all too easy for members of ethnic minorities in France to have the sense that their cultures, languages and values receive no recognition or respect from the republic. Finally, the French political class, reflecting a highly centralised tradition of governance, is itself somewhat remote and divorced from everyday challenges and realities. It is customary in Ireland, for instance, to decry the rather clientelist and localist model of politics which we favour, but sometimes there are advantages. It is quite likely that, faced with events such as those in the *banlieux* in France, an Irish *Taoiseach* (Prime Minister) would have been seen the following day on the front line, talking and seeking to mediate with all sides. This is in contrast to M. Sarkozy, who tends in these situations to be seen in police stations, but not on the streets.

In so far as the French approach has shifted at all, it has moved from an emphasis on *insertion*, an underlying assumption that immigrants would simply arrive and ultimately become assimilated to French identity and French life, with no particular effort being made on the part of the state and/or mainstream society, to *intégration*. This term does not have the same meaning as it does in English but at least implies an active commitment by the state and society to engage with new migrants in a more respectful way, recognising the specificities of their various identities even if there continues to be a certain insistence on the primacy of French culture. The work of state agencies such as the *Fonds d'action et de soutien pour l'intégration et la lutte contre les discriminations* represents a very substantial commitment of state support and state funding – more than €157 million annually – to ethnic minorities and to programmes focused on improving living conditions and opportunities for people from such communities.[24] Nevertheless, traditional universalist republicanism, probably the majority view in France, sees the reification of ethnicity as a major (probably *the* major) danger to social cohesion:

> En fait, l'intégration est le processus en cours ; son aboutissement sera l'assimilation. Si ce mot est, à tort, devenu suspect, il n'a jamais voulu dire que l'on ne garde pas, dans l'ordre du privé, ses fidélités religieuses et la mémoire de ses origines.[25]

> In fact, integration is the ongoing process of which the end-point will be assimilation. Although the word has, wrongly, become suspect, it was never intended to mean that one could not keep, in the private domain, one's religious loyalty and the memory of where one came from.

The arrival of substantial numbers of immigrants in post-World War II France was not in itself a new event. More than any other European country, France had been a country of immigration for a century and a half. But the machine of assimilation had previously proved adept in turning European white Catholic migrants into mainstream French citizens,[26] at least in two generations, in a heavily centralist society with its own key institutions of integration, notably universal conscription, a common Church and a highly centralised and dogmatic statist ideology, which probably found its highest expression in the educational system.

This discourse of universalism was not, however, the only one in nineteenth-century France. A significant element of the French population did not accept the values of the republic more than a century after its creation. Catholic particularism and antisemitism were important factors, but the key one was French colonialism, embraced as much on the left as the right of the political spectrum. The discourse of universalism was soon undermined by an emphasis on the alleged inherent inferiority of France's colonial subjects, who had a separate legal status and limited rights. In the case of Algeria (annexed in 1830) non-white inhabitants were 'nationals' but not 'citizens' even though Algeria was technically regarded as part of metropolitan France and not as an occupied colony.

How was this accomplished and what is its legacy? A newly published collection, *La Fracture coloniale*,[27] throws valuable light on this issue. In the case of Algeria a clear distinction was made in 1862 between *français de France* (French people born in France) and *sujets français* (French subjects). The latter were also referred to as *indigènes* (persons born in the territory), although it is interesting to note that an 1870 decree specifically and exceptionally granted full citizenship to Jewish *indigènes*. From the outset, therefore, French colonialism embodied a differentialist racism which could only subvert French republican egalitarianism, not only in the colonies, but ultimately in the home country as well. Thus a law of 1889 on French nationality was limited to France itself and did not extend, even within continental France, to the children of *indigènes*. An internal 1925 report from the Conseil Supérieur des Colonies was unambiguous:

> On se rend compte qu'un Français, né en France, de parents français, dont les ancêtres sont toujours demeurés sur le sol qu'ont cultivé leur pères, n'est pas de même nature que le sujet qui est né dans un pays nouvellement annexé, bien que ce pays fasse partie intégrante du territoire nationale. Il en diffère par l'origine ethnique, l'hérédité, les coutumes, la mentalité, le caractère et le degré de civilisation. L'un est sujet de la collectivité dominante, conquérante, l'autre sujet d'une collectivité dominée, conquise ... On peut dire qu'aucune des races qui habitent nos colonies ne nous est apparenté et par suite assimilable en masse; toutes appartiennent à ces collectivités présentant des caractères ethniques irréductibles aux nôtres.[28]

> It is noteworthy that a French person, born in France, of French parents whose ancestors have always remained on the soil cultivated by their fathers, is not the same as a person born in a newly annexed territory, even if that territory is an integral part of the national territory. He differs by ethnic origin, heredity, customs, outlook, character and degree of civilisation. One is the subject of a dominant and conquering collectivity; the other is the subject of a dominated and conquered collectivity ... It might be said that none of the races which inhabit our colonies is connected with us (by blood) and thus capable of being assimilated *en masse*; all these collectivities manifest ethnic characteristics incompatible with our own.

The result of this process, at both legal and historical level, was inevitably the creation of a racist and discriminatory culture that had a profound impact on France itself as well as on the colonies and other occupied territories. Yet the attitude to it of a significant part of French officialdom has been one of denial. Article 4 of a controversial law adopted on 23 February 2005 stipulates that:

> les programmes scolaires reconnaissent en particulier le rôle positif de la présence française outre-mer, notamment en Afrique du Nord, et accordent à l'histoire et aux sacrifices des combattants de l'armée française issus de ces territoires la place éminente à laquelle ils ont droit.[29]

> school curricula (will) recognise, in particular, the positive role of the French overseas presence, especially in North Africa, and will allow the history and sacrifices of the French army in these territories the eminent place to which they are entitled.

This astonishing text perpetuates a long-standing denial by many French people of their ignominious role in North Africa and other places.

Dealing with diversity in the new Britain

The opposite end of the spectrum from the French case, at least in theory, may be found in Britain. Here a certain classically liberal viewpoint has been uppermost for some decades. As described in 1966 by Roy Jenkins, the response was to be 'Not a flattening process of assimilation, but ... equal opportunity accompanied by cultural diversity in an atmosphere of mutual tolerance.'[30] A *laissez-faire* approach, based on a tolerance bordering on indifference and embodying legislation and policy designed at most to address the effects of exclusion but not to promote active integration, was held to best recognise a range of differing postcolonial ethnic communities and to provide for spaces of diversity within the broader British polity. There was little pressure to assimilate to mainstream British values and/or society and there was a degree of acceptance of the diverse cultures of which a multi-ethnic Britain, largely reflecting its own colonial past, is composed, even if there was also a partly submerged hierarchicalism within a differentially racialised society. The primary stress of legislation on 'race relations' was to attack blatant forms of individual and later institutional racism, but this was done within a framework which was in itself based on the reification of ethnic difference.

However well-meaning, this policy did not produce the desired results. In part this reflected a set of historical and geographical specificities peculiar to the decline of the British Empire into the postcolonial period. Notably, the arrival from the 1950s onwards of large numbers of immigrants of Asian and Caribbean origin coincided with a period of major change in British society. The positive side of this change was the growth of the welfare state, which itself needed substantial numbers of immigrants to provide new services in health and public transport and to build the houses and motorways of a country which divested itself of the trappings of a Victorian economy and society only in the period after the Second World War.[31] The negative side was reflected in the fact that so many immigrants began working in the factories of the Midlands in an era which turned out to be the twilight days of the country's Victorian industrial infrastructure. From the 1970s onwards the textile factories and other heavy industrial production lines fell silent as winters of discontent gave way to the Thatcherite years. This post-industrial England was a bleak landscape in which two equally disenfranchised and de-skilled communities seemed structurally condemned by changing circumstances to be at each other's throats. It has also been argued that the real failure of British society to integrate immigrants on equal terms impacted less on the *Windrush*[32] generation than on their children, let down by an educational system which denied them equal opportunity and by an ethnic hierarchicalism, already referred to, which continued to pervade British society even as race relations legislation was adopted and the rhetoric of diversity took hold. That very language at times allowed for a form of 'boutique multiculturalism' in which an atomised politics of identity appeared as a pale substitute for a more thoroughgoing challenge to a society which exhibited a severe and structurally embedded inability to move beyond white hegemony to genuine equality. This legacy of implicit racism, combined with the existence of separate ethnic communities which often may have grown up side by side but have had little contact, led to ghettoisation, especially when factors of race, class and economic decline combined to generate strong currents of social exclusion. As in France, these currents sometimes exploded into social violence, in Bristol, Toxteth, Brixton, all in 1981, Bradford and other places in 2001.

British positions have shifted in the recent past, influenced by a number of factors, including the perceived or alleged failures of the British multicultural model. A widely reproduced article by David Goodhart[33] suggested that a fundamental challenge for a multi-ethnic society was the conflict between diversity and solidarity; people are happy to pay taxes for social services provided that those who will receive them share their values. This was denounced by Trevor Phillips, Chairperson of the Commission for Racial Equality,[34] as neo-Powellism, yet Phillips himself dismissed multiculturalism as an outdated doctrine.[35] More soul-searching followed the emergence of a number of native-born suicide bombers on 7 July 2005.

In both Britain and France it is not immigrants themselves who have rioted; rather it is their children and even grandchildren. Social unrest and street violence are not the result of some sudden change, although there is almost always a proximate trigger event. Rather, they result from a build-up of decades of frustration and anger. Clearly neither multiculturalism nor universalism, as least as conceived and practised so far in Britain and France respectively, has been able to address the serious underlying problems of inequality and of perceived challenges to national identities.

The concept of core values: Australia, Canada

There are not many examples of a more radical or thoroughgoing multiculturalism as official policy. The United States moved in the course of the twentieth century from an explicitly racialised policy of immigration and citizenship (e.g. the 1882 Chinese Exclusion Act, while native Americans acquired a general right to citizenship only in 1924) to the comparatively colour-blind immigration policy of the present day. But the United States has no integration policy and the prevailing discourse of individual integration within a *laissez-faire* capitalist society remains the dominant one even though it has been challenged.[36] Modern New Zealand's bicultural integration model is far-reaching, particularly in the way in which it has been grounded in intercultural education and in case law and policy based on overturning the abuses which the 1840 Treaty of Waitangi was designed to prevent.[37] Efforts to promote understanding, good relations and integration between Maori and Pakeha (European settler descendants) have been radical. But they do not address current realities of Asian and Polynesian immigration, and these groups are still strongly excluded and in many cases geographically ghettoised, especially in Auckland, New Zealand's most multi-ethnic city.[38]

Canada and Australia are the only countries in the world which have opted explicitly for a multicultural model and which have introduced legislation and policy to give it effect. Significantly, both countries recognise that it is not possible to have diversity without also affirming core values. For instance, migrants are required to learn an official language – French or English in Canada, English in Australia. Both have also legislated that core values such as gender rights cannot be overridden in the name of cultural diversity. Unfortunately, even though most Australians support the notion of a multicultural society, as borne out by the short and unsuccessful career of Pauline Hanson, a right-wing opponent of the multicultural policy, the Conservative administration has distanced itself to some extent from established policy. Moreover the harsh treatment meted out to asylum seekers who dare to try to make their own way to Australia suggests that it is not a model in every respect.

Kymlicka, looking at Canadian experience, offers interesting evidence to bear out the thesis that public opinion and practice can be influenced by an intelligently led top-down approach combined with effective programmes on the ground. He considers some of the arguments put forward by critics of multiculturalism such as Neil Bissoondath and Richard Gwyn. Examining citizenship, political participation, official language acquisition, and intermarriage rates – four fairly basic measurements, although not comprehensive – he shows conclusively that (1) multiculturalism brought about a change for the better in inter-ethnic relations rather than ghettoisation, (2) Canadian attitudes and behaviour, measured in terms of changes since the introduction of the multiculturalism policy, were substantially better than countries such as the United States and the United Kingdom. If we take, for instance, the measurement of the social acceptance of mixed marriages, whereas 52% of Canadians disapproved of black–white marriages in 1968, 81% approved of them in 1995. In 1988 the approval rate was 72% whereas only 40% of (US)

Americans approved of them and 25% felt they should be illegal. The percentage of people who agreed with the proposition that 'different ethnic groups get along well here' in 1997 was far higher in Canada (75%) than in the United States (58%) or France (51%).[39]

No perfect model has yet been developed for a functioning diverse society. But if one measures the examples just mentioned, one finds that by and large those states which are proactive and which support a policy of respect for diversity are better places to live in. A certain effort and investment, in terms of policy and resources, is required to achieve these practical improvements. Rather than excoriating France for its difficulties, it must be recognised that all European states have had a degree of difficulty in dealing with immigration and diversity. As has been observed, neither the French nor the British model proved adequate to addressing profound problems of alienation, racism and discrimination, although both can also offer examples of good practice. In the face of a moral panic about immigration and about certain serious incidents in a range of countries (e.g. riots in France, bombs in Britain, the murders of Pym Fortuyn and Theo Van Gogh in the Netherlands), it would be inappropriate for governments to be driven into any excessive reaction inspired by a sometimes hotheaded public opinion. Apart from anything else all European societies, for demographic and economic reasons, now need immigrants. They have also undertaken to accept migrants seeking to immigrate for humanitarian reasons through the asylum process, even if, regrettably, they have made it progressively more difficult for such asylum seekers to reach their shores and thus vindicate their rights in international and domestic law.

Towards an EU perspective

The European Union did not become involved in migration and asylum issues for some decades and was silent on the issue of integration. Apart from a single EEC directive of 1977[40] on the education of migrant children) and a 1964 declaration on the status of refugees[41] which has yet to be implemented more than forty years later, migration-related issues were left to member states.

The reasons for this are not difficult to identify. In the first place, nation-states have always asserted that control over who may live within the jurisdiction, or acquire the status of citizen, or visit, is a core issue, as much as a monopoly over the use of force, the national currency and an independent foreign policy. The EU has changed several of these realities too, but it took some time for it to happen. Secondly, migration into and within Europe after World War II was determined to a large extent by bilateral flows, the most important of which were those from former colonies to the 'mother countries' and those from peripheral Europe to core Europe – Ireland to Britain, Portugal to France, Finland to Sweden, etc. At the time there was little perceived need to develop an EEC-level policy. It is noteworthy that the 1977 directive already referred to was designed largely with the children of *European* labour migrants in mind – it was intended to ensure that Italian migrant workers, for instance, could return to Italy and that their children would not be disadvantaged on entering schooling in the Italian language. However, in spite of the good intentions behind this early measure, it remained largely unimplemented.

The key period of change was the mid-1980s. Negotiations on what came to be known as the Schengen agreements began in 1985 and led to their incorporation in 1997 into the *acquis communautaire* as part of the Treaty of Amsterdam.[42] Schengen involved the abolition of border controls and agreement on other forms of co-operation; ultimately the Schengen area expanded from five states to the twenty-six today, including non-EU states Switzerland, Norway and Iceland. The only two EU member states which have opted out of Schengen are Britain and Ireland.[43] More important, the derogation which Ireland and the United Kingdom obtained in 1997 also allows them to opt out of any subsequent legislation in the area of migration policy if they so wish. A number of directives adopted since that time do not apply in either country, a situation which has been criticised by the European Parliament, especially in light of the fact that the new accession states were obliged to accept migration as part of the *acquis communautaire* on joining on 1 May 2004.

The Schengen initiatives coincided with a period when migration-related issues suddenly took on a new political importance. Space does not allow a detailed discussion of the various complex reasons for this new urgency but a few of the central issues are worth mentioning. The Schengen agreements necessitated closer co-operation than before, if only because the new freedoms were intended to benefit only those who were either EU citizens or the possessors of a 'Schengen visa'. There was therefore a perceived need to ensure that those who were not supposed to benefit from the new freedoms did not attempt to avail themselves of them. This led to all kinds of new co-operation in policing, data systems, 'black' and 'white' third-party country visa lists, common asylum rules, etc.

Second, the crisis in Bosnia-Herzogovina in 1991 led to an outflow of refugees of more than 400,000, nearly all of whom went to Germany. The German government promoted the notion of 'burden sharing' for the management of future crises. When the Kosovo crisis blew up in the late 1990s this was actually implemented and EU countries, including Ireland, accepted refugees on a negotiated, shared basis. Third, a general rise in asylum seekers in the 1990s, the uneven nature of their distribution across the European Union and the implementation of the 1990 Dublin Convention[44] (which said one could only apply for asylum in the EU country of first arrival) meant an increased necessity for closer cooperation. As the same time individual member states were implementing various regularisation or amnesty programmes but other states quickly realised there was potential for a knock-on effect in their jurisdictions. Finally, there was increased concern with undocumented immigration, 'terrorist' violence and related or allegedly related issues such as international drug smuggling. Obviously this factor took on a new importance after 9/11.

In addition to the incorporation of the Schengen arrangements as a 'first pillar'[45] area of EU legislation and policy, the Treaty of Amsterdam provided that within five years of its entry into effect – i.e. by May 2004, as it took legal effect in 1999 – responsibility for migration and asylum policy would, in effect, transfer to the European Union and would no longer be purely a matter of national and/or intergovernmental policy. There is a dedicated Directorate General in the European Commission, Justice and Home Affairs, responsible for this and a range of related policy areas under the somewhat Orwellian-sounding umbrella rubric of 'Freedom, security and justice'.[46]

That said, there were a whole set of complex conditions under which this new regime was to come into effect during the five-year transition period and it was clear that it would do so only in so far as there was a unanimous decision by the member states to transfer sovereignty in any particular sector to the European Union. This was in contradistinction to the new regime generally favoured after Amsterdam, which emphasised majority voting in all but a few cases and which gave co-decision powers to the European Parliament. Member states also retained some power to initiate proposals in the field of migration, which is usually the sole prerogative of the European Commission. All this illustrates the highly sensitive nature of the field and the fact that it is, classically, an area of core concern to national jurisdictions, which will not lightly, if ever, cede complete sovereignty even if they are willing to co-ordinate and share some decision-making powers with neighbouring states. What actually happened between 1999 and 2004, but especially after 9/11, is that new initiatives proceeded at a snail-like pace and the caravan always moved at the speed of the slowest wagon. While two important directives were adopted, on family reunification[47] and long-term resident rights,[48] they are rather weak.

A major initiative on integration?

As seen, progress on migration legislation and policy at EU level, in spite of the crucial transfer to EU sovereignty, was in practice slow. This makes recent developments on integration matters, where the European Union had virtually no interest or involvement until the very recent past, all the more remarkable.

This new involvement arose as it became clear that major problems were developing on the integration front in more than one member state. As has been noted, Britain had its riots in Bradford and other places, while the Netherlands witnessed the murders of Pym Fortuyn and Theo Van Gogh. Although the post-9/11 atmosphere has been one of a concern with a security-driven agenda in matters of immigration, it became increasingly clear that there were significant problems of disaffection in Islamic communities in a number of EU member states. This partly explains a particular initiative by the Dutch presidency in 2004.

The 'common basic principles' (CBPs) were adopted at an EU Council of Ministers chaired by the Dutch presidency on 19 November 2004.[49] They were an initiative of the presidency, i.e. not of the Commission, which, as mentioned, is usually sole initiator in policy and legislation but not in immigration, asylum and integration matters. The common basic principles are as follows:

1 Integration is a dynamic, two-way process of mutual accommodation by all immigrants and residents of member states.
2 Integration implies respect for the basic values of the European Union by every resident.
3 Employment is a key part of the integration process and is central to the participation of immigrants, to the contributions immigrants make to the host society, and to making such contributions visible.
4 Basic knowledge of the host society's language, history and institutions is indispensable to integration; enabling immigrants to acquire this basic knowledge is essential to successful integration.
5 Efforts in education are essential in preparing immigrants, and particularly their descendants, to be more successful and more active participants in society.
6 Access for immigrants to institutions, as well as to public and private goods and services, on an equal basis to national citizens and in a non-discriminatory way is an indispensable foundation for better integration.
7 Frequent interaction between immigrants and citizens of the member states is a fundamental prerequisite of integration.

8   The practice of diverse cultures and religions is guaranteed under the Charter of Fundamental Rights and must be safeguarded, unless practices conflict with other inviolable European rights or with national law.

9   The participation of immigrants in the democratic process and in the formulation of integration policies and measures, especially at the local and regional levels, is a key to effective integration.

10 Mainstreaming integration policies and measures in all relevant policy portfolios and levels of government and public services is an important consideration in public policy formation and implementation. The principle of engaging civil society is also endorsed.

11 Developing clear goals, indicators and evaluation mechanisms are necessary to adjust policy, evaluate progress on integration and to make the exchange of information more effective, so as to transfer good experience.[50]

These principles seek to strike a number of balances. The principle of integration as a two-way process is affirmed but so is the insistence that migrants need to engage with the host society, its history and culture. Respect for diversity is affirmed but so is the primary place of core values. Due recognition is given to 'identity' issues, but the more practical issues of employment, education and access to services are also stressed. The achievement of mainstreamed integration in a cross-sectoral way is recognised as a responsibility of the state, but the need to engage civil society is also recognised. Finally, integration is seen as innately intercultural, i.e. there must be active and frequent interaction between migrants and host society.

At the very least the CBPs establish a number of key principles and do set out an agenda to tackle racism, discrimination and social exclusion. An EU Commission 'communication' (equivalent to a White Paper) endorses the principles, proposes funding and an action programme based on those principles and proposes a degree of stakeholder involvement, although the level of minority ethnic representation at any level of the process is minimal.[51]

Unfortunately, there is little sign, since the publication of the Dutch proposals and the Commission communication, of significant early progress in the implementation of these principles. Thus the failure of the EU to adopt a European constitution has deprived the Union of the secure legal basis which it would need to pursue an integration agenda. Moreover, member states are likely to continue to insist on their own sovereignty in this very sensitive policy area and the Commission will necessarily proceed with extreme caution. It is likely that policy initiatives will not attempt to align national policies to some putative common goals; research, evaluation and examples of good practices will constitute the early bases for common action.

That said, integration is now firmly on the EU agenda. Concern will be fuelled, in particular, by the concern of both EU and US governments about 'home-grown terrorists'.[52] After the London bombs, but also British-born shoe bomber Richard Read, Belgian female suicide bomber Muriel Degauque in Iraq, the Dutch murders of Fortuyn and Van Gogh, the growing fear is that European countries now face a threat from highly motivated, alienated young Europeans, of non-mainstream backgrounds but with all the legal rights of European citizenship. Crucially, they may be able to operate with either the indifference, or tacit sympathy, or active support, of a minority of people in every country in Europe. By contrast, the IRA probably never had this level of support since the 1970s, and it still managed to cause devastation in London with the Canary Wharf bombing in the early 1990s.

Seen in that light, the 'depoliticised' nature of the CBPs is problematic. It is nonsensical to deny that there are clear and proximate causes for disaffection among certain migrant and diasporic communities. Most communities are made up of people who do not engage in acts of violence or extremism. But they will be more likely to shelter those who do, if their experience is that they live in societies where they are not treated as equals and are ruled by governments in which they have little visible representation and which implement policies which are deeply hostile to people of their own ethnic backgrounds. One has only to think of some of the more disastrous decisions by the British government in Ireland. After Operation Motorman (internment) in 1971, Bloody Sunday and the fiasco of the hunger strikes, IRA recruitment soared. In the case of present ethnic relations, governments cannot continue to ignore the role of internal racism and discrimination, as well as the actions of certain Western countries in places like Iraq, in the growing confrontation between some European Muslims and host societies. There therefore can be no 'depoliticised' approach to integration. It will hardly prove productive to tell European Muslims how much they are respected if they experience daily racism and discrimination, if the CIA is practising 'extraordinary rendition' in European countries with tacit connivance by governments, or if a US-led coalition is killing civilians in Iraq and ignoring the human rights of Guantanamo detainees.

Conclusion

The lesson of France and other established countries of immigration is that racism and xenophobia can be defeated only if both the state and civil society are actively involved. A multi-faceted approach is required, embracing policy, legislation and the social domains, particularly that of education. Fighting xenophobia and racism is only one part of the equation; the other component is an active commitment to integration.

All EU states have some kind of anti-racist legislation in place. However, these laws need to be strengthened in many cases, enforcement needs to be improved and greater resources need to be devoted to the field. There are some excellent models of good practice, notably in the United Kingdom, which include codified and clear targets for action, with clear benchmarks and milestones and the use of targeted initiatives and mainstreaming, both within organisations employing migrant workers and in terms of service provision for migrants and their families. Recruitment and promotion are rightly seen as key issues.

Policy innovation in Ireland in the field of integration has been limited to date. While the first report on the topic, *Integration: A Two-way Process*,[53] proposed a rather timid definition of integration and a largely aspirational integration agenda, matters have advanced somewhat with the 2005 publication of the *National Action Plan against Racism*.[54] Nonetheless, Ireland has yet to engage proactively with a more fundamental question about what is meant by a politics of integration in the most comprehensive sense of the term, bearing in mind the issues, debates and discourses outlined.

New immigration societies like Ireland can learn from the experience of other countries. There is a precious window of opportunity thanks to a strong and vibrant economy and forecasts suggesting continuing growth and an ongoing need for migrants, but one must also recognise that the result of inaction now will be a form of forced, resented and almost certainly failed *de facto* assimilation over time. The long-term effects of such an approach can be only negative. Ireland has not been inoculated with some kind of unique vaccine against racism. The Irish record to date and its treatment of indigenous minorities such as Travellers (an indigenous partly nomadic community) is poor.

White mainstream anti-racists face a specific challenge. Respect for diversity is not about a token commitment to diversity while remaining embedded in an entrenched position of all that mainstream society holds to be 'normal'. It involves risk-taking and a willingness to give up power. This is a point missed by those who pursue a community relations model, because such a model, as well as reifying difference behind rigid boundaries and eliminating the gradual, the syncretic and the mixed, airbrushes away the reality of power. Who controls the society and who controls the key institutions – media, education, politics? How can decisions be taken about who belongs; whose values, culture and traditions are to be recognised as central and which are to be regarded as marginal?

It is far too early to say what the shape of a multicultural Ireland might be, and indeed it would be foolish to attempt to pre-empt a process which has barely begun. It seems safe to say, however, that, while Black and Asian sports stars may serve as future Irish role models and become a significant element in the process of integration, mainstream society also needs to find ways of building dialogue with new communities where they are respected and accepted on their own terms and not just those of the host society. That society has transformed itself from a one lacking in self-belief and opportunity to a cosmopolitan and thriving community, but it has not done so without considerable outside assistance, including that of migrants. A little less self-congratulation, and a little more stress on openness and long-term thinking, would now be in order if Irish society is not to become rapidly segregated and dysfunctional.

Notes

1 C. O'Brien, 'New figures challenge welfare tourism fears', *Irish Times*, 24 October 2005.
2 G. Fitzgerald, 'Some facts on "displacement" of Irish workers', *Irish Times*, 14 January 2006.
3 Home Office, *Accession Monitoring Report, May 2004–September 2005* (London: Home Office, 2005), p. 3.
4 Migration Policy Institute, *United States: Inflow of Foreign-born Population by Country of Birth, 1986–2004* (Washington, DC: Migration Policy Institute, 2006), www.migrationinformation.org/GlobalData/countrydata/data.cfm.
5 Department of Enterprise Trade and Employment, *Statistics and Company Listings up to December 31st 2005* (Dublin: DETE, 2006), www.entemp.ie/labour/workpermits/statistics.htm, accessed 14 January 2006.
6 A special category of employment authorisation for certain types of employment where there is considered to be a labour shortage in Ireland. For those coming from states for which a visa is required to enter Ireland the term used is 'work visa'; for persons coming from a state for which no visa is required the permit is called a 'work authorisation'.
7 New Zealand Department of Labour/Te Teri Mahi, *Migration Trends, 2004/2005*, www.immigration.govt.nz/migrant/general/generalinformation/research/, accessed 14 January 2006.
8 M. Tracy, *Racism and Immigration in Ireland: A Comparative Analysis*

(Dublin: Trinity College, 2000), www.tcd.ie/sociology/mphil/dwnl/Marsall-Tracey.PDF, accessed 15 January 2006.

9 Waters, quoted in ibid.

10 Tracy, *Racism and Immigration*.

11 K. Malik, 'Born in Bradford', *Prospect*, October 2005.

12 K. Malik, 'Multiculturalism fans the flames of extremism', *The Times*, 16 July 2005.

13 T. Cantle, *Community Cohesion: A Report of the Independent Review Team* (London: Home Office, 2001).

14 Home Office, 'First Citizenship Ceremony', www.ind.homeoffice.gov.uk/british_citizenship/english/homepage/press0/first_citizenship. html, accessed 14 February 2006.

15 Home Office, *Life in the UK: A Journey to Citizenship* (London: Home Office, 2004).

16 G. Brown, 'The Future of Britishness', keynote speech to Fabian Society conference on the future of Britishness, London, 2006.

17 R. Lentin, 'Responding to the Racialisation of Irishness: Disavowed Multiculturalism and its Discontents', *Sociological Research Online*, 5: 4, www.socresonline.org.uk/5/4/lentin.html, accessed 15 January 2006.

18 C. Taylor, 'Multiculturalism and the Politics of Recognition', in A. Gutman (ed.), *Multiculturalism and the Politics of Recognition* (Princeton, NJ: Princeton University Press, 1992).

19 E. Shohat and R. Stam, 'French Intellectuals and the US Culture Wars', *Black Renaissance/Renaissance noire*, 22 March 2001.

20 M. le Comte de Clermont-Tonnerre, *Assemblée Nationale,* 1791, quoted in J. Streiff-Fénart, 'Modèle républicain et discriminations ethniques : un dilemme français', *Faire savoirs*, 1 (March 2002), www.amares.org/revue/01/FSn1. pdf, accessed 15 January 2006.

21 Loi no. 2004-228 du 15 mars 2004 encadrant, en application du principe de laïcité, le port de signes ou de tenues manifestant une appartenance religieuse dans les écoles, collèges et lycées publics, *Journal officiel*, 65 (17 March 2004), p. 5190, text No. 1.

22 Indigenous Algerians who fought on the French side during the Algerian war of independence.

23 Street slang, or *verlan. Beur* is derived from the word *Arabe.*

24 See *Le Fonds d'action et de soutien pour l'intégration et la lutte contre les discriminations,* www.fasild.fr.

25 C. Jelen, *Il feront de bons français* (Paris: Robert Laffont, 1991), p. 217.

26 G. Noiriel, *Le Creuset français : histoire de l'immigration XIX–XX siècles* (Paris: Seuil, 1992).

27 P. Blanchard, 'La France : entre deux immigrations', in P. Blanchard, N. Bancel and S. Lemaire, *La Fracture coloniale* (Paris: Découverte, 2005), pp. 172–82.

28 Ibid.

29 A. Hajjat, 'Une victoire des nostalgiques de l'Empire colonial' (2005), 1libertaire.free.fr/HistoireOfficielle01.html, accessed 20 January 2006.

30 R. Jenkins, address by the Home Secretary, the Rt Hon. Roy Jenkins, MP, to a meeting of Voluntary Liaison Committees, London, 23 May 1966.

31 T. Judt, *Postwar: A History of Europe since 1945* (London: Heinemann, 2005), chapter 1.

32 A reference to the name of the ship which brought the first large group of immigrants from the Caribbean to Britain in 1948.

33 D. Goodhart, 'Too diverse?' *Prospect*, February 2004, widely reproduced under the title 'The Discomfort of Strangers', see *The Guardian*, www.guardian.co.uk/race/story/0,11374,1154684,00.html, accessed 16 January 2006.

34 T. Phillips, 'Genteel xenophobia is as bad as any other kind', *Guardian*, 16 February 2004, www.guardian.co.uk/comment/story/0,3604,1148847,00.html, accessed 15 January 2006.

35 M. Mirza, 'Backlash against multiculturalism?', *Spiked Culture*, 7 April 2004, www.spiked-online.com/Printable/0000000CA4C4.htm, accessed 15 January 2006.

36 R. Takaki, *Strangers from a Distant Shore* (New York: Little Brown, 1989).

37 Government of New Zealand, *The Treaty of Waitangi*, www.treatyofwaitangi.govt.nz/timeline/treaty1800.php, accessed 15 January 2006.

38 M. King, A. Haas and R. S. Hill, *Reconciling Biculturalism and Multiculturalism in Aotearoa/New Zealand* (Wellington: New Zealand Futures Trust, 2004), www.futurestrust.org.nz/NZDiversity.html.

39 W. Kymlicka, 'Immigrants, Multiculturalism and Canadian Citizenship', in *Finding our Way: Rethinking Ethnocultural Relations in Canada* (Oxford: Oxford University Press, 1997).

40 Council Directive 77/486/EEC of 25 July 1977 on the education of the children of migrant workers, *Official Journal*, L 199, 6 August 1977, http://europa.eu.int/smartapi/cgi/sga_doc?smartapi!celexapi!prod!CELEXnumdoc&lg=EN&numdoc=31977L0486&model=guichett, accessed 20 January 2006.

41 EurLex, 64/305/CEE, Déclaration du 25 mars 1964 des représentants des gouvernements des États membres de la CEE, réunis au sein du Conseil, au sujet des réfugiés (2006), http://europa.eu.int/smartapi/cgi/sga_doc?smartapi!celexapi!prod!CELEXnumdoc&lg=fr&numdoc=41964X0305&model=guichett, accessed 20 January 2006.

42 European Union, *Treaty of Amsterdam* (1997), http://europa.eu.int/abc/obj/amst/en/, accessed 16 January 2006.

43 P. Mac Éinrí, 'The Implications for Ireland and the UK arising from the Development of recent European Union Policy in Migration', in *Migration Policy in Ireland: Reform and Harmonisation* (Dublin: National Consultative Committee on Racism and Interculturalism, 2002).

44 *Official Journal*, C 254, 19 August 1997, pp. 0001–12, europa.eu.int/infonet/library/a/97c25401/en.htm, accessed 15 January 2006.

45 'First pillar' means an area of EU competence as opposed to a field of intergovernmental co-operation. Notably, the European Court of Justice has competence for 'first pillar' issues.

46 European Commission, Directorate of Justice and Home Affairs, http://europa.eu.int/comm/justice_home/index_en.htm, accessed 21 January 2006.

47 Council of European Union, Directive 2003/86/EC of 22 September 2003 on the right to family reunification, *Official Journal*, L 251, 3 October 2003, pp. 12–18.

48 Council of European Union, Directive 2003/109/EC of 25 November 2003 concerning the status of third-country nationals who are long-term residents, *Official Journal*, L 016, 23 January 2004, pp. 44–53

49 Council of European Union, *Presidency Conclusions, 4–5 November,* document 14776/04 (2004).

50 Ibid.

51 European Commission, *A Common Agenda for Integration Framework for the Integration of Third-Country Nationals in the European Union*, Com (2005) 389, final.

52 R. Leiken, 'Europe's angry Muslims', *Foreign Affairs*, August 2004, www.foreignaffairs.org/20050701faessay84409/robert-s-leiken/europe-s-angry-muslims.html, accessed 14 January 2006.

53 Department of Justice Equality and Law Reform, *Integration: A Two-way Process* (Dublin: Department of Justice Equality and Law Reform, 1999).

54 National Consultative Committee on Racism and Interculturalism, *National Action Plan against Racism* (Dublin: NCCRI, 2005).

15

Integration and social policy

Bryan Fanning

This chapter considers the role of Irish social policy in promoting the integration of immigrants. Distinctions between integration, defined in terms of capacity to participate fully in society, and assimilation, whereby the surrender of cultural distinctiveness becomes the cost of social membership, have been emphasised in debates about multiculturalism. However, to date the Irish debate on integration has been principally shaped by social policy norms rather than debates about multiculturalism. The emphasis placed here on integration through social policy does not seek to sidestep present-day controversies about multiculturalism. The question of addressing large-scale immigration in the Republic of Ireland has arisen at a time when the politics of multiculturalism in a number of Western countries has become unsettled. Unlike Ireland, many have a long-standing politics of immigration. In Ireland a distinct multiculturalism, or interculturalism, as it is known, has become partially institutionalised within the state, yet this has had limited influence upon Irish responses to immigration. Within Irish social policy debates a family resemblance can be seen between social inclusion goals and prevalent definitions of integration. This has been informed by broadly similar sociological understandings of the inequalities that cause poverty and those resulting from racism. The National Anti-poverty Strategy, since its inception in 1997, has emphasised the concept of social exclusion. In effect social exclusion is understood as a consequence of the relative material deprivation that can result from income poverty and unemployment. The thesis at the heart of Irish anti-poverty policy is that people may be excluded from activities that are considered the norm for other people in society owing to inadequate income and other resources needed to participate in society.

Yet Irish social policy has, as elsewhere, become partially subordinated to immigration policy. Differences between the welfare entitlements of citizens and non-citizen immigrants function as internal borders. At the same time integration can be presented as a functional requirement of social policy in a context where, for example, education is understood as a basis for future societal wealth and economic productivity or where immigrants reduce present or future dependence ratios. In a greying Europe declining birth rates and ageing work forces signal future potential crises in the provision of retirement age welfare. Such provision potentially depends upon the children of immigrants as well as those of present-day citizens. Notwithstanding the focus on culture, and clashes of culture, in European political debates about integration the recipes that emerge to address perceived communal crises are generally social policy ones.[1] That said, the long-term advantages of successfully integrating immigrants have proved difficult to sell politically. In the Irish case debates about integration must contend with political responses to immigration that have removed a range of social entitlements from new immigrants. The social policy integration debate that is the focus of this chapter is about the need to include immigrants within social citizenship. The above-mentioned intercultural one is essentially concerned with differential social citizenship on the basis of ethnicity. Citizenship rights are presumed. New immigrants, that is to say, noncitizens, excluded from social citizenship, often find themselves outside the remit of many intercultural policies. The conundrum emphasised in this chapter is between social citizenship as the basis of integration and political barriers to extending welfare solidarities to immigrants. These barriers are complex ones to do with perceived problems with multiculturalism, the perceived case for ethnic nepotism and the influence of neo-liberal responses to globalisation. In this context responses to immigrants have become a litmus test for the sustainability of the core presumptions within social citizenship.

The dilemma of social citizenship

In Western Europe the notion of 'social citizenship', as it developed in the post-World War II era, remains the primary intellectual framework for thinking about the welfare state. Social citizenship became embedded in a sociological theory that linked welfare state expansion with the progressive advancement of citizenship.[2] Social policy aspirations for the inclusion of vulnerable or unequally treated groups became conceptually framed in relation to the gold standard of full and equal citizenship. As influentially outlined by Marshall in 1950:

> Citizenship is a status bestowed on those who are full members of the community. All those who possess the status are equal with respect to the rights and duties with which the status is endowed. There is no universal principle which determines what those rights and duties should be, but

societies in which citizenship is a developing institution create an image of ideal citizenship against which achievement can be measured and towards which aspiration can be directed.[3]

Marshall, in the immediate post-World War II period, defined social citizenship as 'the right to share to the full in the social heritage and to live the life of a civilised being according to the standards prevailing in the society'.[4] This definition linked rights with welfare goods and services with dominant constructions of social membership on the basis of gender roles and ethnicity. Some welfare theorists subsequently discussed how women experienced lesser or differential social citizenship on the basis of gender.[5] For example, welfare entitlements were typically linked to paid employment. In Ireland, as elsewhere, those of women were subject to their status as dependants of male breadwinners.[6] Theorists have also emphasised how people with disabilities or minority ethnic groups may experience differential social citizenship.[7] Citizenship has tended to reflect dominant 'nation-building' ideologies of social membership on the basis of 'race', ethnicity, language and religion.[8]

Marshall and his successors legitimised 'social citizenship' by embedding the concept in a historical theory of social change as the gradual unfolding of successive stages of citizenship development. This evolutionary conceptualisation posited the eventual completion of 'social citizenship' as an End of History ideal. Social citizenship was depicted as the inevitable culmination – following the development of legal–civil rights in the eighteenth century and political rights in the nineteenth – of the democratic ideal.[9] Yet, since the 1970s, even as social citizenship developed to address gender, 'race' and other inequalities, it fell foul of shifting political and economic orthodoxies. The decline of Keynesian nation-state economics and neo-liberal responses to globalisation have curtailed the development of social citizenship in many countries. Within the new democracies of Eastern Europe social citizenship is as yet exceedingly thin.[10] In practice the ideals of social citizenship have remained aspirations for many citizens of European nation-states. The social, economic, political and organisational settlements that variously shaped their social policies have varied from country to country. The Republic of Ireland, for instance, could hardly be understood to have a welfare state. Its social policies have been institutionally shaped by a legacy of nineteenth-century poor-law liberalism and post-independence Catholic hegemony, both hostile to state dominance of the welfare economy.[11]

Yet the concept of social citizenship serves as a basis for conceptualising the differential access amongst Irish citizens and, increasingly, non-citizens, to welfare goods and services. Examples include universal entitlement to education and universal child benefits for citizens and equality legislation that prohibits discrimination on grounds such as gender, 'race' and 'membership of the Travelling Community'.[12] Goals of reducing inequalities within social citizenship can be identified within social policies that aim to redress social exclusion caused by relative poverty. The specificity of Irish social citizenship can be identified through the concepts, norms, entitlements and policies which define Irish social policy. Many of these, certainly those considered in this chapter, embody presumptions about social solidarity, social cohesion and belonging that expand upon those about legal, political or economic rights.

Social citizenship and immigration

Immigration tests the limits of social citizenship. Christian Joppke argues that in societies with well developed social rights citizenship becomes a precondition of inclusion. Those without such rights become relatively deprived of key resources needed to ensure social reproduction. If, the story of the last few centuries has been the gradual inclusion of more and more members of society within citizenship – for instance, through extending the franchise and the rights of women – in twenty-first-century Ireland there is a growing disjuncture between citizenship and actual social membership. Gradations of rights between citizens and non-citizens, immigrant 'guest' workers, 'illegal' workers, refugees and asylum seekers have emerged in a number of Western countries that as recently as a century ago operated few restrictions on immigration. In such a context citizenship becomes 'not just a set of rights, but also a mechanism of exclusion'.[13] The attempt to exclude immigrants from Irish social citizenship – by the time-limited removal in 2004 of a range of welfare entitlements – can be understood is part of a broader international pattern. As summarised by Klausen:

> In the case of social policy and entitlements, the choice is simple at first glance: either immigrants are treated like citizens or they are considered as foreigners and have no claims. But faced with conflicting interests, governments have done both while trying, with varying degrees of success, to regulate immigration. Employer interests have weighted in favor of admitting foreign labor, while trade unions fearing the diluting effect of a foreign proletariat have strenuously opposed the exclusion of foreign workers from 'social minimum' guarantees. Politicians have weighed economic interests against political and social interests, and charted out policies as conflictual as the various interests they were designed to meet.[14]

The kernel of this has been the exclusion of immigrants from solidarities developed around citizenship. David Goodhart, drawing on what has come to be known as ethnic nepotism theory, has influentially argued in the United Kingdom that that there is an inevitable conflict or trade-off between social solidarity and diversity.[15] Diversity, it is argued, undermines the moral consensus on which a large welfare state rests.[16] Welfare solidarities, it is emphasised, have been most pronounced in ethnically homogeneous states such as France, Germany and Sweden and have proved weak in multi-ethnic societies such as the United States.[17] Ethnic nepotism theory as developed by socio-biologists paints a somewhat determinist picture of the workings of ethnic bonds, emphasising, for instance, how research in the United States indicates that racial considerations are the single most important factor shaping whites' views on welfare.[18] Ethnic nepotism theorists argue that ethnic diversity tends to depress contributions to public goods such as welfare.[19] From this perspective the 'Boston versus Berlin' dualism (one favoured by journalists rather than welfare theorists) suggests that European welfare nepotisms may become more like the United States as European countries become multi-ethnic to the level of the United States. For ethnic nepotism theorists this translates into the proposition that 'more diversity = less welfare' whereby the existence of ethnic prejudice and nepotism becomes mobilised to legitimise ethnic prejudice and nepotism. It is essentially a tautological argument. It recalls claims that the presence of Jews caused antisemitism or that racial problems were caused by the presence of blacks.

The portrayal of ethnic nepotism as 'natural' – rather than as a hypothesis about how groups might behave – is part and parcel of a larger culture of anxiety that now impedes the integration of immigrants. In this context, multiculturalism (a word avoided so far in this chapter) has come in for a rough ride from a muscular liberalism – increasingly pronounced since 11 September 2001– that legitimises cultural intolerance. A liberal rationale for rejecting a universal politics of integration was advanced by Richard Rorty, amongst others, during the 1990s.[20] Rorty described his position as one of anti-anti-ethnocentrism. It scorned efforts by liberals to extend pluralism to include those who do not share their beliefs:

> I have been arguing that we pragmatists should grasp the ethnocentric horn of this dilemma. We should say that we must, in practice, privilege our own group, even though there can be no noncircular justification for doing so … We Western liberal intellectuals should accept the fact that we have to start from where we are, and this means that there are lots of views which we cannot take seriously.[21]

Rorty argued that liberals get themselves into a bind because their beliefs pull them in two different incompatible directions. On one hand they possess no doubts about human equality. On the other they become aware that most of the world does not share their values. They cannot, as he puts it, stick up for their beliefs without getting in a muddle or without choosing to be ethnocentric.[22]

An early definition of ethnocentricism – offered Theodor Adorno – defined it as a tendency to regard one's own group as normal and others, by comparison, as strange and inferior.[23] It is often suggested, in keeping with the ethnic nepotism thesis, that ethnocentricism is natural because human societies tend to be suspicious of outsiders.[24] Ethnic nepotism and ethnocentricism may well be rational under certain circumstances but both, especially the former, can be predicated on a thin account of solidarities and interdependences in complex societies. Goodhart, for instance, notes that 'the diversity, individualisation and mobility that characterised developed economies – especially in the era of globalisation – mean that more of our lives are spent amongst strangers'. However, there is nothing essentially new here. Social interdependences became increasingly complex with the onset of industrialisation and urbanisation. Emile Durkhiem described the result as organic solidarity; a complex interdependence grounded in different functions and lived experiences. He contrasted this with a pre-modern mechanistic solidarity of resemblance, where individual members of society did the same work as each other, lived similar lives alongside one another and shared the same experiences.[25] Similarly Ferdinand Tönnies used the concept of *Gemeinschaft* to refer to traditional forms of community and social relations, characterised by shared values and goals, threatened by industrialisation. Tönnies's ideas have underpinned a modernisation thesis that assumes the decline of community as a 'key fact' about the modern world.[26] Yet it is within this very context of presumed decline that new mass welfare solidarities emerged in areas such as education, health, housing and social security. Within modern societies neighbours are often strangers. Solidarities are as likely to be sustained by dominant *imagined* notions of community and belonging as well as by lived experiences. In this context, ideologies of belonging, such as those vested in citizenship, the state, politics and civil society become crucial.

Robert Putnam, in *Bowling Alone: The Collapse and Revival of American Community*, acknowledges the existence from the nineteenth century of ethnic nepotism in the United States, though it is not a term he employs. He emphasises that the ethnic dividing lines that existed then are not the ones that are prominent now. Asians and Hispanics, he argues, have replaced Jews and Italians as targets of discrimination.[27] This suggests that that there is nothing fixed about the nature and extent of ethnic nepotism. Ethnic nepotism theory, in so far as it focuses upon a single comparative variable, tends to conflate the importance of ethnicity.

Comparative analysis of 183 countries indicates that ethnic heterogeneity (as an index of ethnic nepotism) accounts for a very small part (19 per cent) of the variation in welfare expenditure in Western countries. Ethnic heterogeneity, then, is far from the only factor influencing welfare convergence.[28] Countries at a higher level of socio-economic development and democratisation tend to use relatively more than poor countries and non-democracies. The cleavages affecting welfare solidarities in European welfare economies are not just ethnic ones. These, whether in Europe or America, are also based around social class. For example, John Kenneth Galbraith argued in *The Culture of Contentment* that better-off socio-economic groups, themselves the beneficiaries of a previous generation of welfare solidarity, demonstrate little welfare solidarity with lower socio-economic groups.[29] Class rather than ethnicity comes to the fore in Galbraith's thesis on American welfare solidarity. Arguably, where welfare systems are residual, that is, aimed predominantly at socio-economically marginal groups, they command little loyalty from better-off groups. Conversely, welfare legitimacy in social democratic states has depended on the benefits of social policies to, as Galbraith would have it, the contented majority.

That said, the issue of multiculturalism and its discontents cannot be ignored. Multiculturalism is a term that is employed in a number of ways to refer to a range of ideas and practices that relate to acknowledgements of and responses to social diversity. It is understood to stand in opposition to presumptions of societal monoculturalism. This dualism insufficiently captures the possible array of multiculturalisms. However, multiculturalism, broadly conceived, is understood to be critical of and resistant to monocultural presumptions of social homogeneity where these exist in a society that is actually diverse.[30] Important conceptual distinctions exist between 'weak' forms of multiculturalism that expect out-groups to assimilate into the norms of dominant groups and 'strong' variants which emphasise 'integration', a term used to emphasise a break with acknowledged past failed policies of cultural assimilation in Irish equality policy discourse.[31]

Multiculturalism has been attacked from within and without. In 2004 Trevor Phillips, chair of Britain's Commission for Racial Equality, responded robustly to the ethnic nepotism thesis as advanced by Goodhart – describing the argument as xenophobic and those who advanced it as 'liberal Powellites'[32] – but soon after suggested that the term 'multiculturalism' should be abandoned, declaring, 'The word is not useful, it means the wrong things ... Multiculturalism suggests separateness. We are now in a different world.'[33] Here there was a sense of having to face up a post 9/11 mood but also to criticisms from anti-racist critics of British multiculturalism. Notably, Yasmin Alibhai-Brown has argued that the UK multiculturalist settlement that that emerged out the initial era of post-Wold War II immigration no longer connects with immigrant communities. Multiculturalism, she argues, is seen as 'woolly liberalism'. It is understood to be 'only about ethnic minorities' and, consequently has created a sense of white exclusion. Furthermore, she argues, 'it offered a model of representation that dealt only with elites – celebrating success within immigrant communities and ignoring the institutions that marginalized many members of such communities'.[34] The key political problem identified by Alibhai-Brown is legitimacy. Too few people, she says, from either dominant or minority communities, have bought into it. Some of its presumed beneficiaries have been failed by it. Weak multiculturalism seen to concern marginal ethnic groups seems no more viable a basis for social solidarity than social policies aimed solely at marginal socio-economic groups.

In Ireland, in the case of Travellers, a failure of weak multiculturalism can be identified. For example, legislation designed to address the unwillingness of local authorities to provide accommodation for Travellers was subsequently undermined by legislation shaped by anti-Traveller populist politics.[35] The 'intercultural' policies that developed to integrate (as distinct from assimilate) Travellers failed because they were not robust enough to address discrimination and social exclusion and because they commanded little or no political support. The thrust of political responses to Travellers remained assimilationist. Within these Travellers continue to be defined as a deviant sub-culture rather than as a distinct ethnic group.[36] In this context surrender of cultural difference remained the presumed price of social membership. This has proved a difficult price to pay both because many Travellers have clung to their ethnic markers of distinctiveness and because their presumed deviance from the dominant societal norm has served to justify anti-Traveller politics. Yet, to a considerable extent, responses to Travellers have provided a template for policy responses to new immigrant groups.[37] The existing Irish multiculturalism – grounded in legislation against discrimination in employment and the provision of goods and services but circumscribed by dominant liberal understandings of equality of opportunity and justice – is one that predates immigration.[38] Those failed by this were citizens.

Immigration, economy and society

Alibhai-Brown argues that multiculturalism has always felt like such hard work to many, because it has for too long been presented as 'something that we ought to want'. Instead, she argues, we need to realise that diversity is something that we cannot afford to be without and from which we collectively benefit.[39] The case for integration inevitably rests upon perceptions of the benefits.[40] Within the European Union there has been increasing acknowledgement of the need to compensate for declining birth rates with immigration. Without positive net migration the populations of Germany, Greece, Italy and non-EU Sweden would be in decline.[41] Unlike the United States and Canada, European countries have not traditionally regarded themselves as immigrant societies. Sassen, examining the economic relationship between emigrant and immigrant regions, notes that labour-importing areas experience higher rates of growth. It is better, economically, to be an importer of labour than and exporter of one. Immigrant countries tend to accumulate advantage in terms of levels of growth over emigrant countries:

> History suggests that this is an advantage which labor-sending areas either (a) cannot catch up with and/or (b) are structurally not going to be part of because the spatialisation of growth is precisely characterised by this type of uneven development. History suggests it takes several major economic phases to overcome the accumulation of disadvantage and exclusion from the dynamics of growth. One cannot be too rigid or mechanical about these generalizations. But it is clear for Italy and Ireland, even if they now receive immigrants, the fact of two centuries of labour exporting was not a macroeconomic advantage. Only some individuals and localities may have benefited. Today when a whole new economic era is afoot, Italy and Ireland have become part of the new growth dynamics – each in its own specific manner.[42]

One problem facing advocates of integration is that of overcoming 'zero sum' presumptions and preoccupations about 'immigrant free riders'.[43] These proved central to the politics of the 2004 Referendum on Citizenship, where immigrants were portrayed as exploiting maternity health services (ignoring the contribution of thousands of immigrant nurses and doctors). Another problem is that Irish social policy responses to immigrants must contend with the 'Celtic Tiger' perception that these are (or should be) solely economic actors. This essentially neo-liberal case for excluding immigrants from social citizenship forms part of a broader one about how Irish society should respond to globalisation.[44] It has been marked by an increased emphasis on free-market policy solutions to social problems.[45] However, citizens and non-citizens excluded from social protection are not in the same boat. Nor is this exclusion exclusive to globalisation and the prevalence of neo-liberalism.

To some extent unfolding conditions in Ireland recall those in Germany from the 1950s to the 1970s, when rapid expansion of immigration occurred against the backdrop of the exclusion of immigrants from citizenship and social policy. In particular the political mobilisation of distinctions between 'nationals' and 'non-nationals' in 2004 evoked the pejorative use of the term *Ausländer* in Germany after the Second World War. The Irish national/non-national dualism became institutionalised in 2001; it replaced the term 'alien' in legislation.[46] By 2004 it had become the prevalent commonsense conceptual framework for debates about immigration. For instance, it was routinely used by the Department of Enterprise and Employment to describe immigrant workers. Furthermore some elements of Irish policy towards immigrant workers can further be likened to those towards *Gastarbeiter*, or guest workers, in Germany. From the 1950s the federal government promoted the recruitment of immigrant single male workers on a temporary basis.[47] German rules of limiting the stay of individuals to a three-year rotation and Irish annual non-transferable work permits alike suggested that they could be disposed of when necessary. The German 'rotation principle' functioned as intended in so far as the number of guest workers fell by 30 per cent from 1.3 million to 0.9 million during the recession of 1966 and 1967. Immigrant employment in the construction industry was particularly affected by economic conditions, and guest workers, because of lesser rights and entitlements, were more vulnerable to unemployment. Between 1973 and 1976 redundancy rates for immigrants (some 41%) in this sector were almost three times those of German citizen workers (15%). Active recruitment of such workers ended in 1973, amid rising domestic unemployment, increased industrial militancy amongst guest workers and the expansion of the EU. It remained a necessary political orthodoxy into the 1990s to deny that Germany was a country of immigration. Yet, by the end of the 1980s, some 60% of guest workers in West Germany had been born there.[48] Tighter immigration controls during the 1970s increased the extent to which non-EU established guest workers brought over their families and settled permanently. Writing in 1991, Norman Ginsberg offered the following analysis:

> Partly in response to the firm immigration controls after 1973, many of the established guest workers brought over their wives and children and have settled permanently, if never too securely, into German society. It is a clear paradox that in the FRG, as elsewhere, the tightening of immigration control increased the level of permanent settlement. Federal governments have tried many measures to discourage permanent settlement, including financial inducements to leave and at one point withdrawal of child benefit, and the reality of permanent settlement is still not accepted.[49]

It was only with the passing of the 1990 Foreigner Law that immigrant women and children were granted their own right of residence independently of the head of household.[50] In 1997 paragraphs 85–7 of the Foreigners

Law were amended to allow some *Ausländers* to take out German nationality. The criteria were stringent. Children born in Germany would obtain
German nationality if one parent had been born there or had come to
Germany under the age of fourteen and had a permanent resident permit.
To some extent these citizenship criteria are more generous (in the case
of denizen children) than those introduced in Ireland following the 2004
referendum. In other respects (that of a right to Irish citizenship after
four years of residence) they were less so. In both the German and Irish
cases access to citizenship can be undermined by welfare dependence. In
the German case, eight years of prior legal residence – without dependence on social security or a criminal record – are amongst the conditions of citizenship entitlement.[51] The 1990 law and its 1997 successor
allowed the expulsion of long-term foreign residents if they were deemed
excessively dependent on social security.[52] Immigrants to Ireland become
eligible for non-contributory benefits after two years but – the wording
of citizenship legislation suggests – are warned off claiming benefits prior
to becoming citizens lest they put their applications in peril.

The removal of Irish safety nets for new immigrants presumes to
secure temporary labour without increasing dependence. However,
Germany's experience suggests that such immigration policies cannot
prevent permanent settlement even if some immigrants become displaced
by economic downturns. Policies aimed at treating immigrants as just
economic actors are likely to have unintended consequences. These
include the long-term cost to Irish society of deliberately marginalising
immigrant communities.

The Irish integration debate

Three influential efforts to conceptualise integration within Irish social
policy can be identified. The first of these was signalled within the *Report
of the Task Force on the Travelling Community* (1995).[53] This acknowledged the failure of past efforts to assimilate Travellers and outlined
some 400 recommendations at reducing discrimination and Traveller
marginalisation in areas such as accommodation, health, education and
the economy. The second was a report produced in 2000 by the Department of Justice Equality and Law Reform entitled *Integration: A Two-
way* Process. The understanding of integration it outlined drew to some
extent on conceptualisations of social exclusion set out in the National
Anti-poverty Strategy (1997). The third, the main focus of what follows,
can be identified within policy debates about the inclusion of immigrants
within the remit of anti-poverty and social inclusion policies that have
also been influenced by such conceptualisations of social exclusion.

As defined in *Integration: A Two-way Process* (2000), 'integration means the ability to participate to the extent that a person needs and wishes in all the major components of society, without having to relinquish his or her own cultural identity'.[54] In essence this definition has two components. The first relates to the rights and resources needed to participate fully in society. The second concerns forms of racism which justify discrimination and inequality. *Integration: A Two-way Process* (2000) emphasised the need to promote the integration of refugees and immigrants into Irish society though measures to promote employment, very much along the lines of the National Anti-poverty Strategy, and through additional measures aimed at addressing the specific barriers of discrimination, non-recognition of qualifications and lack of fluency in English:

> The emphasis of integration policy should be on supporting initiatives which enable the preservation of the ethnic, cultural and religious identity of the individual and at the same time remove barriers which affect the refugee's ability to access mainstream service.[55]

> Poor English language skills have been previously identified as affecting refugees' prospects of entering gainful employment. Other barriers to entering gainful employment include lack of knowledge of labour market and skills requirements, lack of recognised skills or qualifications and discrimination.[56]

> Employment is a key factor in terms of facilitating integration. It provides a regular income and economic independence, security, status and opportunities for interaction with people from the host community and for social integration. Employment brings may benefits, including improved income and lifestyle, an increased sense of belonging to the community, better interaction with people outside their own communities and allows refugees to contribute to society.[57]

The case for integration, as set out in the report, draws upon the rationale for addressing social exclusion contained in the Partnership 2000 Agreement (1996), the National Anti-poverty Strategy (1997) and more recently in the Revised National Anti-poverty Strategy (2002). Collectively these have articulated a broad definition of social exclusion that encompasses concerns about 'poverty, deprivation, low educational qualifications, labour market disadvantage, joblessness, poor health, poor housing or homelessness, illiteracy and innumeracy, precariousness and incapacity to participate in society'.[58] Concerns that the exclusion of any segment of the population from the incomes and lifestyles of the majority constituted a cost to society were not originally articulated with ethnic minority groups in mind. However, such concerns were specifically identified within the subsequent Programme for Prosperity and Fairness

(2000). which emphasised the need to address racism as an 'emerging cause of poverty in Ireland'.[59]

Partnership 2000 defined social exclusion in terms of 'cumulative marginalisation: from production (employment), from consumption (income poverty), from social networks (community, family and neighbours), from decision-making and from an adequate quality of life'. This definition emphasised access to employment. At the same time it acknowledged that people in low-paid employment or their dependants could also experience poverty. Income and consumption were seen as linked with social processes. People who experienced material deprivation by comparison with community norms were understood to be at risk of exclusion from participation in societal activities. At the same time this definition recognised that exclusion from community, family and neighbourhood networks was not merely a consequence of income poverty. A similar understanding was articulated in the *National Anti-poverty Strategy* (1997), which discussed the problem of social exclusion in the following terms:

> No society can view without deep concern the prospect of a significant minority of people becoming more removed from the incomes and lifestyles of the majority. It is the tackling of the structural factors that underpin this exclusion which requires the strategic approach set out in this document.[60]

The strategy included the following definition of poverty:

> People are living in poverty, if their income and resources (material, cultural and social) are so inadequate as to preclude them from having a standard of living which is regarded as acceptable by Irish society generally. As a result of inadequate income and resources people may be excluded and marginalised from participating in activities which are considered the norm from other people in society.[61]

The National Anti-poverty Strategy (1997) placed a focus on specific groups suffering from multiple disadvantage and at risk of social exclusion. Travellers were identified as one such group. Amongst the stated principles that underpinned the strategy was one of 'guaranteeing the rights of minorities, especially through anti-discrimination measures'.[62] The need for such a focus was amplified within the framework document for the Review of the National Anti-poverty Strategy published in November 2001:

> There are limited data on the economic and social well-being of ethnic minorities in Ireland. Nevertheless, experience in other countries shows that ethnic minorities experience racism, tend to suffer discrimination, disadvantage, marginalisation and poverty. In particular, racism may limit people's access to resources and services. Migrant workers and refugees,

particularly the unskilled, are also vulnerable. If Ireland is to be a successful modern intercultural society, it must integrate foreign-born residents in ways that respect their social, economic and cultural rights.[63]

A commitment was made under the Programme for Prosperity and Fairness (PPF) to review the existing targets under the original National Anti-poverty Strategy framework and introduce possible new targets. A report by the National Economic and Social Forum (NESF), arising from this commitment, outlined a number of steps required to enhance the 1997 strategy.[64] One of these was to address the links between racism and poverty within the strategy through the inclusion of a new target area.[65] The consultation process undertaken during the review of the National Anti-poverty Strategy (NAPS) undertaken in 2001 similarly identified the importance of a focus on migrants and ethnic minorities.[66] The result of this consultation was the inclusion of 'migrants and members of ethnic minority groups' as a distinct target group within the Revised National Anti-poverty Strategy (2002). Notably, the Revised NAPS report, entitled *Building an Inclusive Society*, identified migrants and ethnic minorities as a distinct target group for anti-poverty policies.[67]

Building an Inclusive Society identified, for the first time, migrants and ethnic minorities as a specific target group for anti-poverty policy.[68] It also set an overall objective of ensuring that they are not more likely to experience poverty than majority group members. This category includes asylum seekers and immigrant 'guest' workers on non-transferable work permits. It includes people with lesser rights to state benefits, education and employment training than Irish or EU citizens. This goal of addressing poverty amongst migrants and ethnic minorities implied a new emphasis on the integration of immigrants, not explicitly stated elsewhere in Irish government policy. This ran contrary to an emphasis (dating from the introduction of direct provision in 2000) on immigration policies aimed at preventing asylum seekers and other migrants from becoming embedded in Irish society. This conflict was not explicitly addressed in *Building an Inclusive Society* but the report noted that the goal of ensuring that migrants and ethnic minorities did not experience disproportionate poverty necessitated 'fair and sensible immigration policies', that racism and related intolerance should be tackled and that the right to equal treatment should be upheld. Beyond such general statements of principle the report set no specific targets. By contrast distinct goals were set for other identified vulnerable 'target groups'. The reason given was that very little information was available about the socio-economic situation of foreign-born residents in Ireland. It was; 'not possible. therefore, to define specific targets for this group as a whole or for a particular ethnic group at this stage'.[69]

However, the revised strategy did not set targets to address these goals. The stated reason for the omission of targets was that 'very little quantitative information is available about the socio-economic situation of foreign-born residents in Ireland' and 'it was not possible, therefore, to define specific targets for this group as a whole or for a particular ethnic group at this stage'.[70] The absence of systematic data on ethnic minorities was identified as a barrier to the development and implementation of social inclusion policies to meet their needs.[71]

But this was not the main problem. Aspirations to ensure that migrants and ethnic minorities did not experience disproportionate risks of poverty clashed with subsequent government policies of removing welfare entitlement from them. Arguments for social citizenship approaches to promoting the social inclusion of immigrants were discounted in the policy debate initiated by the consultation process prior to the publication of the *Building an Inclusive Society*.[72] In April 2004, just one month before it removed welfare entitlements from new immigrants, the Irish government hosted as part of its EU presidency a conference entitled 'Reconciling Mobility and Social Inclusion'.[73] Here for the first time efforts were made by senior politicians and their officials to reconcile the disjuncture between immigration policy and social policy.

The equation emphasised by the conference was between the promotion of mobility for economic reasons and the need to 'specifically promote the social inclusion of these workers and, *where appropriate*, that of their families'.[74] Yet the conference defined social inclusion and integration predominantly in terms of the economic integration of workers.[75] Furthermore, the presumption that immigrants were workers with no dependants living in Ireland was repeatedly stated. As put by Mary Coughlan, Minister of Social and Family Affairs at the time of the conference; 'Immigrants generally move in order to work so that they can have a better standard of living for themselves, their families and relatives back home.' She equated social inclusion with participation in the labour market: 'Work, as we know, is the main route out of poverty and social exclusion.'[76] Yet the social policy case for the social inclusion and integration of immigrants was acknowledged, most notably by Minister Coughlan's successor Minister Seamus Brennan in his foreword to the conference proceedings:

Mobile workers, and especially those who migrate from other regions and countries, are particular vulnerable to social exclusion. Mobility can involve leaving behind the supports of family, friends, local community and one's own culture, and experiencing much difficulty in finding comparable supports in the host country. This demands that, in solidarity, we work to provide them with the supports they need to achieve social inclusion and integration. It is clearly also in our interests to do so. The social exclusion of migrants can result in their working well below their potential as well as high rates of unemployment. This has negative consequences both economically and in relation to social cohesion. Two key goals of the Lisbon agenda, greater economic competitiveness and social cohesion, are well served, therefore, by reconciling mobility and social exclusion.[77]

This limited acknowledgement of the social policy case for integration was important in so far as it came from members of a government that had recently decided to remove immigrants from social policy. How such integration was to be furthered other than through the labour market remained unclear. Migrants and ethnic minorities received just a one-paragraph mention in the 2005 report on the implementation of the National Action Plan against Poverty and Social Exclusion 2003–2005. Crucially this noted the 'need to provide migrants with access to social protection and other services'.[78] However, for specifics it pointed readers to another policy document *Planning for Diversity: The National Action Plan against Racism*. This in turn noted the need to include immigrants within 'national plans and programmes that target poverty and social exclusion'. Again nothing specific was envisaged. The National Action Plan against Racism contained some emphasis on the need to address institutional barriers through 'targeted initiatives focusing on access to key public services for Travellers, refugees and migrants' but placed none on the issue of social rights *per se*.[79] Overall it defined integration in narrow terms. As referred to in the plan it 'simply means a range of targeted strategies for the inclusion of groups such as Travellers, refugees and migrants as part of the overall aim of developing a more inclusive and intercultural society'.[80] For the most part emphasis was on the labour market. Integration was envisaged as occurring through 'macro-economic and social policy planning' through 'employment rights, responsibilities and workplace policy'.[81]

Integration into what?

All this somehow recalls Hal, the rogue computer in Stanley Kubrick's *2001: A Space Odyssey* which goes berserk because it cannot reconcile competing mission imperatives. Yet the workings of competing social policy goals are more complex than Kubrick's conflicted computer. A logic of social inclusion grounded in past experience of promoting social solidarity is at once difficult to express and difficult to discount within official debates. Political obstacles to integration seemingly vindicate some elements of the ethnic nepotism thesis. Willingness to exclude immigrants from social inclusion policies is evident in the Irish case. However, the removal of *jus soli* citizenship rights and of denizen entitlement to some welfare goods and services has not as yet undermined social citizenship for those entitled to it. At the time of writing in 2006 the vast majority of immigrants had not lived in Ireland for long enough (four years) to be eligible for citizenship and significant numbers are not resident long enough (two years in the case of non-EU citizens) to be entitled to non-contributory benefits. For the moment citizenship persists as a perceived ethnic fault line between the existing predominantly monocultural Irish 'nationals' and 'non-nationals'.

Recent anti-immigrant politics in countries such as France and Holland has focused upon the perceived unwillingness of immigrants to participate in the societies of host countries. Similar arguments have been used to justify anti-Traveller racism and policies of assimilation in Ireland. 'Society' in such cases tends to be defined in terms of the culture and values of the dominant ethnic group as these are embedded in the structures of the nation-state.[82] Politicians in a number of European countries have argued that some immigrant groups are unwilling to integrate. Yet it is more generally the case that hostility to immigrants, or indeed excluded citizen ethnic minority groups, translates into unwillingness to pursue integration policies aimed at addressing the inequalities and racism encountered by minorities.

There is a tendency to depict social citizenship as a humanistic project – one 'grounded in universal principles of justice and human dignity'.[83] It is also expressed in social and institutional norms as distinct from principles of right or abstract formulations of some greater good. Rorty's argument that Western liberal democracies can start only from the ethnocentric vantage point of 'where we are' has complex implications for social policy. For social policy 'where we are' translates into what 'we' know about the workings and shortcomings of 'our' particular society. This recourse to the 'we' and 'us' of the dominant community, as distinct from the ethnocentric 'them' of the immigrant others, cannot easily be got round. The 'us' of Irish society has over time developed relatively sophisticated understandings about social problems such as poverty, of the difficulty of achieving the integration or social inclusion of citizen marginal groups. The problem with excluding 'them' from prevailing solidarities is that this breaks with a common sense of who 'we' are and what 'we' do. Rorty was preoccupied with reconciling the dilemmas thrown up by the politics of cultural difference for democratic values and norms. For thinkers such as Marshall social citizenship was a crucial component of a democratic society. Ultimately integration as social inclusion cannot be envisaged without social rights (the necessary entitlements to secure participation) and political rights (the ability to participate fully in social life). From this perspective the description of citizenship in *Integration: A Two-way Process* as the 'most potent measure of integration' was an appropriate one.[84]

To suggest that Irish social policy has a role in the integration of immigrants raises a number of questions, not least what is meant by integration and, of course, integration into what? Much writing about social policy from theory down to the nuts and bolts of specific policies is preoccupied with questions of integrating marginal or excluded groups into some unstated conception of societal normalcy. This in its most limited form amounts to an emphasis on assimilation. Beyond the issue of rights and liberal conceptions of equality there remains the need to address institutional barriers caused by the inability of services to address difference. Here the intercultural debate can deepen a social inclusion approach to integration as long as it does not ignore problems caused by differential rights and entitlements. In the complex stratified societies produced by exclusion of non-citizens from social citizenship this will always be a messy business. On one hand services are encouraged to address institutional barriers experienced by some minorities. On the other they may be required to ignore the consequences of structural barriers that prevent access by those not entitled. Such self-imposed blindness cannot but foster new hidden Irelands for which future generations will have to bear the consequences.

Notes

1 For example, the Brixton, Toxteth and Liverpool riots influenced 1980s British urban policy. See D. Mason, *Race and Ethnicity in Modern Britain* (Oxford: Oxford University Press, 2000), p. 89. More recently the Bradford riots have informed UK social inclusion debates. See Cabinet Office, *Minority Ethnic Issues in Social Exclusion and Neighbourhood Renewal* (London: HMSO, 2000).

2 J. Klausen, 'Citizenship and Social Justice', in E. Oddvar Eriksen and J. Loftager (eds), *The Rationality of the Welfare State* (Oslo: Scandinavian University Press, 1996), pp. 211–21.

3 T. H. Marshall, *Citizenship and Social Class*, in T. H. Marshall and T. Bottomore (eds), *Citizenship and Social Class* (London: Pluto Press, 1996; first published 1950), p. 110.

4 Ibid., p. 8.

5 J. Lewis, 'Gender and the Development of Welfare Regimes', *Journal of European Social Policy*, 2: 3 (1993), pp. 159–73; J. O'Connor, 'Gender, Class and Citizenship in the Comparative Analysis of Welfare Regimes', *British Journal of Sociology*, 44: 3 (1993), pp. 501–18.

6 F. Kennedy, *From Cottage to Creche: Family Change in Ireland* (Dublin: Institute of Public Administration, 2001), p. 92.

7 F. Williams, *Social Policy: A Critical Introduction: Issues of Race, Gender and Class* (Cambridge: Polity, 1989).

8 C. Withol de Wenden, 'Immigration Policy and the Issue of Nationality', *Ethnic and Racial Studies*, 14: 3 (1991), p. 329.

9 G. Esping Anderson, 'After the Golden Age? Welfare State Dilemmas in a Global Economy', in G. Esping Anderson (ed.), *Welfare States in Transition: National Adaptations in Global Economies* (London: Sage, 1996), p. 1.

10 A comprehensive study of the social costs of economic transformation in central Europe funded by the Ford Foundation produced the conclusion that '"social citizenship" stands little chance of shaping post-Communist welfare states'. Institut fur die Wissenschaften vom Menschen (IWM), *Social Costs of Economic Transformation in Central Europe* (Vienna: SOCO Working Papers, 1995), cited by Klausen, 'Citizenship and Social Justice', p. 221.

11 B. Fanning, 'Locating Irish Social Policy', in B. Fanning, G. Kiely, P. Kennedy and S. Quin, *Theorising Irish Social Policy* (Dublin: University College Dublin Press, 2004), pp. 6–7.

12 The Employment Equality Act 1998 and the Equal Status Act 2000.

13 C. Joppke, 'How Immigration is Changing Citizenship: a Comparative View', *Ethnic and Racial Studies*, 22: 4 (1999), pp. 629–32.

14 Klausen, 'Citizenship and Social Justice', p. 205.

15 D. Goodhart, 'Discomfort of Strangers', *Prospect*, June 2004.

16 F. K. Salter, 'Introduction', in F. K. Salter (ed.), *Welfare, Ethnicity and Altruism: New Data and Evolutionary Theory* (London: Frank Cass, 2004), p. 5.

17 T. Faist, 'Ethnicisation and Racialisation of Welfare State Politics in Germany and the USA', *Ethnic and Racial Studies*, 18: 2 (1995), pp. 219–50.

18 M. Gilens, '"Race Coding" and White Opposition to Welfare', *American Political Science Journal*, 90: 3 (1996), p. 601.

19 Salter, *Welfare, Ethnicity and Altruism*, p. 14.

20 R. Rorty, *Objectivism, Relativism and Truth* (New York: Cambridge University Press, 1994), p. 203.

21 Ibid., p. 29.

22 B. Allen, 'What was Epistemology?', in R. B. Brandom (ed.), *Rorty and his Critics* (London: Blackwell, 2000), p. 224.

23 T. S. Adorno, E. Frenkel-Brunswick, D. J. Levinson and R. N. Sanforo, *The Authoritarian Personality* (New York: Harper & Row, 1950).

24 S. Body-Gendrot, 'Now you see it, now you don't', *Ethnic and Racial Studies*, 21: 5 (1998), p. 849.

25 G. Ritzer, *Sociological Theory* (New York: McGraw-Hill, 1996), p. 80.

26 H. Tovey and P. Share, *A Sociology of Ireland* (Gill & Macmillan, 2000), p. 337.

27 R. Putman, *Bowling Alone: The Collapse and Revival of American Community* (New York: Touchstone, 2000), p. 376.

28 Based on correlations between an index of ethnic hetrogenieity (as an indicator of ethnic nepotism) and various dependent variables indicating ethic inequalities and expenditures on social security and welfare in 183

countries. T. Vanhsnen, 'An Exploratory Comparative Study of the Relationship between Ethnic Heterogeneity and Welfare Politics', in Salter, *Welfare, Ethnicity and Altruism*, pp. 105, 111–18.

29 J. K. Galbraith, *The Culture of Contentment* (London: Pelican, 1992), p. 23.

30 D. T. Goldberg, *Multiculturalism: A Critical Reader* (Oxford: Blackwell, 1994), p. 7.

31 B. Fanning, *Racism and Social Change in the Republic of Ireland* (Manchester: Manchester University Press, 2002), p. 186.

32 T. Phillips, in *The Guardian*, 16 February 2004.

33 As quoted in *The Times*, 3 April 2004.

34 Y. Alibhai-Brown, *After Multiculturalism* (London: Foreign Policy Centre, 2000), p. 7.

35 The Housing (Traveller Accommodation) Act 1998 introduced a statutory entitlement to accommodation. This prevented local authorities from using the courts to displace Travellers they were unwilling to accommodate. The Housing (Miscellaneous Provisions) Act 2002 criminalised Travellers engaged in unauthorised halting even where their statutory entitlement to accommodation facilities went unmet. In 2002 'Citizen Traveller', a state-funded anti-racism body, had its funding removed by the Minister of Justice Equality and Law Reform when it described this new legislation as racist. See B. Fanning, 'The political currency of Irish racism, 1997–2002', *Studies*, 91, pp. 319–28

36 Fanning, *Racism and Social Change*, p. 155

37 Notably as institutionalised by *The National Consultative Committee and Racism and Interculturalism*. See www.nccri.ie. Also see Department of Justice Equality and Law Reform, *Plan For Diversity: The National Action Plan against Racism, 2005–2008* (Dublin: Stationery Office, 2005).

38 Fanning, *Racism and Social Change*, p. 183.

39 Alibhai-Brown, *After Multiculturalism*, p. 7.

40 Ibid., p. 74.

41 Eurostat, *The Social Situation in the European Union* (Brussels: European Commission, 2002), p. 65.

42 S. Sassen, *Guests and Aliens* (New York: New Press, 1999), p. 140.

43 F. Salter, 'The Evolutionary Deficit in Mainstream Political Theory on Welfare and Ethnicity' in Salter, *Welfare, Ethnicity and Altruism*, p. 316.

44 W. K. Roche and T. Craddon, 'Neo-corporatism and Social Partnership', in M. Adshead and M. Millar (eds), *Public Administration and Public Policy in Ireland: Theory and Practice* (London: Routledge, 2003), p. 73.

45 G. Taylor, 'Hailing with an Invisible Hand: a "Cosy" Political Dispute amid the Rise of Neo-liberal Politics in modern Ireland', *Government and Opposition*, 37: 4 (2002), pp. 501–23, 521.

46 The Irish Nationality and Citizenship Act 2001 superseded the Aliens Act 1935.

47 B. Marshall, *Europe in Change: The new Germany and Migration in Europe* (Manchester: Manchester University Press, 2000), pp. 11–12.

48 Marshall, *Europe in Change*, pp. 11–14.

49 N. Ginsburg, *Divisions of Welfare* (London: Sage, 1992), p. 80.
50 Marshall, *Europe in Change*, p. 15.
51 Ibid., p. 150
52 Ibid., p. 161.
53 Government of Ireland, *Report of the Task Force on the Travelling Community* (Dublin: Stationery Office, 1995).
54 Department of Justice Equality and Law Reform, *Integration: A Two-way Process* (Dublin: Stationery Office, 2000), p. 9.
55 Ibid., p. 9.
56 Ibid., p. 29.
57 Ibid.
58 T. Atkinson, B. Cantillon, E. Marlier and B. Nolan, *Social Indicators: The EU and Social Inclusion* (Oxford: Oxford University Press, 2000), p. 3.
59 Department of Social Community and Family Affairs, *Building an Inclusive Society: Review of the National Anti-poverty Strategy under the Programme for Prosperity and Fairness* (Dublin: Official Publications, 2002), p. 4.
60 Government of Ireland, *Sharing in Progress: The National Anti-poverty Strategy* (Dublin: Official Publications, 1997), p. 4.
61 Ibid., p. 3.
62 Goodbody Economic Consultants, *Review of the National Anti-poverty Strategy: Framework Document* (Dublin: Goodbody Economic Consultants, 2001), p. 4.
63 Ibid.
64 Government of Ireland, *Programme for Prosperity and Fairness* (Dublin: Official Publications, 2000), pp. 78–9.
65 National Economic and Social Forum, *The National Anti-poverty Strategy*, Forum Opinion No. 18 (Dublin: NESF, 2000), p. 32.
66 Goodbody, *Framework Document*, p. 4.
67 Department of Social Community and Family Affairs, *Review of the National Anti-poverty Strategy*, p. 17.
68 Ibid.
69 Ibid., p. 18.
70 Ibid.
71 Conference of Religious In Ireland, *Review of the National Anti-poverty Strategy* (Dublin: Justice Commission, 2002), p. 5.
72 For example, in 2002 I undertook secondary research funded by the Combat Poverty Agency (CPA), the National Consultative Committee on Racism and Interculturalism (NCCRI) and the Department of Social and Family Affairs on the relationship between racism, ethnicity and poverty in the Republic of Ireland. The resultant peer-reviewed report was not supported by these agencies. The report emphasised the importance of social rights and entitlements to the life chances of immigrants.
73 See Office for Social Inclusion, *Reconciling Mobility and Social Inclusion: The Role of Employment and Social Policy* (Dublin: Stationery Office, 2004).
74 Quoted from the back cover, ibid., italic emphasis added.

75 Ibid., p. 8.
76 Ibid., p. 27.
77 Ibid., p. 6.
78 Office for Social Inclusion, *National Action Plan against Poverty and Social Exclusion: Implementation and Update Report* (Dublin: Stationery Office, 2005), p. 4.
79 Department of Justice Equality and Law Reform, *Planning for Diversity: The National Action Plan against Racism, 2005–2008* (Dublin: Stationery Office, 2005), p. 31.
80 Ibid., p. 39.
81 Ibid., p. 31.
82 J. Rex, 'Race and Ethnicity in Europe', in J. Bailey (ed.), *Social Europe: Unity and Diversity* (London: Longman, 1992), p. 119.
83 E. Oddvar Eriksen and J. Loftager, 'Challenging the Normative Foundation of the Welfare State', in E. Oddvar Eriksen and J. Loftager (eds), *The Rationality of the Welfare State* (Oslo: Scandanavian University Press, 1996), pp. 2–3.
84 *Integration: A Two-way Process*, p. 32.

Index